HOMEFRONT &
BATTLEFRONT

Nelson BC in World War II

Sylvia Crooks

Library and Archives Canada Cataloguing in Publication

Crooks, Sylvia, 1936–
Homefront & battlefront : Nelson, B.C. in World War II
/ Sylvia Crooks.
Includes index.
ISBN 1-894694-38-4

1. World war 1939–1945—Casualties—BritishColumbia—Nelson Region. 2. Soldiers—British Columbia—Nelson Region—Biography. 3. World War, 1939–1945—British Columbia—Nelson Region. 4. Nelson Region (B.C.)—Biography. 5. Nelson Region (B.C.)— History. I. Title.

FC3849.N44Z48 2005   940.53'71162'0922   C2005-904207-9

Editor: Lois M. Bewley
Copy editor: Barbara Ladouceur
Proofreader: Neall Calvert
Book and cover design: Gordon Finlay
with Gary Wilcox and Laura Kinder

First printing August 2005
Printed in Canada

Granville Island
Publishing
212 – 1656 Duranleau
Vancouver, BC, Canada V6H 3S4
Tel: (604) 688-0320 Toll free: 1-877-688-0320
www.GranvilleIslandPublishing.com

DEDICATION

To the memory of the young men

from the Nelson district who sacrificed their lives

for Canada in World War II, and in particular

Pilot Officer Maurice Coupland Latornell,

who was the inspiration

for this book.

Acknowledgements

When I began this project I had no intention of writing a book, but simply wanted to satisfy my own curiosity about the young men from my home town who sacrificed their lives so that the rest of us might continue to live in freedom. I was three years old when the Second World War broke out, and nine when it ended. My early years were immersed in what I have termed "that far-off but ever-present war," when everything stopped each evening at six o'clock for the National News, when almost all our activities were touched by the theme of war. As I delved into the *Nelson Daily News* of those years I began to realize that here was a whole community that went to war. It was, indeed, a people's war. The immersion that I remember as a child was true for adults as well, who not only gave their sons and husbands and brothers and sweethearts, but who also came together, as people do in times of common danger, and found the time, the energy and the dollars to help make victory possible. And Nelson's story, unique in its own detail, is the story of communities across the country. I realized that it is a story that should be told.

I could not have told this story without the help of so many present and former Nelsonites who lived through those years, and who shared their experiences and their family stories with me. They include, in alphabetical order: Norman Ackley, John Barwis, Don Beattie, Gary Bowell, Ray Burgess Jr., Maxwell Carne, George Coletti, Peter Dewdney, Alex Dingwall, Alan Emmott, Phyllis (Gray) Gautschi, H.A.D. "Bud" Greenwood, Florence Hartridge, Audrey (Emery Andrew) Heustis, Fran (Campbell) Horan, Sam McBride, W. David MacDonald, Alyse Mathisen, Bob Morrow, Dawn (Miller) Nelson, John Norris, Dawn (Sharp) and George Penniket, Helen (Ferguson) Poisson, Lillian (Armstrong) Potts, Alan Ramsden, H.W. "Bert" Ramsden, Treve Roberts, Stan Smith, Edna (Steed) Whiteley, Helen (Latornell) Wood, and the late Daphne (Rhode) Wilson.

I am indebted to Anne George (the niece of Jack and Hampton Gray), Corinne Dalgas (granddaughter of Agner Dalgas), Ann Rolfe (half-sister of Bob Andrew) and Tanna Allan (niece of William Allen). I also wish to thank Deborah Thomas and Trish Miller, librarians at the Nelson Municipal Library, and Carol Westmacott, librarian at L.V. Rogers Secondary School. I am grateful for the advice I have had from my brother Tom Shorthouse, my son Brian Crooks, and especially for the editorial assistance and advice from Betty Keller. My research was greatly helped by Janet Mason, BC Provincial Toponymist, Base Mapping & Geomatic Services Branch, Ministry of Sustainable Resource Management. I want to thank Managing Editor Bob Hall for granting me permission to make liberal use of archived issues of the *Nelson Daily News*.

I reserve a special thank you for Shawn Lamb, curator of the Nelson Museum who, at a time of recovery from a disastrous fire at the museum, found the space for me to work and the time to assist me in my research. Above all, I want to thank my research assistant and editorial advisor, Lois Bewley, who encouraged me to write this book and was unfailing with her assistance.

Sylvia Crooks
Vancouver, BC
July, 2005

CONTENTS

Pilot Officer Maurice Latornell
Photo courtesy of Helen Wood

INTRODUCTION

Seventy young men left the small Canadian city of Nelson in the early 1940s, never to return. They died on battlefields, at sea, and in the air, thousands of miles from home. Most of them had grown up together, many had been classmates, close friends and neighbours. Some were brothers or brothers-in-law. Every November 11th they are officially remembered when veterans and townspeople gather around the cenotaph that records their names.

Maurice Latornell is one of those names. He taught me how to skate when I was three years old. He was in his early twenties, fun, and full of life, and his death four years later made that far-off but ever-present war a reality for me. Over the years I remembered Maurice and decided finally to find the answers to my questions of how and where he died. I began with the Nelson Cenotaph to confirm the spelling of his name, and was struck by the other names of men who lost their lives in that six-year-long conflict we call World War II, family names so familiar to me and anyone else who grew up in Nelson. And so began the quest to uncover who they were and how they lost their young lives.

This, then, is the record of what I learned about their short lives and their too-early deaths. Included are accounts of other casualties of that war, young men who had strong connections with the Nelson district but who are not remembered on the Nelson Cenotaph. Some who came home, who survived terrifying experiences, tell their stories. It is also a record of the community itself as it went to war on the homefront, how Nelson sent its young men and women off with patriotic zeal, how it grieved their losses, celebrated their victories, marshalled its resources and devoted its civic life for six tumultuous years to this one purpose—winning.

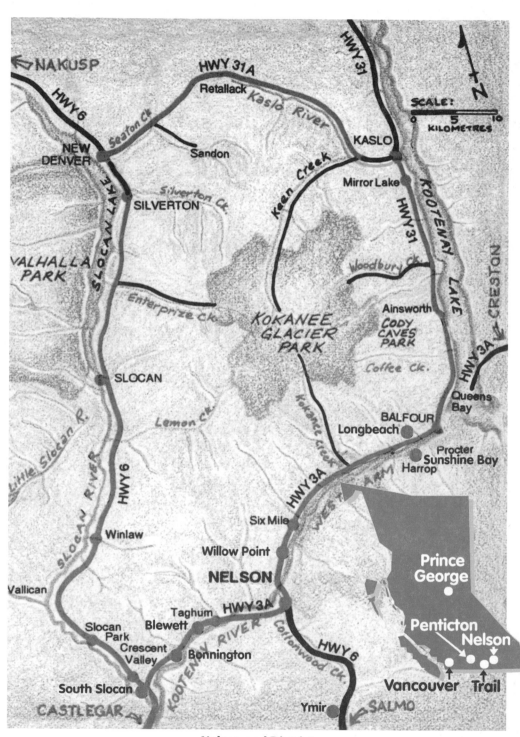

Nelson and District
Map by Barbara Brown

1939
1940

CHAPTER ONE

On September 1, 1939, Hitler's army invades Poland, bringing to an end the "appeasement" policy of Britain and France, who declare war on Germany on September 3. Canada follows on September 10 with her own declaration of war. Prime Minister Mackenzie King promises that only volunteers will be sent overseas. With a regular army of only 4,500 men (augmented by 51,000 partly-trained reservists), an air force with fewer than 20 modern combat aircraft, and a navy with only six destroyers, Canada is woefully unprepared for war. Nevertheless, Canadian troops arrive in England by the end of the year. In the spring of 1940 the anxious calm of the "phoney war" ends when Germany occupies Denmark and invades Norway. The German "blitzkrieg" blasts its way through Luxembourg, Belgium, the Netherlands and France. This leaves Canada as Britain's principal ally against the Axis powers of Germany and Italy. In June some 350,000 British and French troops are rescued from the beaches of Dunkirk. A month later the "Battle of Britain" begins in the air, and the British are threatened with invasion. A desperate need for pilots leads to the establishment of the British Commonwealth Air Training Plan in Canada. Canada sends war materials overseas as rapidly as her depressed economy, factories and shipyards can recover.

Nelson's story is a microcosm of Canadian life in those dark war years, 1939 to 1945, a story that was repeated in hundreds of small towns and cities across the country. Yet each community is unique and has its own tale to tell. Nelson, calling itself the "Queen City of the Kootenays," is tucked into a beautiful, green, narrow valley on the west arm of Kootenay Lake in southeastern British Columbia. In 1939, with a population of some 7,000, it was a distribution centre for a rich mining and logging area, was also a government centre, and because of its scenic beauty, was beginning to be conscious of its great tourism potential. The city had a history of support for the arts, had a thriving little theatre group, a popular boys' choir, a new civic recreation centre which housed a movie theatre, skating rink, curling rink, badminton and basketball courts, and library. The city had only recently lost its opera house to a fire. An article in the *Vancouver Sun* in 1940 described Nelson as "one of the more prosperous interior British Columbia communities...noted for its fine spirit of civic pride." The young journalist, Bruce Hutchison, wrote about the uniqueness of Nelson as he saw it:

> A real city is not built of wood and stone and concrete, but of age, of legends, of experience shared and of joint toil between men. By such a definition Canada has few cities, perhaps half a dozen. Nelson...is one of them.... It is more a city than any point in British Columbia east of Vancouver. It has an atmosphere, a personality, a feeling about it that make it unique. Not just its glorious setting on the hill beside the great lake of Kootenay, its homes scattered broadcast from the water's edge half way up the green mountains. Not just its industries, fine streets and thriving business. Something else entirely that you can feel as soon as you drive over the rim of the hill. Here is a community that has lived long together, which has gathered history and a sense of family.[1]

Nelson also had a military tradition. The city supplied to the Boer War the highest quota of men per capita of any Canadian community its size.[2] During that war some 45 recruits joined the Rocky Mountain Rangers in Nelson. The city could also boast a Victoria Cross (VC) winner in the First World War. He was Commander Rowland Bourke, who came to Nelson as a young man with his family in 1903. He served on motor launches with the Royal Navy Volunteer Reserve, winning his VC for rescuing 38 sailors from a sinking ship. In May 1915 the 54th Kootenay Infantry Battalion was established in Nelson and went overseas as part of the Canadian Expeditionary Force. They took part in the battles of Ypres, Lens, Passchendaele, Arras, Amiens, Bourlon Wood, Cambrai, Valenciennes and Vimy Ridge. In the Battle of the Somme in 1916 some 1,200 men of the 54th Battalion went into action; only 500 survived, many of them wounded. Over 50 of the 251 men listed on the Nelson Cenotaph as World War I casualties were with the 54th Battalion.[3]

The 54th was converted in 1936 into the 24th Field Brigade of the Royal Canadian Artillery, with batteries at Cranbrook, Kimberley, Nelson and Trail. Agner Dalgas, a decorated veteran of the Great War, made his home in Nelson, where he worked as an engineer with the BC Department of Public Works. During the 1930s he ardently advocated revival of the organized militia and formed a military institute of former officers who met regularly to discuss military problems. On September 1, 1939, the batteries of the 24th Field Brigade were mobilized. Captain Dalgas was promoted to major and commanded the 111th (Nelson) Field Battery, oversaw its recruitment and training, and spoke to local organizations about the threat of war and of his pride in the 111th.

By the eve of war in September 1939, recruitment had already begun. Even though Canada was not to declare war on Germany for another ten days, the local newspaper, *Nelson Daily News*, in its September 1 issue was advising Kootenay men who wished to volunteer for service in permanent army units to apply through the Provincial Police office in Nelson. By September 4 there were already 12 new recruits to the 111th Field Battery. The newspaper reported threatened local shortages of flour and sugar in response to extremely heavy buying, and the placing of guards on public utilities to prevent sabotage. An editorial on that day promised that "Canada will throw her whole weight…her industry, her wealth, and her man-power of every kind into the fight against the insatiable aggressor."

Immediately after war was declared, the 111th (Nelson) Battery was advised that it was to be among the first contingent to go overseas with the First Canadian Division. In October the Legion held a "smoker" in which "the old army paid tribute to the new army." It was a stirring evening of music and dedication, accompanied by Mickey McEwen's old-time orchestra. The president of the Nelson Branch of the Legion, James Spencer, urged the recruits of the 111th to keep in mind the reputation made by the Canadian Corps in the last war. "Give them hell and get Hitler. Go out and make a reputation of your own." Major Dalgas, pointing to two flags on the wall, one representing the Legion and one the 111th, declared that one was already covered with honours, and the 111th would follow in that tradition.[4]

Not all of Canada was so eager to fight. Memories of the endless slaughter of World War I remained vivid. Prime Minister Mackenzie

Downtown Nelson in 1940, from Gyro Park Bluff, Looking West
Baker Street is on the left and Vernon Street on the right. The large white building, bottom right, is the Civic Centre where the Boeing plant was housed.
Photo by J.H. Allen, courtesy of Nelson Museum

King recalled parliament and for a week Canada was neutral, wanting to show its independence from Britain, before declaring war on September 10. Many young Canadian men, jobless and hopeless, suddenly found themselves wanted by the armed forces. Some had seen the war coming and had already joined the RAF or the Royal Navy.

One such young man brought the war early to Nelson. The front page of the *Nelson Daily News* on December 11, 1939, featured the picture of a proud, smiling teenager in Royal Navy uniform, the "first Interior boy to give his life." He was ***Ordinary Seaman George Henry Trevelyan Rasmussen***, 18 years of age, who died of burns he suffered in an accident while on patrol with HMS *Woolwich* in British waters. His family lived at Willow Point on the north shore of the lake; his father was a constable in the BC Police detachment at Nelson. George was born in Nelson in 1921 and attended elementary and junior high schools there, before attending St. George's School in Vancouver. He was a popular boy who was a strong swimmer, "spending hours in the lake at a time, and taking his dip in the winter as regularly as in summer."

A schoolmate of George's, Dawn Penniket, remembers that "he hated school...and had no yearning for book learning. Loved Latin and was good for a laugh." Before he was 17 he went to England to join the Royal Navy. He wrote to his parents about his life aboard the training ship HMS *Ganges*:

> We were issued with a lovely kit...learned how to march in squads...go to school 1½ hours daily...rifle drill...over 2500 boys in training school...I am taking up wireless telegraphy... three boys here from Canada...we get bread, margarine, eggs, tea, cocoa, stew, beef, rabbit meat which I am sure is rat meat...we get five shillings and three pence a week...[5]

After his training period he served on the battleship HMS *Ramillies* and on the destroyer HMS *Sikh* in the Mediterranean before being transferred to HMS *Woolwich*. His last letter home, received by his parents about three weeks before he died, was dated September 9, aboard the HMS *Sikh*:

> Please excuse me for not answering your letters for so long, but no one knows how hard we have been run for the last six weeks in order to work up to a very high standard of efficiency, so that now that we are at war no one can touch or even try to come up

to a height nearly as good as ours...far better to be charging through the thundering seas than to stay in harbour and work about the ship in the scorching sunshine, as it doesn't get hot MUCH out here, only a hundred and ten in the shade.... I have very little news to write as we cannot give the slightest information concerning the Navy, as it is most important that everything be kept a secret in time of war. I can say that we have been on a lovely cruise this summer all up through the Greek Islands, calling at various ports and seeing marvellous sights. Of

George Rasmussen of North Shore First Interior Boy to Give His Life

GEORGE H. RASMUSSEN, Jr.
·who died Saturday night in Gosport Hospital, of burns received presumably on sea duty in British waters.—This picture was taken at Christmas, 1938.—For full story see page two.

Front-page Article
Nelson Daily News, *December 11, 1939*

course you have heard about the old ruins in Greece. I have got a very quiet job on the *Sikh*. I am Captain's Coxswain, and take him wherever he wants to go in his car—What do you think about the war? Isn't it terrible? But still, it has to come some day, so why not get it over with now, as keep on having these crises? We know just how and where we stand now that war has been declared and you can be sure that it won't last more than a couple of months as the people in Germany are starving now, so God knows what it will be in a month or two.

When the cable was received telling of George's serious injuries from burns, his mother cabled her sister in Pangbourne, England, about 50 miles from Gosport where George lay in the naval hospital. She was able to visit him before he died on the evening of December 9. She cabled her sister in Willow Point: "... saw George, who sends his love. Heartfelt sympathy." George would have turned 19 on January 15.

For seven months after war was declared the only action that took place was sporadically at sea. This "phoney war" came to an end on April

9, 1940, when German forces invaded Norway and Denmark. But the so-called "sitzkrieg" in the west, with a focus on the Maginot and Siegfried Lines, continued for another month. On May 10 the German "blitzkrieg" struck against Belgium, Holland and France. The Royal Air Force, which had until then been busy on coastal patrol, doing aerial surveillance and dropping propaganda leaflets on German cities, responded.

Among the first to go into battle were the fighter squadrons stationed in France. One of these was 87 Squadron, which had been posted to France as part of the air component of the British Expeditionary Force. It saw little of the enemy throughout the "phoney war" months of September to April except for occasional reconnaissance missions. On April 10 it went into action, and among the fighter pilots was *John Alexander Campbell*, a 27-year-old native of Nelson.

On May 12 a force of RAF bombers was attacking bridges near Maastricht in Belgium in order to stop advancing German troops. Ahead of the bombers were eight Hurricane fighters. The Royal Air Force's web diary tells the story:

> Suddenly, the fighter pilots saw the sky fill with German Bf109s—120 in all. Despite the fearful odds, the Hurricanes fought as best they could, accounting for three Germans but losing six of their own.[6]

Jack was among the fighter pilots lost that day. The next day he was recommended for the Distinguished Flying Cross (DFC). The citation reads:[7]

> This officer succeeded to the temporary command of a flight just before the German invasion of Holland and Belgium and during the two following days led it with great courage and determination. He set a fine example by destroying four enemy aircraft. On one occasion, when leading a flight of seven aircraft in protection of Blenheim bombers, he showed great personal gallantry in leading his squadron to an attack against 40 enemy aircraft.

He was the first Nelson man to be decorated in the war.

Like George Rasmussen, Jack Campbell was born in Nelson but lived with his family at Willow Point, five miles along the lake from Nelson. His grandparents were pioneers in the Nelson area. He was the son of a First World War veteran who had been badly wounded and gassed, and on his return home "suffered the effects of service." He had died 15 years earlier, leaving his widow with seven children. Jack's sister, Fran Horan, recalls

"Jack loved tennis and golf, was good to our mother who became a widow when Jack was about 12." He attended school in Nelson and according to the high school annual was "an ardent student and a very clever one." While working at the COMINCO smelter in Trail, Jack decided in 1937 to take Royal Air Corps training in England. He qualified very quickly and eventually became a flight commander with the 87th Fighter Squadron.

Jack's mother told the Nelson newspaper how she learned of his DFC:

Flying Officer Jack Campbell, DFC
Photo Courtesy of Nelson Museum

> I was sitting by the radio, listening to the war news, when John's name came over.... It made me very proud to be his mother, especially when one thinks of the wonderful work that the Air Force and the Navy have been doing.[8]

Like so many mothers during those terrible years, she was to live anxious days, with three other children in the services, one son and two daughters in the Air Force.

In June 1940 the Canadian parliament passed the *National Resources Mobilization Act,* which gave the government powers over property, industry and manpower, including conscription for home defence only. All persons over 16 years of age were required to register for war service. It seems that the young men of Nelson were more than ready for the call. An editorial on May 25 urged action:

> Let's go! What are we waiting for? This is the spirit of the Kootenay young men who are waiting for the recruiting call. Presumably the Third Division, which the Government announced to parliament would be raised, will be, like its elders, representative of all Canada, and in that case there should be a Kootenay battalion

or a Kootenay brigade of artillery. Whichever type is allotted to this loyal territory, the allotment will be quickly filled, whenever recruiting starts. The Nelson Armoury has been maintained during the entire winter and spring, in readiness for use again.

The armoury, or Nelson Drill Hall as it was called, was soon to be busy. General recruiting "to swell the ranks of Canada's men in khaki" began in Nelson on June 13. Built in 1902, the Drill Hall had been the centre of recruitment and basic training for the 54th Battalion in World War I, and was to become a hub again as recruitment accelerated. Nelson archivist and historian, Shawn Lamb, has written, "There are many veterans who remember standing shivering in the hall waiting for Doctor Borden to test their physical fitness in their first introduction to army life."[9]

Members of the 111th Battery had already left Nelson in October 1939 for intensive training at Edmonton, and were among the first Canadian soldiers to go overseas in May 1940. It was disclosed four years later that among them was a 14-year-old Nelson boy, Gunner James Norman Ackley, who managed to slip by the recruiting officer, even though he was a slight lad, only five feet, eight inches in height, and weighing 116 pounds. "I was pretty sly," is his explanation today. Norman survived "five years and five days overseas," including the bloody Italian campaign, where he served with the Lanark and Renfrew Scottish Regiment.

The first Nelson district draft of recruits under the National Resources Mobilization Act, consisting of 27 men, left Nelson on June 19, 1940, for the regimental depot at Vancouver where they would be assigned to various units of the Canadian Active Service Force. There was no delay once the men had made the commitment. Recruits were to be prepared to leave for their various depots the day after being accepted and attested. Typically, the recruits were paraded from the Drill Hall through the city to the CPR station, with the Nelson Bugle Band in the lead, and accompanied by the Nelson platoon of the Veterans Guard. Family and friends gathered to see them off, and members of local organizations distributed chocolate bars and cigarettes among the men. The mayor or a member of the city council would be in attendance to extend official best wishes and encouragement. This kind of rousing send-off was a Nelson tradition, going back to the Boer War. In the seven-week period between June 19 and August 3, 1940, nine drafts of recruits left Nelson with such a fanfare for an indefinite tour of military service.

The Veterans Guard of Canada was formed on May 24, 1940, its purpose being to guard vital installations such as bridges and power plants, and eventually to guard prisoners of war interned in Canada. They were veterans of the First World War now too old for active service, many of them with sons and daughters in the military. Author Barry Broadfoot has called the Veterans Guard "the most unsung of the 750,000-man Canadian Army."[10] In the Nelson area they were used especially to guard the power plants on the Kootenay River between Nelson and Castlegar, but they were also front and centre in any military parade or patriotic ceremony, such as seeing off the new recruits. T.J. McBride commanded the Nelson platoon.

Patriotic exercises were the order of the day in schools as well, especially to celebrate May 24, Empire Day. In 1940 Reverend J.C. Holmes urged the junior high school students to support the men in France and Belgium:

> …to build their characters by living up to the great British ideals, put a portion at least of their spending money to the purchase of war stamps instead of to pleasure, and be loyal to their country, reporting to their parents when unfavourable remarks were made by others against their country.

This was followed by the singing of *The British Grenadiers*, *Ye Mariners of England*, *The Marseillaise*, and *God of the Nations*. At one of Nelson's two elementary schools, Central School, C.B. Garland advised the children of "the difference between the subjects of the British Empire and those of other countries."

> …just the difference in the point of view of the people. The British think in a British way, that stands for freedom of speech, freedom of religion and freedom of the press, while others think in a way of personal fulfillment.

This was followed by the singing of *The Canadian Boat Song*, *Bluebells of Scotland*, *Land of Our Birth*, and *Land of Hope and Glory*.

The purchase of War Savings Stamps was one of the ways that children were recruited to support the war effort. Stamps were sold in schools, and often classes within a school or schools themselves would compete to raise the most money. The stamps, called "silver bullets," cost 25 cents each. On May 27, 1940, War Savings Certificates were issued by the government, and a call went out to "Canadians of small means" to support the war effort by their purchase; they were sold in denominations of $5, $10, $25, $50 and $100. In August 1940 it was reported that Nelson was

The 111th (Nelson) Battery, Royal Canadian Artillery

On training in Edmonton, about a month before they left for overseas. Many of the men had autographed the back of the picture. *Photo by McDermid Studios Ltd., Edmonton, courtesy of Royal Canadian Legion, Branch 51*

O's AND GUNNERS
ERY R.C.A. C.A.S.F.
RIL 15th 1940

among the leaders in BC in sales of War Savings Stamps and Certificates. The four banks and post office had sold over $5,400 worth in the last two weeks of July alone.

By mid-1940, after Germany had scored crushing victories in France and the Low Countries, many Canadians were feeling jittery about security at home, and the local Nelson newspaper echoed this concern in the many articles about the danger of enemy aliens and fifth columnists. In May the Nelson City Council joined municipalities throughout the country in urging the federal government to take action against potential fifth-column activities. Mayor Norman Stibbs expressed this concern:

> Nelson City Council is not only heartily in accord with the internment of all enemy aliens, but we would go a step further; we would examine all foreigners of that class who have been naturalized within the last year or two, and if they were not able to give a fully satisfactory account of themselves we would intern them also.[11]

Alderman G.M. Benwell expressed his concern about sabotage, and added:

> The Dominion Government doesn't seem to be making any effort to pep up enthusiasm through the country like there was in the last war. The first thing we know Fritzie will be knocking at our front door.[12]

The council passed a resolution asking the government to organize a voluntary defence corps similar to that in Great Britain.

Anxiety was compounded when Italy declared war on the Allies on June 10. Nelson residents of Italian descent "voiced keen disappointment and regret, and all of those contacted by the *Daily News* were sure that Mussolini had made the wrong move." The next day the newspaper quoted several responses:

> "That crazy Mussolini. I don't know what he can be thinking of," declared Louis Coletti. "I enlisted for the last war—the 11th Canadian Artillery—and I'd do it for Canada again. Most of the Italians here are completely faithful to Canada." Ralph deGirolamo, nearly 38 years a resident of Nelson, asserted: "I never thought Mussolini would do it. He talked a lot, but I never thought he would help Germany. I've got a boy. If he should be needed to fight for Canada I won't hold him back for one minute." From D. Maglio's family came an expression of deep sorrow that Italy had thrown in its lot with Germany, and a declaration of

loyalty to the British Empire. "Our family has been here over 40 years," they said. "Our hearts are here." Angelo Vulcano wished vehemently that "somebody would give it to Mussolini, the bum." He declared, "The working people don't want to fight."

The government proclaimed that all persons over the age of 16 of German or Italian origin who had become British subjects by naturalization since September 1, 1922, must register. Registrations were to be made at Trail at the Provincial Police office.

The war was not the only interest of Nelsonites during that first year of the war. Even under increasingly dark clouds, life went on. In May 1940 the city celebrated two technological advances. Through the fundraising efforts of students, citizens, teachers and the school board, a moving-picture projector and sound machine were purchased for the junior high school and demonstrated to the Junior Chamber of Commerce. And there was another war going on—the apparently unwinnable fight against poliomyelitis. When an outbreak of scarlet fever threatened Nelson's children, parents were filled with dread that it might be polio. The big war momentarily took second place. At a special ceremony attended by 250 citizens, two iron lungs, one for an adult and the other for a baby, were presented to the Kootenay Lake General Hospital by Mayor Stibbs. "At a time when men are bending every effort on machines to deal death and destruction in war, it is a fine thing to have an event like this occur," declared Hospital Board Chairman J.B. Gray, who was to lose two sons in the war.[13] Long-standing interests such as fishing were not forgotten. C.F. Kearns, the game branch inspector, announced that Kootenay Lake's fishing was the best in North America. "There are Rainbows elsewhere," he said, "but they are larger and better fighters in this lake."[14]

The war, however, was the consuming interest and its support came from every corner of the community. The Great Depression had left few financial reserves available on the homefront, but individuals and community groups had resources of energy and determination just waiting to be tapped. In Nelson the response was "total mobilization." On July 20 the *Nelson Daily News* published a feature article outlining the multiple war activities in the city. "On dozens of home fronts—in the kitchen, the parlor, in work rooms and in work shops, in offices and factories—Nelson folk are marshalling their funds and the labor of their hands and hearts to aid Canada's war effort," it pronounced. The list of activities covered a whole page of the newspaper.

One of the first organizations to spring into action was The Women's Auxiliary to the 111th Field Battery. It had been formed before war broke out and was composed of wives, mothers, other relatives, and sweethearts of enlisted men. It later enlarged its scope and name to Women's Auxiliary to the Active Forces (WA). With a mission "to supply all comforts and needs to the boys overseas and to relieve distress of families of servicemen at home," it set about shipping socks (with cigarettes tucked in) to the boys in England, and barrels of apples to the men of the 111th Battery in training at Edmonton. "Knitting needles clicked incessantly" and "tag days" were held to raise money for more wool. The WA also sent Christmas parcels to each Nelson and district man overseas. Like so many organizations, it raised funds for War Savings Certificates or other war-related causes through public teas at Lakeside Park and private teas in members' homes, through bake sales and card parties.

Church organizations of all denominations were busy knitting and sewing as well as fundraising. The St. Paul's United Church Boys' Choir donated the proceeds from a concert to the Refugee Fund, and the Catholic Women's League offered to take refugee children into their homes. Both the Salvation Army and the Knights of Columbus raised funds for army huts, to be used for recreation and comfort for servicemen training in Canada and in England. The First Presbyterian Church Women's Association was later to "adopt" two soldiers overseas with whom they corresponded and supplied with packages from home.

The Red Cross Society, whose ranks swelled with volunteers, played a leading role in homefront activities. Supplies for servicemen and women, civilians and hospitals were prepared by women who worked daily to assemble "V" Bundles, which were shipped to the Vancouver headquarters. Many district auxiliaries were also formed at small communities surrounding Nelson: Willow Point, South Slocan, Blewett, Bonnington, Sheep Creek, Salmo, Ymir, Thrums, Queens Bay, Procter, Balfour, Sunshine Bay and Longbeach. Women organized themselves into knitting and sewing groups with names such as the Spitfires. Mrs. M. Brattle, one of the most active members at the "V" Bundles headquarters in Vancouver, told *The Family Herald and Weekly Star* that Nelson was the most patriotic town in BC. She stated that she heard almost every woman in Nelson sewed for the "V" Bundles or was engaged in some sort of patriotic work. Citizens donated some of their handiwork to the Red Cross Shop, opened in 1940, with sales going to the war effort. Among the contributors were elementary school children, who donated articles they had made in J.M. Morley's woodworking classes at Central School.

Another very active organization was the Kokanee Chapter of the IODE (Imperial Order of the Daughters of the Empire), a Canadian women's service club, which in early 1940 collected money for the National Bomber Fund's purchase of a plane for the air force. The women took part in the sewing activities for servicemen and refugees, and sent books and magazines to men on active service. In 1940 the Nelson Women's Institute concentrated its war effort on "the preparation of comforts" for the Women's Auxiliary Territorial Service, in which 40,000 women were serving in Great Britain. There was a pressing need for stockings, scarves, gloves, bedsocks, bedjackets, sweaters and cushions.

Members of the Rotary Club, Gyros and Kinsmen set up competitions among the clubs to sell the largest number of War Savings Stamps and Certificates. The Kinsmen concentrated their main efforts on a "Milk for Britain" campaign, and raised funds through tag days, bingo evenings, and the popular *Kinauctions of the Air*, where donations from local citizens and businesses were auctioned off over the local radio station, CKLN.

The wartime activities of many other organizations were detailed in the newspaper article of July 20. These included the Junior Chamber of Commerce, whose entire membership volunteered to assist with the national registration of men and women; the Soroptimists, who were supporting a War Ambulance Fund; the Joymakers and Eagles Lodge, whose whist drives and dances supported a Cigarette Fund for servicemen; the Finnish Relief Committee and the Norwegian Civilian Relief Committee, who were providing help to the Red Cross; the Board of Trade, which took a leading part in the promotion of War Savings Stamps and Certificates. The Nelson Graduate Nurses Association taught home nursing courses, rolled bandages and prepared dressings for the Disaster Relief Committee of the Red Cross.

The first concerted fundraising effort by the Nelson district was the Bomber Fund drive in mid-1940. Donations to the fund were still coming in when on October 9 a cheque for $5,166.98 was cabled to "The Rt. Hon. Winston Churchill." An accompanying letter read: "Please accept this gift as an expression of the loyalty and confidence of the people of the City of Nelson and District, British Columbia. It is their desire that it be made available to Lord Beaverbrook to aid in the purchase of military aircraft as he sees fit." The cheque was signed by the fund trustees, R.A. Peebles, F.F. Payne and E.S. Planta.

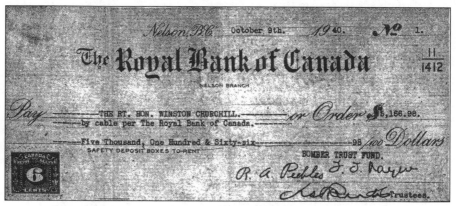

Cheque sent to Winston Churchill from the people of Nelson and district, 1940

The financial contribution to the war effort by Nelson's young people was not only in the purchase of War Savings Stamps through the schools. The Junior Girls' War League was busily engaged in knitting wristlets, socks and hot water bottle covers. Two of the girls raised funds by renting out their bicycles, "a real sacrifice during the fine weather," and two others were cutting lawns. A candy sale to support the IODE War Fund netted $9.00. "The girls are anxious and eager to do anything to contribute to the war effort," said the League's sponsor, Mrs. J.H. Argyle. The Nelson Boy Scouts and the 32nd IODE Company of Girl Guides worked as ushers at patriotic concerts and programs, and were acting as messengers for the Red Cross. The Nelson Girl Guide company took part in a week in May that was set aside as a "Guide Gift Week," in which Guides past and present throughout the British Empire gave a half day's salary (or the equivalent) toward the purchase of a motor life boat and an air ambulance service, including the first specially constructed ambulance aircraft to be used by the Royal Air Force during the war. In charge of the local campaign was Mrs. W.C. Motley of Bonnington, who was to lose a son in the Royal Canadian Naval Volunteer Reserve.

One 14-year-old contributed to the war effort in a novel way. Alan Ramsden, who had a hobby of making exploding devices by following instructions in the *Encyclopaedia Britannica*, came up with an idea for an aerial bomb using infrared guidance, which he sent off to the Government Inventions Board in Ottawa. The local newspaper interviewed him:

> Well, I just sorta had an idea it might work, so I talked it over with Mr. Chamberlain [his science teacher at the junior high school] and he thought I should go ahead. So when I went home I made a drawing and sent it to Ottawa. Gee, wouldn't it be swell if it worked out!"[15]

Young Alan got into trouble for granting an interview about his highly sensitive invention which had interested the inventions board, so nothing else was to appear in the press about it until after the war. In fact, Alan later learned that the idea had been taken up by General Electric in the United States and developed into a bomb-dropping mechanism called the "Mickey Mouse."

A number of local orchestras, dance bands and choirs donated their services for fundraising events. Nelson's two theatres raised almost $1,000 when they charged admission by War Savings Stamps. There were benefit softball, baseball and lacrosse games. This was a community campaign; everyone who had something to give, gave it to the cause. By the end of 1940 the Nelson district had collected over a half million dollars from its various fundraising campaigns. The popular CBC radio program *Carry On, Canada* made specific mention of Nelson's "magnificent achievement" in its broadcast of October 20, 1940.

Members of the Canadian Legion who raised money to support the gifts of cigarettes they made to each recruit as he left from the Nelson train station, also offered assistance to dependents of enlisted men. Another contribution of the Legion was the collection of field glasses from citizens for the Department of National Defence, a glaring indication of how unready Canada was to go to war.

Unreadiness was not confined to Canada, however. In the late summer and autumn the Battle of Britain filled the sky above England. At one point every plane that the RAF could fly was in the air; there were no reserves of either aircraft or pilots. This near-disaster spurred on plans for one of the timeliest activities of the war—the British Commonwealth Air Training Plan, with schools established on the Canadian Prairies and in Ontario. In all, 131,553 airmen were to graduate from the program, some 73,000 of them Canadians.

Five of the men listed on the Nelson Cenotaph from World War II died on home soil while in the service, somewhere in Canada, either from accident or illness. The first of these was 27-year-old *Private Terence Butler "Harry" Rowley*, who was serving with the Canadian Scottish Regiment, 2nd Battalion, when he died on October 4, 1940, from injuries suffered in an accident on BC's Island Highway. He was riding in the sidecar of an army motorcycle when it collided with a car. Harry, who had worked as a labourer in Nelson in the late '30s, had been in the service for only two and one-half months. He left a wife and three children as well as his parents in his hometown of Iffley, Saskatchewan.

1941

CHAPTER TWO

Germany responds to British and Australian successes in North Africa by sending its crack Afrika Korps under General Rommel, who manages to push the Allied forces back into Egypt. Germany is victorious in Yugoslavia and Greece. In June Hitler begins his invasion of the USSR, but the drive towards Leningrad and Moscow is halted by the Russian winter. Britain and the United States swap bases for ships under the American Lend-Lease Act and President Roosevelt and Prime Minister Churchill announce their joint opposition to fascism in the Atlantic Charter, effectively ending American neutrality. U-boat successes against Atlantic convoys increase and Britain is desperate for food and supplies. Mass bombing raids continue on British cities. The war becomes truly global when, on December 7, Japan attacks the US naval base at Pearl Harbor, and American and British bases in Siam, Malaya and the Philippines. In support of its Axis ally, Germany declares war on the United States. Canada declares war on Japan and sends raw recruits of the Royal Rifles of Canada and the Winnipeg Grenadiers to Hong Kong, where they face well-trained and equipped Japanese forces in December, resulting in 290 Canadians killed and 493 wounded and taken prisoner. Canada is on a full wartime footing, and has several Commonwealth Air Training Schools in operation. Roosevelt calls Canada "the aerodrome of democracy."

The Second World War was to bring new horrors to warfare, but it was no different from other wars in that it inflamed and consumed the young, and coloured the lives of a generation forever. Boys barely out of high school joined up in their thousands. Phyllis (Gray) Gautschi, the sister of two young Nelson boys who were killed overseas, described how her brothers and others who went with them "left smiling, laughing and eager. They were all young men going off to save the world."[16] The average age of the young men from the Nelson district who lost their lives was 25, meaning that the average age at enlistment would have been at least a year or two younger. Many had younger brothers and sisters still in school and likely to join them in the services later. In February 1941, RCAF recruiting officers visited Nelson and interviewed 50 Nelson district men, among them 20 senior high school students.

Daphne (Rhode) Wilson, who was a Nelson High School student during those early years of the war, has described how the war brought excitement and romance to girls in their teens:

> It was very exciting to be in a war. It was only 21 years since the end of the Great War. Many of our fathers had fought in the Great War and we had grown up hearing stories of bravery in the trenches, had memorized *In Flanders Fields* and had sold poppies on Armistice Day. Our school library had a book [about] "Count Luckner, the Sea Devil," a famous German naval captain who had sunk a record number of Allied ships. He made the chasing and sinking of submarines seem like an international sport. We read the translation of the German novel *All Quiet on the Western Front* and saw its movie, where our Brave Boys and their Brave Boys came out of the trenches on Christmas Eve to sing *Silent Night* and fraternize together before resuming the war the next morning. *It was so romantic!* Black and white movies didn't show red blood.... The boys in grade ten were too young to join up and "get in the fun." They envied their older brothers who were rushing to join the air force and the navy before they got their call at 18 for military conscription in the army. Young men in uniform began to appear on the streets of Nelson. It was so exciting![17]

The Nelson High School annual, *Mountaineer*, reflected how the war was at the forefront of students' minds and activities. An editorial summarized "Our War Effort":

> Since the beginning of the war, we, the students of Nelson High School have done as much as we can to help the Allied war effort. It is our duty to do as much as we can, however little that may be. The Red Cross and cadet activities have met with considerable success while the inter-division War Saving Stamp race has had admirable results.... The usual Monday morning flag exercises

have been held each week. For St. George's Day our flag exercises were postponed until Thursday so that a patriotic program could be presented. Participants in the program were Mona Scott who recited, Bob Wilson who spoke on "St. George's Day" and the renowned NHS orchestra which, under the direction of Miss Cottingham, played *Land of Hope and Glory* and *There'll Always Be an England*. Such things may seem small when mentioned as "our war effort" but if it is our best it is creditable.... We hope that future students may equal and surpass our efforts as long as such activities are necessary in our school. We trust that it will not be too long.[18]

An item in the 1941 annual was typical of how the war was predominant. It had the title "Patriotic Menu":

Chungking's Young Men's Club kept up with modern times at a recent dinner party by serving this menu: Bomb Splinters (Hors d'oeuvres), Japan in the Bog (Thick Soup), Albanian Entanglements (Italian spaghetti), Ghandi Gives Up Hunger Strike (Indian Curried Chickens).

In both the junior high and high schools, boys, and later girls, signed up in large numbers for the cadets; in the 1941–42 school year well over 100 students had joined. Instruction was carried out by teachers as well as officers from the local Veterans Guard. The training included shooting practice at the Legion Hall, courses in small arms, field craft, scouting, map reading and guerilla tactics. During the warmer weather there were weekly parades and rifle drills, often held during regular physical education periods. The cadets were included in many patriotic civic ceremonies, along with the Junior High School Bugle Band.

In April Nelson became the sixth BC community to participate in the War Emergency Training Plan. Men ranging in age from 18 to 54 (excluding 21-year-olds, who were the first to be called for army training) attended classes in electronics, mechanics and metal work at the junior high school, under the instruction of B.B. Clark and A.J. Cornish. Once they had completed the course, the men were subject to a call to any part of the country where their skills were needed in war industries.

On a daily basis people were reading in the newspaper and hearing on the radio about the bombing raids against British cities and the threat of an imminent invasion by German forces. They read about the damage inflicted on such famous and beloved London landmarks as the British

Museum, Berkeley Square, Buckingham Palace and Westminster Abbey. Letters from loved ones stationed in Britain often told of the bombing, the destruction, and the stoicism of the British people. A five-year-old child evacuee from England had arrived in Nelson to live with her aunt and uncle, and the local newspaper told the poignant story of how she had pointed to concrete remains of a zinc refinery near Lakeside Park and exclaimed, "Look, Auntie, there's an air raid shelter."[19]

Nelsonites came out in force on April 23, St. George's Day, to show their support for the battered British people. Businesses and schools, even beer parlors, closed in the afternoon so citizens could take part in a "monster parade" through the city to Lakeside Park, where a ceremony of "Salute to Britain" took place. Train whistles and the Fire Hall bell rang at 1:30 to call people to the centre of town to begin the parade, led by the Veterans Guard, the Women's Training Corps, Canadian Legion, school cadets, Salvation Army Guards, Pythian Sisters and their auxiliary Nomads of Avrudaka, Graduate Nurses, and students from five Nelson schools. Seven bands took part and "special parade units" included a Chinese group and a number of "New Canadians" in costume.

The high school annual for 1941 listed 38 Nelson High School alumni who were in active service at the time, among them five who would not survive the war. One of these was **_Sergeant Henry Percival "Hank" Hartridge_**, a pilot with RAF 21 Squadron. In their Blenheim IV bombers, the squadron played a prominent part in the offensive against enemy shipping in the English Channel, the North Sea and German installations on the Continent. Only 21 years of age, Hank was an acting squadron leader when he set out on July 23 on a mission over occupied Holland. The air correspondent for _The Daily Mail_ described it as "one of the most daring and successful daylight attacks ever made by the RAF."[20]

> Reconnaissance pilots had picked out a large concentration of shipping in Rotterdam harbour, chief supply port for garrisons in Hitler's occupied territories. They made detailed reports as to the positions of all ships. It was decided to "get them" at all costs, and several squadrons of Blenheims crossed the Dutch coast about tea-time on Wednesday. As they flew over the coast in a victory "V" formation Dutch people cheered them. Debris from one ship flew high into the air; two supply ships, each 4,000 tons,

Sergeant Henry "Hank" Hartridge
Photos courtesy of Florence Hartridge

blew up and the flames licked high above the diving Blenheims.... Besides the 17 ships put out of action, five more totalling between 40,000 and 45,000 tons were severely damaged. On land two warehouses and a factory were left burning fiercely.

The Daily Mail correspondent described the feat of a Canadian flyer, later identified as Henry Hartridge, who was killed in this operation:

It was wonderful flying. The Canadian captain of one machine flew between a high wireless aerial on the quayside and the mast of the 17,000 ton Rotterdamsche Lloyd liner *Baloeran* [which had been taken over by the German Navy]. The liner received direct hits, one bomb falling right between the funnels.

His plane was hit as it gained altitude. The crew bailed out, but were hit by gunfire as they were coming down in their parachutes.

Henry Hartridge was born in Murree, India, in 1919. The family moved to his parents' native England, where they lived until 1929 when they immigrated to Canada. They resided for a short while in Crawford Bay on the east side of Kootenay Lake, and settled finally in Balfour, 20 miles along the lake from Nelson. In a memorial page of the Nelson High School's annual for 1942, Hank was described as "an all-round athlete, well known for his proficiency in boxing, hockey, swimming and lacrosse." He held a parchment certificate from the Royal Canadian Humane Association, awarded to him and two other young men for saving four lives on the lake. While at a beach party in Balfour they had heard cries across the water and had rowed out with a flashlight to find and rescue four women whose boat had filled and overturned as they were rowing from Procter to Balfour.

After graduating from Nelson High in 1939, Hank was working in the Gold Belt Mine at Sheep Creek when he enlisted in the RCAF in June 1940. He was one of the earliest recruits from the Nelson district, and was among the first to arrive overseas. He had received his wings only five months before he was killed in combat. Only a short while before he was reported missing he had sent his father, a captain in the First World War, photos of Piccadilly Circus and Trafalgar Square in order to disprove German claims of damage from the Blitz to these two famous London landmarks.

The first anniversary of Henry's death was to be marked by a solemn high requiem mass at the Cathedral of Mary Immaculate in Nelson, conducted by the Redemptorist fathers. A mountain behind Procter, just a few miles from Balfour, has been named Hartridge Mountain in his memory.

A Nelson man was among the Canadian soldiers who took part in an early, successful commando raid in August 1941. A combined force of Canadian and Norwegian infantry and British commandos carried out *Operation Gauntlet* on the Norwegian island of Spitsbergen, some 600 miles south of the North Pole. The object of the raid was to destroy the rich Soviet-owned coal mines to keep them from German hands and to evacuate the population. Lance Corporal William Swain of Nelson was one of the hand-picked men of the 2nd Canadian Infantry Brigade who took part in the raid, which succeeded in destroying the mines and coal and oil stocks, and in evacuating the Russian miners and the Norwegian population. A veteran of the First World War, William Swain had left Nelson for Edmonton with the 111th Battery in 1939, and was among the first Canadians to arrive in Britain. Shortly after this operation he was re-posted to duties in Canada.

Nelson was widely known for its community spirit and enterprise, as Bruce Hutchison had pointed out. Gary Bowell, a veteran of the war who grew up in Nelson, recalls many community projects during the 1920s and '30s which brought together service clubs, church groups and school children in a special cause. During the 1930s, for instance, several churches organized work parties of young people to pick and pack apples at a fruit farm and packing plant at Balfour, to ship the apples as a gift to Prairie communities especially hard hit by the Depression. Service clubs routinely banded together to provide fun for the kids at such events as a Hallowe'en Jamboree at the Ball Park (featuring greasy pig, greasy pole and pie-eating contests) and, as I recall, day-long celebrations on Dominion Day, culminating in a community picnic at Lakeside Park. It is no surprise, then, that this spirit should come to the fore during the crisis years of war.

Men in the services, particularly airmen, whether local boys or not, captured the hearts of Nelson's citizens. A novel program Nelson introduced to the war effort was an organized plan of entertaining servicemen on leave from the Commonwealth Air Training Schools, established in mid-1940. The program got underway in April 1941 after a Nelson boy in the RCAF brought some of his chums home for a short holiday. "The vacation was so successful the public-minded citizens saw the opportunity for the major war effort which they had sought so long."[21] The program was truly a community effort. Taking part in the original organizing meeting, led by Mrs. George Lambert, were the Nelson City Council, eleven ladies' organizations and six men's organizations. Widely publicized by the RCAF, the program was to be copied by other Canadian communities.

In September 1941 the CBC radio program *Carry On, Canada* paid high tribute to Nelson for its program of entertaining airmen on leave from their training stations on the Prairies. The text read, in part:

> Here is a story of war industry new and quite unique. It comes to *Carry On, Canada* from Nelson, in British Columbia, the Queen City of the Kootenays. Nelson is a serene and lovely place, far removed from signs of war. It possesses no war industry as we know the term. No ships are built in Nelson, no forges clang and clatter as some weapon or munition of war is beaten into shape. But it has its own particular surprise. The citizens of Nelson are fighting the war by giving holidays worth having to the Empire's fighting men. Not long ago they had a weekend party for 40 airmen from Australia.... There is a citizens' committee which has a list of all those persons willing to take the boys from the nearest Commonwealth Plan training depots into their homes when they get leave. There is community entertainment, trips to places of interest, dances, and picnics. There are NO formal functions and NO speechmaking. Nelson's war industry builds morale. Canada expects, and Nelson fulfils. Carry on![22]

Author Frederick Niven, who resided in Nelson, described the program for the Glasgow *Herald*:

> The Air Force uniform takes them free of charge on the street car, into movie theatres, into badminton courts, skating rink or curling rink, and to a performance at the theatre. When their leave is over their hosts and hostesses go down to the station to see them off, a well-filled lunch box is handed to each man to save the dining car costs on the way back to the training camps. Not so much as a nickel or dime need they spend while guests here unless they want to, but the citizens don't want them to. "Your money is no good here," I have heard remarked to more than one who wanted to play host on an outing.[23]

Anzac Airmen on Leave in Nelson Parade into Town from the CPR Station
Nelson Daily News, April 26, 1941

The program continued throughout the war. Typically, the airmen were met at the station by their hosts and hostesses, and were paraded through town behind the Junior High School Bugle Band to the Legion Hall, where they registered. Mayor Stibbs would deliver a welcoming address before they went off with their billets for a few days' rest and recreation, often at summer homes and cottages along the warm, sandy beaches of Kootenay Lake. I remember one young New Zealand airman who was billeted at a neighbouring summer cottage, who spent his leave, led by me, his seven-year-old guide, searching in the reeds and amid the rocks of the shoreline for snakes, which he claimed were unknown in New Zealand.

British and Anzac airmen often spent their Christmas and New Year's leaves with Nelson families. They enjoyed skating at the Civic Centre, skiing and sledding on the mountainous Nelson Golf & Country Club course, New Year's parties and dances, and presentations in their honour by the Nelson Little Theatre. Many of the airmen spent more than one leave in Nelson, and some, like New Zealand airman George Penniket, married a Nelson girl. Airmen who arrived in Nelson by accident were

Commonwealth Airman Weds Nelson Girl

Nelson's program of entertaining airmen on leave resulted in some marriages, such as that of New Zealand airman George Penniket and Nelson girl Dawn Sharp.

Photo courtesy Dawn and George Penniket

also welcomed and roundly entertained. In October 1941 two RCAF Stranraer Flying Boats, en route from eastern Canada to the Pacific Coast, made emergency landings on the arm of Kootenay Lake, about six miles from Nelson, and tied up at Lakeside Park and Walton's boat houses. During their short stay the crews were given free admission to facilities and were taken to a dance at the popular Playmor Dance Hall, 13 miles from the city.

The Nelson newspaper recorded many letters of thanks from the airmen. In a letter to Mrs. George Lambert and E.A. Mann, who co-chaired the organizing body for the program, the Nelson Citizens Committee, the commanding officer of the Air Training School at Medicine Hat wrote: "Never in my years of command of a unit has any city come forward with the outstretched hands of hospitality as that of the City of Nelson."[24] In January 1942 an eight-piece orchestra from the school at Medicine Hat arrived in Nelson to "play for the entertainment of citizens on any occasion desired." A letter explained: "It is hoped to make some small repayment for what Nelson has done for the men."

In October 1941 recruitment began for Nelson's new Reserve

Army unit, No. 17 Platoon of the 2nd Battalion, Rocky Mountain Rangers. The Rangers were a historic BC unit, dating back to the Northwest Rebellion in 1885, and had served in both the Boer War and World War I. Recruits for the Nelson platoon were sworn in by Lieutenant Colonel D. Philpot, officer commanding the Kootenay units of the Rangers. Platoon commander was Lieutenant C.H. Hamilton. Men between the ages of 18 and 50 in good physical condition were eligible to join.

Patriotism was running high, and with the war going so badly for the Allies throughout 1941, many men, both young and old, were anxious to "do their bit." There are many stories of boys sneaking into the ranks before their 18th birthday, and of men trying more than once to meet the physical requirements of enlistment. On September 6, 1941, the *Daily News* reported the determined effort of James Dawson, a Nelson street-car conductor and veteran of the Great War:

> A sergeant in the 111th (Nelson) Field Battery during the years it operated as a non-permanent militia unit, he was declared unfit when the battery mobilized at the outbreak of the war and had to drop out. Subsequently he tried to enlist but again was declared unfit. Mr. Dawson determined then that if it was possible he would make himself fit. A former holder of the British Army swimming championship and always a swimmer, he turned to Kootenay Lake. Daily, for the past two months he has taken a 600-yard swim—300 yards from Lakeside Park, westward toward the City Wharf, and 300 yards back against the current. When he appeared again for medical examination, he passed with flying colours.

The collection and creation of items for the "V" Bundles became evermore urgent with news of war refugees and the homeless survivors of the Blitz. The Nelson Centre of the National Committee on Refugees was in full swing in 1941 and, together with Red Cross volunteers, sewed, mended and repaired items sent in by citizens from all over the district, and sorted and packed them for shipment overseas. In the last two months of 1941 alone the Refugee Committee shipped out 1,500 pounds of articles.

The *Nelson Daily News* recorded many stories of citizens doing what they could to help the war effort. The issue of February 19, 1941, related the contribution of one Nelson couple:

> Too old to fight, but not to serve—Mr. and Mrs. John Russell, elderly Granite Road couple, knitting side by side since December 1939, have turned in over 190 pairs of sox to the Nelson Red

Cross Society. At present the couple are turning out about four
pairs of finely knitted sox every week. Some months ago Mrs.
Russell enclosed a note in a pair of sox and the sox bearing the
note ultimately reached a sailor in West Hartlepool, England, who
sent a letter acknowledging receipt of the sox....

In the same month Mrs. McHardy of the IODE spoke of the fine
contributions of Nelson's women:

All women want to be able to do more and many of them envy the
sturdy women of Greece who are carrying stones to the mountain
tops for their men to roll down on the enemy. Lacking that kind
of opportunity, the women of Nelson could help in the sale of
War Savings Stamps.[25]

Satenig Papazian, an orphan of the Armenian massacre of 1915 and
adopted by a Nelson family, had joined the Canadian Women's Training
Corps. But wanting to do even more to end this war, she spent almost all
her savings on Victory Bonds.

Victory Loan campaigns, which had proved such a potent source
of funding for World War I, were inaugurated in May 1941. The first
campaign was to raise over three-quarters of a million dollars from the
Nelson district, and eight more campaigns in the war years would each
raise close to a million dollars or more. The value of those eight million
dollars raised from Nelson and smaller neighbouring communities
(Salmo, Sheep Creek, Kaslo, Nakusp, New Denver and Slocan), which
had just emerged from the Depression years, can be appreciated when
one reads an advertisement for New Year's dinner in 1941 at Nelson's
Star Cafe. The price for the dinner was 75 cents for adults and 50 cents
for children.

And the Victory Loan drives were only one of many fundraising
campaigns that citizens were called upon to support. The campaign
to sell War Savings Stamps and Certificates was ongoing. In February
1941 a dramatic opening for a major drive, called "Hammer Hitler and
Mussolini," was planned for the centre of town. Effigies of the two were
to be paraded through town in coffins to the corner of Ward and Baker
Streets. There, by the purchase of War Savings Stamps, people could drive
nails into the coffins. At the end of the day the effigies would be burned.
For some reason, unexplained in the local newspaper, the event was
replaced by a "Sing the Dictators Down" program at the Civic Theatre,
where some 500 people joined in a community sing-song of patriotic

Hors D'oeuvres
Crisp Celery, Ripe Olives, Head Lettuce,
Salted Almonds, Fresh Fruit Cocktail,
Hot House Tomatoes, Strawberry Punch

Soup
Consomme Brunoise, Chicken a la Monaco

Fish
Boiled Fraser River Fillet of Salmon, Sauce Nantaise

Salad
Combination Vegetables

Sweet Entree
Peche Beignets au Nadere

Boiled
Young Capon, Sauce Toulouse

Entrees
Filet de Mignon, Maperty; English Mutton Chops;
Rasher of Bacon;
Fried Spring Chicken, Unjointed Maryland

Joints
Prime Rib of Beef, horseradish;
Domestic Duck, sauce pomme;
Stuffed Young Turkey, cranberry jelly

Vegetables
Steamed or mashed potatoes, green peas

Desserts
New Year's Pudding, hard sauce; Vanilla ice cream;
Apple, hot mince or pumpkin pie;
Fancy fresh fruits; Fruit cake; Assorted nuts

Tea, Coffee, Milk, Cocoa

Menu for Star Café's 1941 New Year's Dinner

and religious songs, interspersed with inspirational messages.

In the same campaign a "Klondyke Night Gold Rush" was held in the Civic Centre, where the medium of exchange was War Savings Stamps. A stamp was the cost of admission and stamps were the prizes for the many games. In one game a dollar of "Klondyke money" purchased a supply of "hand grenades" to hurl at a dodging Adolf Hitler (played by Alderman H.H. Hinnitt) or Benito Mussolini (played by Bill Freno). Like most of Nelson's war efforts, this was truly a community event. The IODE had charge of the barbecue stand, Red Cross girls served the sandwiches, the Soroptimists operated a bar of soft drinks, the Gyro Club kept the crown-and-anchor wheel turning, the Junior Chamber of Commerce operated a "hilarious housie-housie" booth (a British Army name for Bingo), and the Kinsmen, assisted by the Boy Scouts, sold the "grenades." The Rotary club operated a "jitney dance" where dancers paid with "Klondyke" stamps per dance. There were two orchestras: Mickey McEwen's Old Timers in Klondike regalia and the Harrison Brothers played "old time numbers". Decorations were by the Nelson Fire Department, and the mayor pulled the winning raffle ticket.

Clearly, Nelson had a flair for the dramatic during the war years. As part of the War Savings Stamps campaign that February, the city staged a demonstration blackout, "the first in Western Canada and the third in Canada." It brought nation-wide publicity to Nelson's war effort. Hundreds of people gathered downtown to experience complete darkness. At 9:30 on that night sirens wailed their warning and the Nelson platoon of the Veterans Guard, headed by piper and drummer, marched through the business section of town. The *Daily News* described the drama: "When the lights came on again a public address system rang out the song that has gripped millions in the past few months, *There'll Always Be An England*." At the Civic Theatre, C.B. Garland, spotlighted by a flashlight as he stood on the stage, told the audience that the blackout was "symbolic of the lights of Europe being extinguished by the foul cloud of Nazi terrorism and conquest."[26]

The goal of the district's war savings efforts was to collect enough each month to purchase two universal gun carriers, worth about $5,000 each. In November a gun carrier was exhibited at the corner of Baker and Ward Streets, in the heart of downtown. Hundreds of children and a number of adults had the exciting chance to ride in the carrier as it was paraded to

Nelson Blackout

Tomorrow, Friday Evening, 9:15-10:15

EACH RESIDENT in City and surrounding District to black out their premises and shut off all outside lights.

Business Firms and Merchants to turn off all lights in warehouses and stores including Neon signs and turn on again after "all clear" has been sounded.

Keep autos off the streets except when absolutely necessary. If you must drive, screen car lights except for ¼x3-inch vertical slots and do not exceed 15 miles per hour.

Everyone urged to stay off the street, avoid using the phone except in emergency from 9 till 10:30 p.m. and cooperate to the full with the Wardens all of whom carry their credential cards.

Essential services will be maintained, such as Street Cars, Power for heating, cooking, refrigeration, etc., and places of amusement will be open as usual.

The wholehearted assistance of everybody in making this a real test will be appreciated and help considerably in perfecting further plans for dealing with this great and imminent danger.

BLACKOUT SIGNAL—5 blasts (3 times) of C.P.R. whistle and sirens.

ALL CLEAR—3 blasts (3 times) of C.P.R. whistle and sirens.

H. E. Thain, Chief A. R. P. Warden

Announcement in the *Nelson Daily News*

the Recreation Grounds several blocks away. Every effort was being made to make everyone feel closer to the war that was raging so far away.

It did not seem quite so far away when on December 7 the Japanese bombed Pearl Harbor. A Nelson boy, Bob Crerar, was a survivor of the attack. He had joined the United States Navy to take medical training after he graduated from Nelson High School. Shortly before the attack, he had been on leave in Nelson when he was recalled by telegram to report back to base in California. At the time of the attack he was a pharmacist mate on a warship in the harbour. Bob told his story in a letter to the Nelson High School Red Cross Committee:

I was in the midst of all but the first few minutes of the attack... and I didn't get a scratch. Don't think the attack was a raid in the sense that the enemy flew high overhead and dropped their bombs and flew away again—it was not so easy as that. They came in low, dropped their bombs on specific objects and then returned to machine gun the defenders on the ground.... My greatest impression was the shock of being plunged in a twinkling from the peace and calm of a Sunday morning into the midst of a pitched battle.... I was on my feet continuously from Sunday morning…until Tuesday afternoon—on our second day at sea looking for the enemy. Those three days seemed to be a bad dream from which I will awaken.[27]

Bob was to survive the war, including action on Guadalcanal.

The Japanese attack spurred on home defence activities in British Columbia. The day after Pearl Harbor, Nelson's Air Raid Precaution Committee (ARP) and the Civilian Protection Corps began preparing for a possible attack. Plans were made with the schools for evacuation of children in the event of a daylight raid. Householders were told they must have a box of dry sand on hand at all times to be used in smothering incendiary bombs, and they "should be prepared in an alert to start filling bathtubs, kettles, pots and pans, buckets and tubs with water to be used in fighting fires if water mains were broken." The Nelson Red Cross began plans to receive evacuees from Trail in the event of an attack on that neighbouring industrial city, and the Nelson City Council urged provincial and federal governments to designate the Kootenay district from Trail to Kimberley a vulnerable area in which blackout regulations could be enforced.

1942

CHAPTER THREE

Japanese forces sweep through the Pacific, winning major battles in Singapore, the Philippines, the Solomon Islands and Burma. In June the US Navy wins the Battle of Midway, effectively ending Japanese eastward expansion. Canadians of Japanese origin are removed from the West Coast to internment camps in the BC Interior, Alberta and Ontario. The Alaska Highway is built. Canadians vote three to one for conscription, but Prime Minister Mackenzie King promises "conscription if necessary, but not necessarily conscription." In August 5,000 Canadian troops and 1,000 British commandos raid the French port of Dieppe; about 60 percent of the men who reach the shore are killed, wounded or captured. On the Russian front the Battle of Stalingrad begins. In North Africa, Montgomery's forces defeat Rommel's Afrika Korps at El Alamein and retake Tobruk. Submarine warfare is at its peak in the North Atlantic with disastrous losses in men and ships; 46 percent of all Allied tonnage sunk in the war is lost in 1942. The Royal Canadian Navy responds with increased convoy patrols. Destroyers, minesweepers and corvettes, many built in Canada, begin to make a formidable antisubmarine force.

Early in 1942 Nelson was to lose another of her vibrant young men to the war. He was *John Balfour Gray, Jr.*, the younger son of a prominent Nelson jeweller and watchmaker. Jack was a flight sergeant with the RCAF, flying as a wireless operator / air gunner with RAF 144 Squadron. At 3:00 a.m. on February 27 his Hampden I bomber was returning from a mine-laying operation over the Kiel Canal in the Elbe Estuary when the aircraft ran out of fuel. It crashed into a railway crossing near Hexthorpe in the southern outskirts of Doncaster,

Yorkshire, near their home airfield, killing all four crew members. Jack was thrown from the aircraft and died on impact. He had turned 21 six days earlier.

Jack Gray was the first overseas casualty of the war to reside within the city limits of Nelson. He was born in Trail, BC but grew up in Nelson. Jack was nicknamed Bull-Dog or J.B. in high school, and at six feet two was a popular young athlete, starring with the high school's Blue Bombers basketball team. He also excelled at hockey and lacrosse. He had a "cheery, mischievous nature," and as his mother said of her two boys, Jack was "more apt to be stirring up the fireworks." In fact, the story goes that Jack was the last student to be given the strap in the old Nelson High School, and that punishment was meted out by a teacher who was the sister of Jack Campbell, the young airman from Willow Point who was lost in 1940.[28] A verse in the high-school annual for 1939 suggested how Jack was vulnerable to "detentions":

Our friend Jack Gray has quite a line
Especially when teacher gives him "time."

Jack joined the RCAF immediately after graduating from high school in June 1940. He was the first Nelson airman to graduate from the Commonwealth Air Training program, and he sailed for Britain in April 1941on the SS *Georgic*, the last liner built by the White Star Line, in a convoy escorted by HMS *Rodney*. He was thrilled to be seeing his father's native land for the first time, and wrote home enthusiastically about the adventure of crossing the Atlantic:

It was really a thrilling sight when we went up on deck, to see green hills of Scotland about which I had heard so much. No fooling Dad, I really fell in love with Scotland right from the first. It was a beautiful spring day when we first saw land.... The voyage across was quite uneventful and smooth. We saw no submarines and if we had I need not say that we were well protected.... We had second class quarters as the first class were for officers. The bunks are not bad although when the mighty Atlantic gets rough you toss about like a cart. It was amazing to see the other troop ships bounding around in the heavy seas while the battleship hardly wavers.... There were all sorts of new things which I had never seen—such things as whales blowing and porpoises roaring and playing about.[29]

According to a buddy of Jack's who was with him in training and on the same ship across the Atlantic, the young airmen spent most of the long voyage shooting craps.

Jack wrote admiringly about the spirit of the British people, and the welcome they gave to the servicemen from overseas.

> Soon after we got ashore we boarded a train. The next six hours were the most pleasant I ever spent on a train. The trains, as you know, are not the same as ours but have little compartments seating about six—I like them. The first city we came to was Glasgow and the trip from [censored] to there was a revelation to me. All the way people were out waving and cheering us on—and they did mean it. The people here know there is a war on. I hate to say it but I have never seen anything like it in all my time in Canada. I felt like cheering myself when I saw these women and men in Glasgow standing by ruined homes but still waving us on.

He wrote also about life during the Blitz in London and witnessing its devastation:

> I have been in London twice already now. It is a wonderful experience to see all these places about which we have heard so much. It is impossible to imagine the size of London until you have been there. We are 15 miles from the heart of London yet you can see no spot that isn't jammed with houses all the way. London at night is something too. There are a few weak lights around to guide you but when an alarm sounds it becomes pitch black there. It is queer when you think of being in the heart of a big city yet there is not a light to be seen. The Piccadilly Circus used to be an absolute blaze of lights but not one is to be seen now.... You never saw anything like the spirit of the people here. They just laugh and say he will get it all back and then some. It looks as though, to me, that the Nazis care little what they bomb as there are wrecked buildings all over London. Another thing that amazes me is the way they clean everything up after a raid. Buildings which have been ruined are cleaned up and fenced off—it is really amazing. It would do a lot of people in Canada good to see London in an air raid—they would know then what we are fighting a war for.

Jack's close friend, Flying Officer Henry "Harry" Humphries, recalled the wireless air gunner training they received together at Oxbridge in 1941, while the Battle of Britain raged.[30] Many of the men were "washed out" by air sickness, although they did little flying—"not more than twenty hours." Partly because of the changeable weather, the Hampden planes in which they were training suffered many accidents. "The undercarriage would burst into flames on touchdown. Every other week we were on funeral parade." There were 16 Canadians in their training group, fellows who had been together from the start. But because they became notorious for going AWOL while on leave in London, each of them was eventually assigned to different squadrons—a form of punishment for their misbehaviour. Jack spent his last Christmas in Edinburgh, on leave with his buddy Harry Humphries. Every day they visited the Castle, and would stop in at pubs to play darts all the way back to their lodgings at the George Hotel on Princes Street.

In 1941 they had both been in a documentary film, *Target For Tonight*, which received a special Academy Award certificate "for its vivid and dramatic presentation of the heroism of the RAF." Made at Elstree Studios, the film follows one crew in the planning and execution of an actual bombing raid over Germany. Harry Humphries remembered that "every night they gave us a pound. That was beer money." The documentary was shown as a main feature and was seen by an estimated 50 million people in North America alone, where its popularity was a propaganda coup, especially for the Victory Bonds campaign. Jack Gray was prominent in one of the promotional posters made for the film. In Nelson the film was shown in December 1941, just two months before Jack was killed.

Jack had a flair for life that was evident in his letters. He was anxious to share his adventures with the folks at home, and to report his meetings with fellow Nelson servicemen. He wrote about spending his first night on British soil at a canteen with Davy MacDonald, a Nelson boy with the Canadian Forestry Corps, who eventually came home from the war, and of meeting Jim Hughes, also of the Forestry Corps, who did not return.

The Gray family was very close. Jack's older brother Hampton, or Hammy as he was called, was in the Royal Canadian Naval Volunteer Reserve in the Fleet Air Arm and was also stationed in Britain. The two brothers were able to meet occasionally, the first time shortly after Jack arrived overseas. He wrote to his parents:

> I wrote [Hampton] a letter as soon as I got to London. Next I went to Canada House and learned his whereabouts. Of course on learning he was only 30 miles from London...I got on a train

and went there. I was sitting in the mess having a cup of tea when he came in. It was wonderful meeting so far from home.... Boy, I'm sure proud of my brother now. He had about 45 hours in the air but the real thing is to have a brother who is a pilot in the Fleet Air Arm. Those fellows have to be really good.... He still has lots of work ahead before he gets his wings but I am sure he will. Hope to get up to see him again.

The last time they met was in January 1942, about a month before Jack was killed. The telegram from his father telling of Jack's death was misdirected and reached Hampton after the funeral in Doncaster had taken place. Hammy visited Jack's grave in Yorkshire on more than one occasion. He wrote to his parents on his first visit about how the grave was "covered with turf and was tidy and neat. There was a card on top which I presume had been with some flowers 'from the Officers and NCOs of 144 Squadron.'" Later he wrote, "Jack's grave…is with a fairly large group of service graves and they all have nice white crosses up and a few flowers on each one."[31] Hammy was to lose his life three years later, and although he had no white cross to mark his grave, the Victoria Cross that he won would bring him many more memorials.

Jack's father, J.B. Gray, was broadcasting a speech over Radio CKLN advocating the purchase of Victory Bonds only hours before he received the telegram announcing the death of his younger son. He spoke of a young man's "great decision to enlist and fight for the defence of his country and the protection of the dear ones he left at home."

It [motivation] may spring from the spirit of adventure which caused our forefathers to sail the seas and seek new lands and new opportunities. Or we can imagine that somewhere within the heart of these young men there is a stirring of a spirit that has come down to him from generations of men who in the past gave their all in the fight for freedom.[32]

At every turn citizens were being bombarded by requests to support fundraising campaigns for the war. New causes were constantly emerging and Saturday "tag days" on the corners of Baker Street were weekly events. There was the Bomber Fund, the Army Huts Fund, the War Ambulance Fund, the Cigarette Fund, the Refugee Fund, Canadian Aid to Russia Fund, and the Greek Relief Fund. In Nelson, Dorothy Todd was organizing a local branch of the International Dorothy Spitfire

CANADIAN PACIFIC
TELEGRAPHS
World Wide Communications

CANADIAN PACIFIC COMMUNICATIONS
STANDARD TIME INDICATED

C.D. 13

W.D.NEIL, General Manager of Communications Montreal

3 VR B 68/67 VIA CABLE BGOVT COML

GLOUCESTER FEB 28 1010A

IMPORTANT PRIORITY
   MR GRAY,
      815 BAKER ST,
      NELSON BC

DEEPLY REGRET TO INFORM YOU THAT YOUR SON CAN/R58225 FLIGHT SERGEANT
JOHN BALFOUR GRAY IS REPORTED TO HAVE LOST HIS LIFE IN ACTION NEAR
WARMSWORTH DONCASTER YORKSHIRE ON 27TH FEBRUARY 1942 LETTER CONFIRMING
THIS CABLEGRAM AND GIVING ALL AVAILABLE INFORMATION FOLLOWS THE AIR
COUNCIL EXPRESS THEIR PROFOUND SYMPATHY AIR OFFICER IN CHIEF RCAF OVERSEAS
0358.   R C A F RECORD OFFICE GLOUCESTER

4.15 AM
Come on Canada! — Buy the New Victory Bonds

BUCKINGHAM PALACE

The Queen and I offer you our heartfelt sympathy in your great sorrow.

We pray that your country's gratitude for a life so nobly given in its service may bring you some measure of consolation.

George R.I.

John Balfour Gray, an Early Nelson Casualty

Left top: Jack Gray (front row left) on the set of the Academy Award–winning documentary, *Target For Tonight*. Beside him is his buddy, Harry Humphries.

Left bottom: The telegram received by Mr. and Mrs. J.B. Gray telling of their son Jack's death in February 1942.

Above: The letter of condolence from the King.

All, courtesy of Phyllis Gautschi

The Funeral of Flight Sergeant Jack Gray and one of his Crewmates
A bleak February day of 1942, in Doncaster, Yorkshire.
Photo courtesy of Phyllis Gautschi

Fund for women with the first name of Dorothy; its purpose was to raise money for fighter planes.

In May 1942 the newly-formed Kinette Club, wives of the Kinsmen, staged a novel fundraising event in support of the Kinsmen's ongoing "Milk for Britain" campaign—an Air Raid Shelter Tea, in the basement of Wait's News Stand in the centre of town. My mother, Agnes Shorthouse, was one of the organizers. I remember advertising the event along the main street of town, wearing a sandwich board in the shape of a milk bottle. Since I was only five years old I had to peer around the sides of the milk bottle to see where I was going. Sand bags were piled up around the door to the tea, sirens sounded, and a recording of exploding bombs simulated the experience of a real air raid. Miniature sand bags were distributed, with a lucky number for a door prize. While the patrons made their contributions to the Milk for Britain Fund and sipped their tea, they watched first-aid demonstrations. According to my mother, the realism was too much for one elderly woman: she fainted and was carried out on the demonstration stretcher.

It was not only in their pocketbooks that people were feeling the effects of the war at home. In March the federal Wartime Prices and Trade Board, which had been set up in 1939, established an office in Nelson on Baker Street, their mandate being to enforce the prices and rationing regulations that were imposed, "not to persecute and prosecute, but to help the Canadian public" avoid inflation and war profiteering. Sugar was the first food staple to be rationed, along with alcohol, and that was followed shortly by tea, coffee and butter. Ration application forms for all residents were collected throughout the city, and in June women volunteers took over the library at Central School and worked in three shifts to make out ration cards for each applicant. Frugality was the order of the day. Volunteers were told to bring filled fountain pens. Daphne Wilson recalled how liquor rationing was a boon to some Nelsonites:

> You had to apply for a permit, which allowed two bottles of liquor per month. The local taxi companies all ran a lucrative bootleg business, borrowing permits for two dollars a bottle. I sold my permit plus my mother's to the bootleggers and used the money to buy hard-to-come-by towels, sheeting and blankets from Eatons catalogue whenever they became available. By the end of the war I had quite a stash.[33]

In March 1942 restrictions were put on the sale and purchase of tires. People who were in an "eligible class," such as doctors, nurses and policemen, were allowed to buy a new tire and tube if a used set was turned in. Others must "get by" on the best used tires and tubes they could find. New cars could not be purchased for private use. In April restrictions on gasoline began, and the public street railway system in Nelson became more popular than ever. The annual gas allowance was 120 gallons. Gas stations could be open between 7 a.m. and 7 p.m. on weekdays, but closed from 7 p.m. on Saturday until Monday morning. And taxi drivers faced a fine for driving more than 15 miles beyond the city limits.

Brass and bronze articles, such as doorbells, nameplates, hat and coat hooks, were banned. Between sundown and sunrise no verandah lights, neon and other illuminated signs were allowed, including the big illuminated clock on the Medical Arts Building in the centre of town. Only street lighting was permitted.

Restrictions extended to clothing as well. In January 1942 the Wartime Prices and Trade Board announced that the manufacture of corsets, girdles and other articles made of all-elastic was banned. "Regulations completely changed the look of fashion, banning certain design elements that took lots of cloth, such as French cuffs. 'Frills and furbelows' were out, replaced by slim, spartan designs."[34] On March 5 the *Nelson Daily News* announced:

> Double breasted suit coats and Norfolk jackets will be a thing of the past when strict clothing regulations designed to conserve Canadian wool and textile supplies, come into effect. Men's vests, sometimes colourful and sometimes ornate in the past, will be conservative. The back strap on vests, the inside breast pocket and special pencil pocket will disappear. The ornamental buttons on suit coat sleeves will be limited to one.

Cosmetics were affected also. Lipstick, rouge and face powder were to be manufactured in four shades only, and nail polish shades would be reduced from as many as 23 to 6. Silk was needed for parachutes, so silk stockings became unavailable. Women painted their legs and drew seams with eyebrow pencil.

Nelson's bakers agreed to "cut out frills" in their products and to cut down on bread wrapping. Bread deliveries were reduced to three days a week; it was pointed out that fewer deliveries would "reduce the unhealthy habit of eating bread fresh from the oven." Meat rationing and price controls were to begin a year later, and "Meatless Tuesdays" were enforced in restaurants, hotels and institutions other than work camps and hospitals. Once tea and coffee were added to the rationing list, one cup per sitting was the rule for restaurants. There were even regulations governing the amount of ice cream that could be served in a cone, and the size of milk shakes.

In 1941 the government had launched the National Salvage Campaign, with slogans such as "Dig In and Dig Out the Scrap," and "Get Into the Scrap." When the call went out for scrap metal, Nelson was quick to respond:

> Old German guns from the last war which have decorated the boulevard on Vernon St.... for some years are soon to go into the scrap pot and be melted down for making munitions to be turned against the enemy.[35]

Newspaper stories throughout the war reported the success of various salvage campaigns. School children were among the enthusiastic workers and prolific collectors. In May 1942 members of the Veterans Guard and

Wartime Restrictions

When tea and coffee were rationed in August 1942, restaurants were not allowed to serve a second cup. *Cartoon by Charles Knight, courtesy of* Windsor Star

the Junior High School Cadet Corps sorted and packed bottles from the Red Cross bottle drive. In June Central School won the cup donated by Fire Chief G.A. MacDonald and jeweller E.E. Collinson for the greatest quantity of rubber and aluminum collected per capita in a school salvage competition. The newspaper reported that Central School had turned in close to 3,000 pounds of rubber; St. Joseph's Academy, the local Catholic school, came in second, with 925 pounds, but its grades 3-4 and 5-6 classes led all other grades in the city in individual class returns.

Salvage drives were spurred on by a press release from the Department of Munitions in Ottawa, stating that enough steel could be salvaged from an old car to make 25 heavy machine guns. An editorial in the *Nelson Daily News* estimated that "based on that calculation, the 400 derelict cars in Nelson's dump could produce 10,000 machine guns."[36] The Red Cross, church organizations, service clubs, veterans' groups and school children all took part in the salvage efforts. They collected pots and pans, glass, old batteries, bones and fat, rubber, tin foil from cigarette packages, and scrap paper by the ton.

For young children like myself growing up in those years, war was the natural condition. When there was talk of the war coming to an end in 1945 it seemed logical that news broadcasts would come to an end as well. The predominant theme of everything was war: toys and board games such as "Blitz" and "Flying Aces," comic books in black and white that featured Johnny Canuck and caricatures of the merciless German and Japanese enemy. My brother collected comic books that were mini-biographies of the Allied leaders: Churchill, Roosevelt, Chiang Kai-shek and de Gaulle. "Big-Little books" featured corner pictures that when flipped showed diving Spitfires. Making balsa models of fighters and bombers was a popular hobby of the boys. Instead of baseball cards, cigarette packages had warplane cards. One favourite Christmas toy in my family was a toy battleship, spring-loaded so that if the torpedo shot by the accompanying submarine hit the target, the battleship would explode into several pieces; my brother added a thumbtack to the torpedo to give it more heft. Candy was in short supply, chocolate bars were generally unavailable, and grocery stores sold soybean spread instead of peanut butter. In school, children knitted khaki-coloured squares, ostensibly to be made into blankets, and in order to conserve paper, wrote in the margins of their notebooks when the pages were full. The Junior Red Cross group hand-hemmed dozens of "ugly khaki handkerchiefs for servicemen." We

HOUSEHOLDERS! *THESE ARE YOUR*

WAR WEAPONS

Save them, Give them, and help WIN THIS WAR

We cannot **all** march into battle—but **we can** march into the attics, the cellars and store-away places in our homes.

There are war weapons in these places—and in your household waste, which can be turned into a valuable contribution to Canada's war production and into funds for war auxiliary services.

Many local volunteer organizations have already completed plans for a Salvage Campaign in their districts. More will follow. Quickly, we hope, all Canada will be organized to "**clean out** and **clean up** on Hitler"!

Every day of **every** week until this war is won, **every scrap of material** which can be profitably salvaged in the area in which you live must be saved, collected and turned into war production material and money.

A careful study and survey is being made throughout Canada by this Department as to the type and class of salvage which will realize the greatest return in your community. If this information is not now in the hands of your local Salvage Committee or your Municipal Council, have them communicate with the Supervisor, National Salvage Campaign, New Supreme Court Building, Ottawa.

The complete facilities of the Department are at the disposal of local community organizations to aid in making their Salvage Campaigns a success.

When the Campaign starts in **your** community, we ask that you give it your unqualified support.

EVERY SCRAP COUNTS

* Put Them Out Carefully
* They Will Be Collected
* They Will Be Used

Issued by authority of Honourable James G. Gardiner, Minister

DEPARTMENT OF NATIONAL WAR SERVICES

An Advertisement in the *Nelson Daily News*, 1942

kids played a lot of commando games and watched a lot of movies where the bad guys were Germans. In the 1929 musical *The Desert Song* the villains had been Arabs; in the 1940s version they were Nazis. Even the dance reviews and Nelson Skating Club carnivals had war themes. In our tap-dancing debut my brother and I did a military number to *Anchors Aweigh*. Dozens of Nelson children performed regularly in the annual skating carnivals; in 1942 the theme was "St. George and the Dragon," an allegorical story of the ultimate triumph of outraged Britannia and her allies over the Hitler Dragon.

Special ceremonies were conducted in Nelson's public schools to stress how each family must contribute to the Victory Loan campaign. On February 16, 1942, at the start of the second Victory Loan drive, Central School pupils were told:

> Mighty enemies, strong and swift and cruel, are trying to come nearer to our country; to pull down our flag, tear it in shreds and trample it in the mud. Brave men have gone from this city, from all over Canada and the British Empire, to stop that enemy. You know some of the men—fathers of some, brothers of some, and friends. They are fighting hard, long battles, holding on as best they can.

Their parents were to pledge themselves anew to the war effort a few days later on February 25, during a special ceremony that began with "Beacons of Freedom" being lit across the country, province by province. Due to inclement weather the Nelson ceremony was conducted over radio CKLN with citizens tuning in to participate in the pledge:

> With the message of this Beacon Fire of Freedom burning in my heart, I hereby solemnly re-affirm my belief in Almighty God and again declare my loyalty and allegiance to His Majesty the King. I pledge myself to do all in my power to support all undertakings to insure victory for our arms and a just and lasting peace.

The Nelson High School annual in 1942 was dedicated to one of the teachers, Flying Officer Gerald H. Lee, who had left in 1941 to join the RCAF and eventually was put in charge of air-sea rescue for the west coast. He was to return after the war and become principal of the school. Among other NHS teachers who left in 1942 for the armed forces were James Fraser and Derek Tye. They too returned home. In the summer 50 Nelson cadets from the junior and senior high schools attended a two-week training camp at Vernon, with teachers Roy Temple and Floyd

Fund-raising Cartoons

Cartoons urging the sale of War Savings Stamps and Victory Bonds ran regularly in the *Nelson Daily News. Cartoon by Jack Boothe, courtesy of* Vancouver Province

Irwin in charge. Among the cadets at camp that summer was Jim Hoover, who was to lose his life in Holland three years later.

In late June 1942 the city observed Army Week with a parade "three blocks long," led by the Kootenay Kiltie Band, the Junior High School Cadet Corps Bugle Band and Salvation Army Band. They were followed by members of the Veterans Guard, Rocky Mountain Rangers, the Canadian Legion, the Girl Guides, Boy Scouts and Cubs, and the Nelson detachment of the Canadian Women's Training Corps (CWTC), led by Major Winnifred Kinahan. Various stores on the main street had special window displays for Army Week, and a Drumhead Service was held at Lakeside Park, where Reverend H. Stewart Forbes spoke of the three requisites of heroism—"great thinking, high associations, and deep devotion." Rev. Forbes had lost a son in the merchant navy a few months earlier.

The summer months brought more tragic news to the Nelson community. In a two-week period of late June and early July three Nelson district young men were to lose their lives overseas.

The first was *Pilot Officer Francis Larry Flynn*, age 26, who lived in the Vallican-Passmore area of the Slocan Valley. Larry was with the #1651 Conversion Unit of the RCAF, which was a tutoring unit for crews of the Stirling bomber. During an air operation on June 26 his aircraft went missing and was never found. Larry was the only Canadian in his crew. He was raised in Lethbridge along with his brother Ralph, who was also with the RCAF and who survived the war. Larry joined the RCAF in January 1941 and went overseas the same year. The previous November he had been among servicemen who sent messages home from Britain over CBC radio. Like the thousands of young Commonwealth airmen who have no known grave, his name is engraved on the Runnymede Memorial at Englefield Green in Surrey, 24 miles west of London. Of the 3,050 names of Canadian airmen on the memorial, six of them are also commemorated on the Nelson Cenotaph.

A second casualty that summer was a young man, described by one of his high-school classmates and fellow airman as "the all-Canadian boy." *Pilot Officer Richard Sydney "Syd" Horswill* was with the RCAF's #14 Advanced Flying School stationed in the Midlands of England. On July 2 his crew of three was on a wind-speed and direction-finding exercise when their Oxford aircraft broke up in midair and crashed near the railway station at Carlton on Trent in Nottinghamshire. Syd and his English and New Zealand crewmates were all killed. He was 24 years old.

Born in Hedley, BC, Syd attended school at Naramata and Penticton before moving with his family to Nelson when he was nine years old. He was a natural leader and excelled as a musician, an athlete and a scholar. His death was front-page news in Nelson and his obituary in the *Daily News* on July 4 summarized his many talents:

> ...in junior high school he was a member of the Student Council and took part in dramatics, in high school was a member of the debating team, elected president of House B, was chairman of the School Sports Committee, was a successful track competitor, captain of the basketball team, coach of the girls' basketball team, a member of the school's Music Club, was chosen to represent the Nelson district among Empire youths at the coronation of King George VI, and won the Willingdon Prize in an Empire-wide essay-writing competition.

Pilot Officer Syd Horswill
Photo courtesy of Phyllis Gautschi

Outside of school Syd was especially known for his beautiful singing voice. He had early training as a member of the St. Paul's United Church Boys' Choir under Mrs. Amy Ferguson, as did many of the young men who took part in the war. He often was a soloist in local concerts and church services, and in 1940 travelled with the choir to Vancouver to compete in the BC Music Festival. That year the choir featured a senior quartet in which he took part with his close friend, Leonard Stewart, who was to lose his life in Europe nine months later. He sang also with school choirs and the St. Saviour's Anglican Choir, and was a winner in both solo and duet classes at Kootenay Music Festivals.

Obviously Syd was enthusiastic about life and joined in school and community activities with boundless energy. He was also known as a prime athlete. Outside of school he played lacrosse, rugby, hockey and badminton, and carried off many prizes for diving and swimming at Kootenay regattas. He was a popular leader among the students. When he left for England to represent the Nelson district at the coronation of King George VI and to claim his prize in the Empire-wide essay-writing contest, he was given a grand send-off by his high school classmates, who paraded him to the CPR station. In the summers he attended Camp Koolaree on the west arm of Kootenay Lake, along with hundreds of other Kootenay kids, and they had elected him "Big Chief." During that summer of 1942 Camp Koolaree flew its flags at half mast in his honour. Dawn Penniket, who attended high school with Syd, remembers, "He was a leader all through school. Well liked—the girls all were mad about him."

As a freshman student at the University of British Columbia, Syd won critical praise for his performance of "Captain Corcoran" in the Musical Society's presentation of *HMS Pinafore*. It was while he was at UBC that he joined the RCAF and won his wings at the Commonwealth Air Training School at Claresholm, Alberta. Twice during his training he headed his class, winning a gold bracelet at an early stage, and heading the class on graduation. A few days after winning his wings, in January 1942, Syd married a Nelson girl, Margaret "Peggy" Gibbon at St. Saviour's Pro-Cathedral. They were to be married only four months before Syd left for overseas duty. Peggy, who also joined the air force, was to lose a brother as well as a husband to the war.

Just a week after news of Syd Horswill's death was received, Nelson residents learned that another of the city's promising young men had fallen. *Lieutenant Robert Clifton "Clifford" Craufurd*, age 28, was serving with the Royal Canadian Engineers, 18th Field Company, when on July 9 he died of wounds, presumably from an accident, in Britain. At the time his company was stationed at Battle, East Sussex, near Hastings.

Cliff was born in Nelson in 1913 and attended Central elementary, junior high and high schools there. While in high school he often represented the school in oratorical contest with other Kootenay schools. The NHS *Mountaineer* for 1927 records how he was a member of the winning team in answer to a challenge from the Kaslo High School Literary Society, to debate whether or not physical education should be part of the school curriculum. He was a popular entertainer with his classmates, and also in the community when he sang comic songs with his father, Leslie. Cliff won a scholarship to take his final year of high school at Upper Canada College in Toronto. From there he entered the University of Toronto and graduated with a Bachelor of Science degree in chemical engineering. He worked as a supervising chemist for Proctor & Gamble in Hamilton, and there too he was a popular entertainer and song leader at factory social functions. Shortly after war was declared, Cliff joined a militia unit and soon went on active service with a commission as lieutenant in the Royal Canadian Engineers. He had been overseas about a year before he was killed.

The country went into shock and mourning when it gradually became clear that the first battle of the war in Europe involving large numbers of Canadian troops had resulted in disaster. Of the 6,000 servicemen who raided the port of Dieppe on August 19, 1942, 5,000 were Canadians. Over 900 were killed and 1,800 were taken prisoner. Only 236 of the men who made it back to British shores had not suffered wounds. There were no Nelson district men among the fatalities, but there were some who took part and survived. These included Gunner Bryan Ryley and Captain George Wallach, who made it back to England. Gerald McEwan Ross, Elmer "Lefty" White and Fred Makaroff were among those taken prisoner by the Germans, and spent three years in captivity. Three Nelson sisters, Alma Smith, Mrs. Leslie Bealby and Mrs. Ivan Lewis, lost a brother at Dieppe, Private Leonard Smith of Chelan, Saskatchewan.

In February 1942, in the wake of the attack on Pearl Harbor, the Canadian government had invoked the *War Measures Act* to uproot and relocate thousands of Japanese, most of them Canadian citizens, from their homes on the Pacific Coast. Their houses, fishing boats, businesses, cars, even cameras and radios were confiscated. Many internment camps were built in the West Kootenays, at Slocan City, New Denver, Kaslo, Lemon Creek, Roseberry and the ghost town of Sandon. The CPR brought the Japanese-Canadian families to Nelson en route to internment camps in the Slocan Valley. Some were ferried from Nelson by sternwheeler up the arm of the lake to Kaslo.

That first harsh Kootenay winter was especially desperate for the internees, some of whom were forced to live in tents until enough houses could be constructed. The houses, built without insulation, were occupied by sometimes as many as ten families, sharing a single stove. There are stories of people putting lanterns under their beds to try to keep warm, and of icicles hanging from the ceiling. It was the Doukhobors who farmed in the Slocan Valley and along the Kootenay River who came to the rescue of the Japanese-Canadians in the winter and spring of 1942. They brought wagon loads of fresh vegetables, a dietary staple for the Japanese-Canadians, before the internees were able to grow their own. As a young child, BC geneticist David Suzuki was interned with his family in Slocan City. In his autobiography he describes that winter:

> A world war was raging, and for everyone in Canada there was rationing and sacrifice. But we were considered enemy aliens, and fresh food was even less easy to come by in remote areas like Slocan. The people who saved us from malnutrition were the Doukhobors. They…came into town with wagonloads of fresh vegetables and meat…. My father always speaks gratefully of the Doukhobors because they were friends of the Japanese-Canadians.[37]

Local businesses in the Nelson area profited from the relocation of the Japanese-Canadians: suppliers of foodstuffs and all manner of consumer goods, as well as lumber mills and contractors involved in the construction of hundreds of houses. Although the internees were treated with suspicion and racial prejudice by some of the locals, there was also admiration for how well they managed to survive their harsh conditions. My father owned a meat market in Slocan City which he periodically visited. I must have been only six or seven (actually the same age as David Suzuki) when I accompanied my father on one of his visits, and I recall how impressed he was with the hard-working Japanese-Canadian people. As we walked along a row of small houses he pointed out to me that they were the cleanest people he had ever seen, even scrubbing their front steps.

While the war brought personal tragedy to many Nelson citizens, it also brought economic prosperity. As one Nelson journalist of the time wrote,

"...the war effort spreads through the district like roots of a tree.".... Mines of other years have been re-opened, mills re-built, and an increasing flow of lead and zinc concentrates is moving to United States smelters.... Lumbering's part is evidenced by trainloads of forest products.... Spruce for airplane veneers made at Vancouver; cottonwood for locally-made veneers that find a hundred war uses; spruce lumber and cottonwood for wartime packaging; cedar poles for power lines in place of steel; lumber for Alaska Highway construction, for barracks, internment camps and wartime housing—this is the picture of West Kootenay lumbering in wartime. Increased railway traffic has resulted in expansion of shop facilities at Nelson, a CPR divisional point....[38]

The mining industry close by was booming in the Ymir–Sheep Creek area and in the Ainsworth, Slocan and Lardeau areas. Wholesale firms were settling in Nelson and industries such as iron works, a soap factory, a shipyard and sawmills had located there. The city boasted more than 260 retail outlets. Over 90 mills were operating. A match block factory was producing the pine for about 90 percent of the matches manufactured in eastern Canada. There were two jam factories operating at full capacity, and in September 1942 the McDonald Jam Factory received an order for 6,000 cases of jam for the crews building the Alaska Highway.

As the war raged on, manpower was becoming more of an issue. In late 1942 it was announced that married men between the ages of 19 and 25 were to become subject to compulsory military service, and 17-year-olds would be permitted to join the army with the consent of parents or guardians, allowing more time for basic training.

The British had been recruiting women for the armed forces since 1938, but it was not until 1941 that the Canadian government followed suit. In July 1941 the Royal Canadian Air Force Women's Division (WD) had been established, followed a month later by the Canadian Women's Army Corps (CWAC). Recruitment advertisements emphasized how each woman in the CWAC "relieved a man for active service," while the motto of the Air Force Women's Division was "They Serve that Men May Fly." Airwomen replaced men in aircraft maintenance, on desks and in meteorological services. They packed parachutes, took aerial surveys and plotted air manoeuvres. The women in the Women's Army Corps or CWAC performed a full range of tasks.

Naturally, they were assigned traditional duties (laundry, household chores, cooking, sewing). Those who had some inclination for the stage took part in shows prepared for the troops, such as the Canadian Army Show. They were also assigned clerical work, and many served at the National Defence HQ in Ottawa. Women served in health and communications services as well. They were medical assistants, dental assistants, switchboard operators, radar operators, cipher clerks. And others found themselves in traditionally male jobs: driving cars, trucks, ambulances, as mechanics, or radar operators.[39]

It was not until almost a year later that the Women's Royal Canadian Naval Service (WRCNS or Wrens) was founded. The story goes that the Royal Canadian Navy (RCN), presumably knowing how valuable the British Wrens were to the Royal Navy, sent a signal to the British Admiralty with the urgent request, "Please send us a mother Wren." The response from the Canadian government was the creation of the WRCNS in the spring of 1942. Many Wrens were stationed at Halifax, where thousands of sailors and merchant seamen came and went. Among them was Margaret Colley of Balfour, a member of the *Nelson Daily News* editorial staff before joining the service. She worked with many other Wrens as a "writer" or "supply assistant," handling all the paperwork for the service, the leave papers, draft forms, transportation chits, and other myriad service documents that kept the navy going.

Canadian servicewomen were stationed also in the United States, to work as stenographers and file clerks in Canadian Armed Forces liaison offices there. Corporal Edythe Thomson, described as "one of the outstanding women mining experts of the world,"[40] was assigned to the RCAF Financial Liaison Office at the British Air Commission in New York, its purpose being to facilitate movement of needed war materials to Great Britain. She had worked in a metallurgical laboratory in Nelson and for 16 years had been secretary of the Chamber of Mines of Eastern British Columbia. Now she worked as a stenographer.

Dozens of young Nelson women joined the forces and many served overseas. Among the first to enlist in the Air Force WD were Jill Wigg (later Blakeney) and Peggy (Gibbon) Horswill (later McLeod), who served in England. Jill rose in rank from private to flight sergeant during her three years overseas, and was to be awarded the British Empire Medal for meritorious service. Peggy's sister, Leading Wren Ruby Gibbon, served in Halifax and later in London with the RCN Communications Branch as a coder/teletype operator. Life was not entirely war-related for the servicewomen overseas. Ruby Gibbon joined a group of Wrens in taking a Canadian Legion–sponsored course at Oxford University on the life of Shakespeare.

Mary Soles of Sunshine Bay was the first woman from the Kootenays to enlist in the Canadian Women's Army Corps. She signed up in 1941 as a telephone operator and served for a time at the Signal Centre in Vancouver before going overseas in 1943, where her son, Kenneth, was serving with the RCAF. In 1940 a Nelson unit of the Canadian Women's Training Corps (CWTC) had been organized under Major Winnifred Kinahan and Captain Dora Perasso, in which the women were taught first aid and motor mechanics, skills that would be needed in a local emergency. Many of the members went on to join the active forces. Jessie Harrop, the first CWTC member to join the Women's Army Corps, was given a ceremonial send-off with a parade through town and farewell wishes from the mayor. By July 1943 all three Scott-Lauder girls of Queens Bay were to be sergeants in the armed forces, Esme in the CWAC, and Joan and Sybil in the RCAF.

Canadian Nursing Sisters had served in wars since the Northwest Rebellion in 1885. In May 1942 Canadian nurses became the first in any Allied country to receive officer status. Thousands served close to the battlefields in Europe. The first Nelson nurse to go overseas on war service was Elizabeth Stewart, who served with the Red Cross. Another former Nelson nurse at Kootenay Lake General Hospital (KLGH), Muriel Ahier, was one of the first Canadian nurses to serve in the Middle East. During the Blitz, Kitty (Johnstone) Ridley, Nelson native and award-winning graduate of KLGH, was lady superintendent of a Fire Service and First Aid Red Cross post, with a mobile unit in London.

Private Charles Henry Lequereux, age 46, was the only member of the Veterans Guard of Canada to be listed on the Nelson Cenotaph. He died suddenly on October 30, 1942, presumably of natural causes, while on duty at Seebe, Alberta, acting as a guard at the internment camp built there in the foothills of the Rockies between Calgary and Banff. The camp was used first for alien internees and pacifists and later German officer personnel. A Swiss by birth, Charles served in World War I with the French army. He immigrated to Canada after the armistice and worked in the forest industry, first in Quebec and later in Cranbrook. He had made his home in Nelson since 1931. There were two other Nelson district men who were on active service with the Veterans Guard when they died in 1943, but whose names are not on the Nelson Cenotaph. *Private Theodore Benjamin Beninger*, age 55, a rancher at Perry Siding in the Slocan Valley, was stationed at Ross Barracks in Moose Jaw when he died suddenly on July 17, 1943. *Corporal William Brown*, age 50, a resident of Nelson, was on duty with the Veterans Guard at South Slocan when he died suddenly on September 18, 1943.

Nelson Unit of the Canadian Women's Training Corps in March 1941
Front row from left: Mary Talbot, Margaret Morrow, Mrs. Eric Ramsden, Jill Wigg, Satenig Papazian; **Second row:** Greta Curwen, Mrs. O.G. Gallaher, Lieutenant Dora Perasso, Mrs. J.C. Muir, Marian Bradshaw; **Back row:** Winnifred Kinahan, Jessie Harrop, Mrs. E.C. Hutchinson, Jean Burgess. *Photo courtesy of Nelson Museum*

1943

CHAPTER FOUR

Even though losses on all fronts are very heavy, 1943 sees the war beginning to turn in favour of the Allies. German forces surrender at Stalingrad and also in North Africa. Losses by U-boat "wolf-packs" lessen attacks on Atlantic shipping. At the Casablanca Conference, Churchill and Roosevelt announce that the Allies will accept only "unconditional surrender." The Japanese navy is defeated at the Battle of the Bismarck Sea and the Americans re-take Guadalcanal. In Poland the Germans finally crush the uprising of inhabitants in the Warsaw Ghetto and kill thousands of Jews, sending the rest to die in concentration camps. "Canadianization" of squadrons in the RAF finally takes place in Coastal, Fighter and Bomber commands. No. 6 (RCAF) Group in Bomber Command, flying heavy-bomber night raids over Germany, sustains staggering losses. Between March and June alone, No. 6 Group loses more than 100 aircraft and crews. In July the 1ˢᵗ Canadian Division takes part in Operation Husky, the invasion of Sicily, and in September is part of Montgomery's 8ᵗʰ Army that invades Italy. Mussolini falls from power and the new government of Italy declares war on Germany. The Canadians fight fiercely against German defensive lines at the Sangro and Moro Rivers. After a week's vicious fighting, the 2ⁿᵈ Canadian Infantry Brigade captures Ortona; its losses are 1,372 killed. Production of war materials and ships escalates on the home front.

The fourth year of the war began in Nelson with servicemen at the centre of activities. One hundred visiting airmen took part in dozens of civic functions and private parties. Among them was a group of Norwegians who were feted by the Nelson Scandinavian Association at the Eagles Hall. On New Year's Day a hockey game between Nelson's Home Guard and a team composed of Nelson servicemen on leave drew the biggest crowd of the season. Among the players for the armed forces were John Dingwall and Harold Breeze, neither of whom would survive the war.

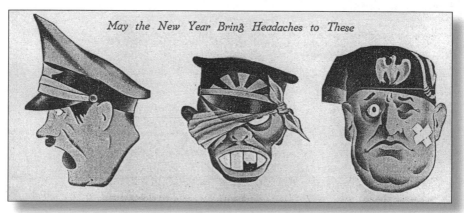

May the New Year Bring Headaches to These

New Year's Wish by the *Nelson Daily News*, New Year's Day Issue, 1943

In April 1943 personal tragedy struck again for the people of Nelson. On April 9 **Leonard James Stewart** went missing, presumed killed, when the Stirling aircraft he piloted was lost in a night raid over enemy territory. Flying Officer Stewart flew with the RAF's 7 Squadron, part of the Pathfinder Force that Bomber Command had assembled in August 1942. This force consisted of a *corps d'élite* of crews hand-picked for their high navigational ability. Their role was to precede the main bombing attack and light up a target area with incendiary fires. It is not surprising that Leonard Stewart should be picked for this strategic force. Twice during his RCAF training he had headed his class, and he received an engraved gold identification bracelet for topping the graduating class at the Flying Training School at Currie Field in Calgary.

Like his close boyhood friend, Syd Horswill, Len was a member of the critically acclaimed St. Paul's United Church Boys' Choir and was soloist in many concerts and church services. In fact, 65 of the Nelson boys who served in the war, and six who died, were members of Mrs. Amy Ferguson's remarkable choir.[41] The choir members formed a bond with their choir leader and with each other. At the choir's annual banquet in May 1941, both Len Stewart and Syd Horswill, about to leave for the RCAF, were honoured, and were presented with a Bible by choir member

Don Beattie, who was shortly to go off to war himself. Often, as the boys were leaving for military service, Mrs. Ferguson would slip them a note of encouragement. Many continued to write to her. In July 1941 while at an RCAF training camp at Edmonton, Len wrote to Mrs. Ferguson of the happy times he and his fellow choir members had spent at her home:

> I only wish we had some such place to go here but I'm afraid there is none just like it. But here's wishing you strength and inspiration to carry on with those lucky fellows in the choir....[42]

It was his last letter to Mrs. Ferguson. In September 1941 Syd Horswill had written his last letter to her as well:

> Dear Mrs. Ferguson. Greetings from Boundary Bay! I often think of the days when we would arrive en masse at your front door and be welcomed with a broad smile and a cheery greeting. Those were the days and I would love to be able to have just one evening around your piano with yourself, Mr. F., the choirboys and stacks and stacks of duets, quartets and solo arrangements. What a swell evening that would be! I really enjoy flying and I hope I am good enough to complete everything satisfactorily to the end. While I am up in the air above the cloud layers, I often think of that passage you told me about some French aviator writing about his emotions while soaring alone up in the blue heavens.... Len has completed his course at Sea Island and now has 48 hours leave.... Pass on a hearty greeting to the members of the swellest boys' choir in Canada.[43]

The boys of the choir were to pay a special tribute to Len Stewart in the choir's 21st anniversary booklet in 1952:

> To Leonard Stewart our boys have always put it "Hats off." We remember gratefully his untiring assistance with the young boys of the choir. He was our accompanist until he left to further his studies both at Normal and at UBC. His talents as a musician and also as a public speaker will long be remembered in St. Paul's. In him we saw the spirit of The Christ, translated into action.

Len was also active in sports throughout his school years in Nelson, as were most of the young men who served in the forces. He was attending the University of British Columbia when he enlisted in the RCAF in May 1941. His name is inscribed on the Runnymede Memorial, among the airmen with no known grave. He was 27 years old.

TOP ROW, Left to Right:
John Beattie,
John Dingwall,
Robert Ludlow

SECOND ROW, Left to Right:
Sydney Horswell,
Leonard Swewart.

THIRD ROW, Left to Right:
Walter Thompson,
Jerry Wallace.

Memorial Page for Nelson Choir Members
Six members of the St. Paul's United Church Boys' Choir were killed in the war. Actually, Walter Thompson, third row left, died in 1950. A total of 65 former choir members served in World War II. *Courtesy of Nelson Museum*

U-boat action in the North Atlantic took the life of another of Nelson's young airmen, who never made it to British shores. ***Pilot Officer Robert Stewart "Bert" Jardine*** was one of 37 RCAF officers lost at sea en route to overseas service. They were aboard the freighter MV *Amerika* when it was sunk by a German submarine on the night of April 22, 1943, in a blinding snowstorm. The freighter was positioned near the end of the convoy when it was torpedoed 12 miles south-east of Cape Farewell, Greenland. The captain of a Danish liner that witnessed the event described how "in a little more than a half hour nothing could be seen except wreckage and red lights indicating people swimming about in the water."[44] Sixteen of the 53 RCAF airmen aboard were rescued by a Royal Navy corvette after spending four frigid hours in a damaged lifeboat.

Bert Jardine was educated in Nelson schools and, according to the news story reporting his death, "was widely popular and a natural leader in sport activities." He played lacrosse, hockey and softball, and was a swimmer, a strong skater and a hunter. His sister, Winnifred Linville, recalls how he loved climbing the hills around Nelson, and each spring would bring home a bouquet of dog-tooth violets for his mother.[45] He left high school before graduating and joined the thousands of young men who rode the rails looking for work. He found work at the Trail smelter and later as a linotype operator at the *Nelson Daily News*. He enlisted in the RCAF in 1941. Bert's name is inscribed on a memorial in Ottawa commemorating airmen of the British Commonwealth who lost their lives while serving in units operating from bases in Canada, the British West Indies and the United States, or while in training in North America. Bert was 28 years old.

The need for manpower was growing ever more urgent. Since late in 1942, all women aged 20 to 24 were required to register with the National Selective Service for war work. In early 1943 the federal Department of Labour ordered men in specified occupations to register for transfer to essential war industry. Some of these occupations seem now to be somewhat surprising. For instance, café waiters, "regardless of nationality," were required to register by June 15. The newspaper reported that in May, nine Nelson men had registered under this "Compulsory Employment Transfer Order," and had been referred back to their present jobs until a call for their services was made.

Recruiting parties for the armed forces were again visiting high schools in the spring of 1943 to enlist both boys and girls who would be graduating at the end of June. The students could enlist immediately, and would be given leave until July in order to complete their education. In May a RCAF mobile recruiting unit visited Nelson and interviewed 12 young men who applied, only five of whom were accepted into the RCAF. There was a special need for women to serve as operations-room clerks, and six young Nelson women applied. The recruiters visited high-school senior classes and showed films depicting the work of ferrying planes and other activities of the Women's Division. A newspaper story outlined the recruitment requirements of the RCAF's WD:

> To qualify candidates must have senior matriculation and must be of high character and integrity, since the work is of a secret nature. They must be intelligent, alert and accurate, must not be highly strung nor nervous, must have good hearing and must have no impediments in their speech. New trades for women are aircraft helper, aircraft recognition instructor, and hairdresser.[46]

By the end of 1943 the Nelson district had sent nearly 1,000 men and women to the forces. The local Women's Auxiliary supplied each recruit with a special Christmas parcel.

The high school annual proudly announced that the Nelson Senior High Cadet Corps had become a branch of the services during the 1942–43 school year. They were now a unit in the Royal Canadian Army Cadets. There was great excitement when the new uniforms arrived in October 1943, followed by a steady flow of new pieces of equipment: field telephones, signalling lamps, pistols and gas masks.

Once again, the high school annual is peppered with war humour and war sentiment. One little verse referred to the disappearance during the war of silk stockings.

Farewell to Silk Hosiery
Farewell, dear silk, and fond good-bye,
Your other uses now I see,
As a parachute you'll land some guy.
That's more than you ever did for me.

Another sentimental little poem, with the title "Our Sailor Boy" by student Rowena Coleman, likely written for the Victory Bond campaign, reflects the anxiety that families suffered day by day:

He's tall, dark and well!! handsome too.
He wears the navy uniform so blue.
And when he's far, far out to sea
I hope he sometimes thinks of me.
I think of him throughout the day
And every night for him I pray.
We love him truly, his Mom and I
So for his sake War Bonds we'll buy.
Now just in case you take things wrong
This sailor boy so big and strong
Is my brother, my pride and joy
And mother's great big "handsome" boy.

The war created many major disruptions to everyday life, not least of all to young couples and newlyweds. The story of a young Nelson couple, Maisie Grimes and Miles Riddle, is typical.[47] High school sweethearts, they married in May 1941. Miles was a university student about to enter the RCAF. For the next two years Maisie moved around the country, following her husband from base to base, until he was transferred overseas to fly troops and supplies into Karachi, India. Like many young wives, Maisie returned to her parents' home in Nelson to wait for her husband's return. Daphne Wilson has described the anxiety and heartache of the time:

With the threat of imminent separation, many people made hasty marriages. Young husbands left young wives, often pregnant or with small babies, and went overseas, never dreaming they would never see each other for four or five years. No commercial long distance telephone in those days, no commercial airlines, only heavily censored letters and parcels that had to go through a shipping blockade to reach Britain or to be forwarded to Holland, Italy, or India or Burma.[48]

The local newspaper's syndicated medical column offered advice about coping with the stress and strain that was part of daily living for most families:

What we don't always remember is that the civilian stay-at-home's nervous system is under a strain as well as the soldier's under combat duty.... So, if during this period some member of your family rather suddenly begins to develop symptoms never exhibited before, don't necessarily take it too hard. And also be sympathetic and kind with them. They should be examined by a competent physician, of course, but if he can not find any physical cause for the trouble, try to see if you can determine whether or not it is related to the difficult times we are passing through.[49]

Some of the advice must have been most difficult, if not impossible, to follow:

> One of the ways in which every parent and grandparent, every wife, other relative or sweetheart can help is to boost the morale of our soldiers and sailors.... [In letters] we won't tell him of our fears and anxieties about him. We won't tell him what a hole his going left in our hearts nor how we miss him. We won't be so selfish. There will be no weeping in our words, no tears between our lines.[50]

Radio soap operas also depicted the difficulties for families with loved ones in the services. All activity stopped in my home so my mother and grandmother could listen to the popular CBC radio soap opera, *Soldier's Wife*, which dealt with the anguish and the complications caused by the absence of the men.

City councils too faced a whole set of special problems during wartime. In the spring of 1943 Nelson's Mayor Stibbs attended a conference of the Canadian Federation of Mayors and Municipalities with the theme "The War and Cities." Topics under discussion included civilian defence, salvage, local ration boards, wartime housing, conservation of materials, problems of local transportation (brought on largely by gasoline rationing) and shortage of manpower.

No single person in Nelson contributed more to the war effort than Norman Clarence Stibbs. As mayor of the city during all of the war years, he worked tirelessly on fundraising campaigns, especially as chairman of Nelson's War Finance Committee, chaired

Mayor Norman Stibbs
Photo courtesy of Nelson Museum

countless other committees, and was ever present to lead patriotic exercises, greet the servicemen and women going out and coming home, and always to sing the praises of Nelson. He was first elected mayor in 1938, and after he retired from the Canadian Pacific Railway in 1940 he devoted himself full-time to civic affairs. Four times during his 11 years as mayor he was returned by acclamation, setting a record in Nelson politics.

In the spring of 1943 Mayor Stibbs set the motto for the Fourth Victory Loan Drive—*Keep That Nelson Touch*—calling on the patriotic persona of Admiral Lord Nelson and his cry, "Engage the Enemy More Closely!" Along with a portrait of the admiral in the full-page newspaper promotion of the drive was a stirring message from the mayor to the citizens of Nelson:

Fellow Citizens
"The Word 'Nelson' Has a Great Tradition"
Let us honour the memory of the man, Admiral Lord Nelson. Let us honour our city which bears his name, the City of Nelson. Let us honour Nelson's Flagship the *Victory*. Let us honour Churchill's "V for Victory." Let us honour our boys and girls on active service. Let us honour Montgomery and all our gallant comrades who are now moving forward to Victory at Tunis and Bizerte. Let us help bring them back victorious.

Nelson, the man, never failed. Nelson, the city, has never failed up to date. We shall not fail in this supreme effort, provided every citizen measures up to his responsibilities.... Do you know that if the "cease fire" had been sounded at 6:00 a.m. on November 11, 1918, instead of 11:00 a.m., there would be five thousand less Canadian and United States soldiers buried in France today?

If the average man realizes the importance of the time factor surely he will open his heart and purse to give generously. No doubt he has tried to do his BIT in the past. This time he must do his SHARE.

I make this solemn appeal to my fellow citizens that it is the sacred duty of each one of us to put Nelson, the city, over the top. Thus we do our part and hasten the return of our boys and girls. WE DARE NOT FAIL!
"Back the Attack" and "Keep That Nelson Touch"
N.C. Stibbs, Mayor of Nelson and Chairman, National War Finance Committee

The Fourth Victory Loan Drive was to raise over one million dollars, surpassing all the previous campaigns. Perhaps some of this success was due to the personal tie that was made during the drive to Nelson's servicemen overseas. A few names of Nelson district men in active service were drawn at random by the Victory Loan Committee at regular intervals and published in the local newspaper, with such banner appeals as these:

District men who have joined the Royal Canadian Air Force...will not look for excuses when called to face the enemy and they have every reason to believe that folks at home will do their share in supporting the Victory Loan.

These boys from Nelson are attacking the most ruthless forces the world has yet experienced, fighting for the way of life that we know and want to live. They can only carry on if we on the homefront keep up the steady stream of supply. Our dollars furnish this needed supply.

Corvettes need men to man them. They are getting them from this district. These are only a few of the many from this district who have joined the Navy. The Nelson district quota will build a corvette. We must do our part.

These boys from our district are in the Royal Canadian Air Force and are all serving overseas at the present time. They require planes and blockbuster bombs. Will your money supply them?

Among the names listed in these little boxed appeals, published on the front page of the newspaper, were several of the young men who would not come home: John Dingwall, Bob Andrew, Bud Ruppel, Maurice Latornell, Chub Greenwood and Jerry Wallace. During the campaign the Women's Auxiliary to the Active Forces featured a photo library of Nelson district servicemen and women, as part of their fundraising tea and bake sale. Members were invited to bring photos of relatives and friends on active service. There were so many pictures that shelves, bookcases and even chairs were used to display them.

A special feature of the Fourth Victory Loan campaign was a Nelson Victory Loan song, written by two prominent Nelson citizens, music by Robert E. Fleming and words by Lillian A.H. Dill. It was one of the highlights at the Fireman's Ball at the Civic Centre on May 10, when it was sung "in a rousing solo" by Percy Young. The song was also performed

A Patriotic Tribute

The window of Wood, Vallance Hardware store during a Victory Loan drive, with pictures of Nelson and district servicemen and women. *Photo courtesy of Nelson Museum*

over Nelson's radio station CKLN, and later recorded for broadcast at Trail and Vancouver.

Nelson's Victory Loan Song

Are you doing your part to win the war,
    You, and the folks at home?
Do your dollars fight with all their might
    To bring back the boys who are gone?

Chorus:
Do you lend your dollars for Victory Bonds?
    Is your shoulder at the wheel?
Do you spend your dollars for ships and bombs
    And tanks and planes and steel?
Do you save your dollars for Canada
    And work for a world that's free?
Do you Back the Attack to the Last Red Cent?
    And pull for Victory?
To bring back our sons facing enemy guns
    It's up to the old home town
While our boys from home are counting on us
    Are you going to let them down?
No, No, No, NO – SO, So, So, SO

We'll lend our dollars for Victory Bonds
　　With our shoulders at the wheel!
We'll spend our dollars for ships and bombs
　　And tanks and planes and steel.
We'll save our dollars for Canada
　　And work for a world that's free!
And Back the Attack to the Last Red Cent
　　And PULL, PULL, PULL, for Victory!

Are you doing your job to pull your weight
　　You who are waiting here?
How deep do you dig, how tight is your belt,
　　As you stand in line and cheer?

Chorus

By 1943 some 1,500 airmen from the Commonwealth Air Training Plan had taken part in the Nelson district's unique entertainment program. Many of the airmen made a real effort to join in community life in the city during their short leaves. Forty-eight airmen billeted with Nelson families on a three-day leave in the spring of 1943 were special guests at the Fireman's Ball, where a group of New Zealand airmen treated the crowd to "a novel, and certainly new-to-Nelson" Maori dance. The newspaper account praised their "peppy interpretation of New Zealand jive routines [which] added merriment and laughter to the gay fun-fest." Another group of airmen visited classrooms at Central School, played softball with the children and took part in their Empire Day ceremonies.

On May 14, the eighth Annual Army Day, the campaign took as its theme "Over the Top with the 8th Army!" With only two days to go in the drive, Nelson residents were reminded of General Montgomery's stirring message to his troops as they launched their final victorious drive: "I... told you that if each one of us did his duty and pulled his full weight then nothing could stop us. And nothing has stopped us.... The triumphant cry now is: Forward to Tunis! Drive the enemy into the sea!"

Two Nelson lads, Clive Fleming, age 10, and his 15-year-old brother, Gordon, were so stirred by such messages that they each bought Victory Bonds with the earnings from their *Daily News* paper routes. Clive was buying his bond on the installment plan. The boys had three brothers in the RCAF. Fourteen-year-old John Leeming, who also had brothers and a sister in the services, bought a bond on his earnings as a telegraph delivery boy. They were following the example of 12-year-old Roy Langill, who in the first Victory Loan campaign in 1941 had walked into the Nelson Victory Loan headquarters office and bought his own bond with money he had saved since early childhood.

Children were expected to pull their weight in support of the city's wartime activities, whether in raising funds, collecting scrap, joining cadets, performing in patriotic ceremonies, or planting Victory Gardens. In March 1943 over 350 children attended a special morning matinee at the Civic Theatre, bringing cans of fat as the price of admission. A total of 650 pounds of fat was collected and shipped to Calgary to be made into glycerin for munitions. That spring 75 boys and girls from Central, Hume, St. Joseph's and the junior high school entered the Rotary Club's Victory Garden Contest. Prizes totalled $40. The newspaper reported on June 16:

> A dozen students of St. Joseph's have plotted out Victory Gardens on a couple of lots at the corner of Robson and Ward and their work is impressing passers-by for its neatness and the showing of vegetable plants. Among the judges is the City Gardener, Jack Holt. The mother of one boy told [organizers] Mrs. Dawson and Alderman Hinnitt that all the vegetables used in their home this spring had come from the boy's Victory Garden.

In the school year 1942–43, children raised over $1,000 in Central School alone from sales of War Savings Stamps and contributions to the Red Cross, Greek War Relief, Canadian Aid to Russia, and the Navy League of Canada. My father, T.S. Shorthouse, chairman of the Nelson Kinsmen Club's Milk for Britain campaign, commented:

> A large percentage of the donations have come from school children throughout the East and West Kootenay. These children have been consistently giving up their spending pennies, placing them in Milk for Britain bottles on teachers' desks.[51]

Nelson residents had concerns other than fundraising during this fourth year of the war. Forest conservation and health insurance were front-page stories. Athletic competitions, concerts and plays were also important in people's daily lives. But the boys in the services were never far from mind. In a special Mother's Day service at Trinity United Church in May, red, white and blue corsages were presented to about 50 mothers and wives of servicemen. That spring the Nelson Gyro Club abandoned its customary social hour following their weekly dinner, and donned old clothes for a "mass assault" on the garden of the home of an airman whose wife was unable to manage it on her own.

During a short, tragic six-week period in late spring and early summer of 1943 the Nelson district was to lose five of its young airmen and one soldier, some to combat and others to accident or illness: Chub Greenwood, John Grant, Robert Main, Harry Warner, Tommy Wallace and Oscar Dorval.

On May 31, 1943, *Warrant Officer George Evelyn "Chub" Greenwood*, age 28, was aboard a Wellington aircraft that failed to return from a night antisubmarine patrol over the Bay of Biscay. He was a wireless air gunner with 407 Squadron of the RCAF, called the Demon Squadron. The crew was made up of men from Vancouver and Vernon who had been together since training in Canada. They had distinguished themselves several times for their exploits in raids on shipping and on German-held ports. They were officially credited with sinking two enemy ships in 1942, and on one occasion had managed a near escape from a German fighter plane during a raid on the Frisian Islands.

Chub Greenwood grew up in South Burnaby and graduated from high school in Vancouver. He worked for a few years for Union Steamships on Bowen Island, but in the mid-1930s he followed his brothers, Jack, Les and Bud to Nelson. There he worked as an accountant and clerk for the Star Grocery, run by his brother Bud. He was a member of the Nelson Little Theatre, and was also an active member of the Nelson Rowing Club. He is buried in France in the Cherbourg Old Communal Cemetery, his body having been recovered from the sea, the only member of his crew whose body was found.

Two of the young men listed on the Nelson Cenotaph grew up in the small mining community of Ymir, 18 miles south of Nelson. One of them was *Flying Officer John William Grant*, who was with the RAF's #52 Operational Training Unit when he was killed in a flying accident in England on June 11, 1943. Experiencing bad visibility, the 22-year-old pilot crashed his Spitfire into a hill one half mile east of Asterton, near Shawbury in Shropshire. John Grant was educated at Ymir and also in

Wallace, Idaho and Longview, Washington. He enlisted in the RCAF in July 1941 and was overseas a year later at the age of 21. His brother, Signalman Jim Grant, was also overseas in the Canadian Army and survived the war. John is buried in Shawbury (St. Mary) Churchyard.

On the same day that John Grant lost his life in a flying accident in England, another young Nelson district man, also in the RCAF, was to die in Edmonton's University Hospital from complications following an attack of pneumonia. **Robert Lindsay Main** had transferred from the Canadian Officers Training Corps (COTC) to the RCAF only seven months before his death, and had been training in navigation at Calgary and Edmonton. He held the rank of aircraftsman second class.

Robert was born in Nelson but had lived for several years at Bonnington Falls, ten miles southwest of Nelson on the Kootenay River, where the City of Nelson operated a hydroelectric power plant. His father was the owner of the Pop-Inn at Corra Linn on the road to Nelson. Robert's mother came to Canada from England as a war bride after World War I, and this may explain his interest in cricket, as divulged by a little verse in the Nelson High School *Mountaineer* for 1939:

A more studious lad is Robert Main.
Daily he comes from Pop-Inn in sunshine or rain.
He's the only claimant to High School fame
As a great enthusiast of the cricket game.

He was, indeed, a "studious lad." After attending St. Joseph's Academy and Nelson High School, he graduated with a Bachelor of Arts degree from St. Michael's College in Toronto in June 1942. The Cathedral of Mary Immaculate in Nelson was filled on June 16 for his funeral, a solemn requiem mass with full military honours. Robert Main was 22 years old.

The day after John Grant and Robert Main lost their lives, another Nelson airman was killed in combat, on June 12, 1943. **Pilot Officer Harry Dale Warner** was a wireless air gunner with the RCAF's 432 Squadron. On the night of June 11/12 Harry and four other crewmen joined 782 other bombers and fighters to attack the city of Düsseldorf on the Rhine. Their Wellington aircraft failed to return and was lost without a trace. He was 24 years old when he was killed, and is listed on the Runnymede Memorial. Shortly before they went missing, Harry and his crew had been honoured by a ceremonial parade for "an exceedingly good show on operation." Harry had been working in Nelson at the time of his enlistment with the RCAF, but his family home was in Vancouver.

Later that month, on June 28, another flying accident took the life of 19-year-old *Sergeant Thomas "Tommy" Wallace*, a wireless air gunner with the #111 Operational Training Unit, stationed at Nassau in the Bahamas. The crew was flying a Mitchell aircraft on an exercise at sea when they met with an unknown mishap. Searchers found an empty, damaged dinghy and a wheel that belong to the aircraft, floating in deep water, but no sign of the men.

Tommy Wallace grew up in Nelson and was "widely popular with his schoolmates," according to the local newspaper's account of his death. He was obviously keen to get into the war. In 1940 he had enlisted in the Canadian Army, and when it was discovered that he was only 16, he was discharged. Not discouraged, after a little more time at school, he enlisted again in the army, and was again discharged on account of his age. Finally, when he reached the eligible age of 18, he enlisted successfully in the RCAF. He spent his final leave in Nelson just three months before his death. Tommy's mother and young brother had moved to the Coast earlier in the year. Along with the name of Bert Jardine from Nelson, Tommy's name is inscribed on the special memorial on Green Island in Ottawa that commemorates the Commonwealth airmen who have no known grave, killed while serving from bases in Canada, the British West Indies and the United States.

Another serviceman from the Nelson District who died of natural causes during the war was *Trooper Oscar Anthony Dorval*, who died at the age of 29 of an aneurysm of the heart on July 3, 1943, while stationed in Surrey, England. He was with the 3rd Army Tank Brigade, Royal Canadian Armoured Corps. Oscar had settled in Willow Point in 1935, had worked as a truck driver and in the silver-lead mines in the Nelson area. He left Nelson on August 3, 1940, with 17 other recruits in Nelson's ninth draft. He originally joined the British Columbia Regiment (Duke of Connaught's Own Rifles), but later at Halifax he transferred to the Tank Corps and went overseas with the regiment in November 1942. Oscar was a native of Morden, Manitoba.

It is not difficult to imagine how exciting it must have been for families of servicemen and women overseas to hear each other's voices during this prolonged and anxious separation. Before the ease and affordability of trans-Atlantic long distance telephone service, this could be done only by recorded messages over the radio. The CBC regularly carried messages from servicemen and women overseas to their families at home. I remember listening to greetings, not only from servicemen to their families, but also from evacuated English children in Canada to their parents at home.

In June and July 1943 the Women's Auxiliary to the Active Forces brought together a large number of parents, wives, brothers, sisters and sweethearts of Nelson and district servicemen and women to record messages to "loved ones in uniform overseas." The recordings were made at radio station CJAT in Trail. After they were cleared by official censors in Ottawa, they were passed along to the BBC, and those addressed were notified of the date and time of the broadcast. Messages went out to over 50 Nelson and district men and women. General greetings were recorded by Mayor Stibbs and the president of the Women's Auxiliary. A Nelson soldier who was home after nearly four years overseas sent "a breezy message to his comrades." Two of the mothers, Mrs. J.C. Forbes of Nelson and Mrs. E.D. Rutherglen of Willow Point, each had three sons to send messages to.

The "sense of family" that Bruce Hutchison wrote about in his article on the city of Nelson is evident in the letters home of the men overseas. They wrote excitedly about the other Nelson servicemen they met in Britain, and about their hunger for news from home. Many of the boys who had served under Major Dalgas in the 111th Battery in Nelson prior to and in the early days of the war, made a point of looking him up when word got around about where he was stationed in England. Lieutenant Bill Myers wrote to the *Nelson Daily News* from a hospital in Britain where he was recovering from wounds:

> It has been quite a time since I was last in Nelson but my heart is still there and I am impatiently waiting for the day that I will be able to return.... I have been laid up for several weeks here but hope to be back to my unit in a couple of weeks. Today I got a very pleasant surprise. I was in the Red Cross library and I found a large stack of the *Daily News*. I haven't seen any for a long time and spent the remainder of the time catching up on the local

news. It was really just like being back home…just like "a breath from home" to be able to read them.

On his return to Nelson, RCAF Sergeant Don Beattie told of how the men overseas always thought of home, and of the pleasure it gave him to be able to read the Nelson newspaper at the Beaver Club in London. It was clear that other Nelson servicemen looked forward to the newspaper also. On one visit to the club Sergeant Beattie was unable to find the Nelson paper. The librarian told him he was the fifth man that day to ask for it.

Overseas Subscriptions
are Permissable

To conserve space in ships the shipment of bundles of newspapers and magazines to persons overseas by private individuals has been restricted. Postal authorities suggest that clippings of articles of interest be sent instead.

This restriction does not affect newspaper and magazine subscriptions sent direct to the addressee from the publishing office.

The Daily News is being dispatched every day to persons overseas who are on the subscription list, whether civilians or members of the armed services.

Nelson Daily News
CIRCULATION DEPARTMENT

Popular Newspaper
The Nelson newspaper was greatly enjoyed by servicemen and women overseas. Families ordered subscriptions for loved ones "over there."

Clearly, the citizens of Nelson had a deep affection for their city, and Mayor Stibbs seldom missed an opportunity to show it off. He brought several nationally or internationally prominent people to the city, including Lord Halifax, a former viceroy of India and British foreign secretary. Lord Halifax was then serving as British ambassador to the United States, and in the summer of 1943 was touring parts of Canada and the US. Mayor Stibbs persuaded the ambassador and his wife to stop their train in Nelson for a whirlwind tour of the city. An embarrassing moment for the mayor came during the welcome at the CPR station when the diminutive mayor, standing on the steps of the ambassador's coach to deliver his welcoming address to his very tall guest, found himself in mid-speech being shunted along the track onto a siding. In a gracious thank you letter to the mayor some days later, Lord Halifax wrote, "It was a great relief that your sudden disappearance at the outset of the proceedings had no serious consequences."[52]

Throughout the war years, community efforts to raise funds and "support the boys" grew and diversified. In July 1943 the Nelson chapter of the IODE became the first in BC to "adopt" a ship, the frigate HMCS *Kokanee* (appropriately, the name of the Nelson chapter). The IODE would contribute needed materials to the crew, send parcels and exchange letters. They set about collecting gifts from Nelson citizens to be included in individual parcels, and the donors of the gifts were identified in the packages sent to the men. Ten-year-old Bert Young received a thank-you letter from a sailor on the *Kokanee* for his gift of a pack of aircraft identification cards. The letter included pictures of the crew's two mascots, Kooty, the kitten, and Bilge, the puppy.

HMCS *Kokanee* was a River Class frigate, built at the Yarrows shipyards in Esquimalt. The ship's name had been suggested by the Nelson City Council upon request of the Department of National Defence. With a complement of 140 men, it was one of 67 River Class frigates used by Commonwealth forces as antisubmarine escorts for trans-Atlantic convoys. The ship's crew and the Nelson IODE chapter were to exchange many gifts, among them a picture album of Kokanee Glacier sent to the crew. The flag of the frigate and the case of the first shell fired from its guns was presented to the Nelson chapter. The flag was placed in St. Saviour's Anglican Pro-Cathedral in a solemn ceremony in which Petty Officer Dick Hornett of the Royal Canadian Navy mounted a ladder to place the flag in its receptacle.

There was no let-up in public pressure to support such well-established fund drives as War Savings Stamps, Victory Bonds and Milk for Britain, while at the same time new fundraising campaigns came on stream. Bingo nights and raffles helped boost the funds of the Kinsmen's high-profile Milk for Britain campaign. In July 1943 the first prize for their raffle was a "beautifully furnished house in Vancouver." The public was advised of how crucial support for this fund could be. A letter received

by the Kinsmen from the matron of Arthur's Home for Girls in Bognor Regis was published in the *Daily News* on July 16:

> Please convey my warmest thanks to the Kinsmen of Canada for their welcome gift of powdered milk. It came at a time when we were really short of fresh milk and we use it in many ways. For milk puddings, blanc manges, custards, soups, stews, fish pies and in mashed vegetables; sprinkled in powered form on stewed fruit it is excellent.

A "monster dance" was held at the Civic Centre on Dominion Day, July 1, as a fundraiser for the Greek Relief Fund. There were also active campaigns in 1943 for a Cypriot Prisoners of War Fund and a Chinese Relief Fund. A dramatic approach to selling more War Savings Stamps was the "Stamp Out The U-Boat Campaign," also launched in July. Buyers of four stamps from the "Miss Canada" girls (high school girls who sold stamps on the corners of Baker Street) were promised that their names would be attached by a sticker to a depth bomb thrown at a German U-boat.

Considering the enormous community commitment to support of the war, Nelson citizens must have been a little surprised, if not chagrined, to be told by the manager of the Vancouver *News-Herald* that "while Nelson might feel it was far removed from Canada's war effort, it should not feel and could not feel it was out of it." Addressing the Nelson Rotary Club in August, he urged Nelsonites to "take pride in the contribution it was making in war industry workers, in enlistments and in war savings."[53]

Employees of the Boeing Aircraft Plant
Workers pose in front of the Civic Centre Badminton Hall where they assembled fittings for Catalina (Canso) flying boats. *Photo courtesy of Nelson Museum*

Indeed, first-line war industry came to the city in the fall of 1943, when Boeing Aircraft of Canada Ltd. established a satellite manufacturing plant in Nelson to assemble belt frames and other small fittings for Catalina Flying Boats. The plant took over the Civic Centre's badminton hall, said to be the largest hall of its kind in western Canada. It was to employ about 150 workers. A novel and common sight on Nelson streets was women in white overalls, bandanas and safety boots, on their way to work. The plant's establishment in Nelson was largely the work of the mayor, who had spearheaded negotiations with Boeing more than a year earlier. Apparently, Boeing required a work force that was comprised of 65 percent women. Mayor Stibbs made the commitment for the City of Nelson:

> I guaranteed the 65% because I was convinced that if such a plant were established our young women, single and married, would not hesitate for a minute to make their contributions to the war effort in this way.… The City would go out of its way to facilitate the establishment of a plant here.[54]

The plant continued in operation until November 1944, when the demand for Catalina bombers fell off.

On September 20, 1943, the Royal Canadian Navy suffered a serious loss with the sinking of the destroyer HMCS *St. Croix* by a U-boat, while it was on convoy escort in the mid-Atlantic, just south of Iceland. Five officers and 76 men were rescued by the frigate HMS *Itchen*, but when the *Itchen* was sunk by a German U-boat a few days later, only one of the *St. Croix*'s crew survived. The *St. Croix* was considered one of the most successful of the Canadian destroyers, having two U-boat kills to its credit. It was one of the first victims of the newly developed acoustic torpedo, which homes in on the sounds of a ship's propellers. Among the 148 men lost from the *St. Croix* was ***Able Seaman William Donald "Bill" Barwis*** of Nelson.

Bill Barwis was born in Mandalay, Burma in 1921, which at that time was under British colonial rule as part of India. Bill's father, a Canadian Army officer, had been on loan to the British to assist in military training. In 1923 the family crossed the Pacific in the *Empress of Canada* to settle first in Vancouver, then in Harrop on the west arm of Kootenay Lake, where Bill's grandparents operated a fox farm. Bill's family moved often because of his father's position as sergeant with the BC Police, which he had joined in the mid-1920s. Bill's brother, John, recalls how the two boys were always a year behind in school because of their frequent moves. Their father, Sergeant C.W.A. "Bert" Barwis, an outstanding athlete, was in charge of the West Kootenay District for the BC Police during the early years of the war.

Bill received his junior high and high schooling in Nelson, except for one year in Prince George. After high school he worked for the Royal Bank in Nelson. He was an excellent musician, a talent that ran in the family. His Italian maternal grandfather had been conductor of the symphony orchestra in Port Said, Egypt. Bill sang, played the guitar and the saxophone, and had performed over the local radio station, CKLN. The Nelson High annual for 1940 called him "a crooning caballero." According to his brother, John, himself a professional musician, Bill was also a promising artist with a special talent for drawing. High-school classmate Dawn Penniket tells of how she ran into him in Victoria in 1940 when he was stationed at Esquimalt and she was attending Normal School:

> I was down town in Victoria; I knew that a guy was following me; I hurried, he hurried. I went faster, so did he, then he grabbed my arm and I whirled around to look into Bill Barwis's smiling

face. We had a great laugh and he said something like, "Did I scare a small town girl who is just away from home in Nelson?" We chatted and went for a soda or something and talked about Nelson.[55]

Bill spent his final evening on Canadian soil visiting with his Nelson friend, George Coletti, whose ship HMCS *Acadia* was docked next to the *St. Croix* in Halifax harbour. Bill's last correspondence with his brother John was in October 1942 when John was in training with the RCAF at St. Thomas. Bill had sent his brother a bag of jelly beans, his favourite candy, as a birthday gift. Bill had turned 22 just two months before his death. His name is inscribed on the Halifax Memorial in Point Pleasant Park, along with the names of nearly

Bill Barwis, lost on HMCS *St. Croix*
Photo courtesy of John Barwis

2,000 sailors of the Royal Canadian Navy who were lost at sea in the Second World War. The monument stands over 12 metres high, and is clearly visible to ships approaching Halifax harbour.

A fifth Victory Loan campaign was launched in the fall of 1943, and in the Kootenay-Boundary area took as its motto "Replace the *St. Croix*." The objective was to raise $2,725,000, the estimated cost of replacing the destroyer. Advertisements in the *Daily News* stressed the loss of the local sailor, Bill Barwis, who "typified the thousands of Canadians battling the Axis at sea wherever it can be engaged." The battle ensign from the *St. Croix* was presented to the city, and "stained, wind-shredded, a corner missing," it flew over the city during the fall campaign.

There is nothing to indicate that the citizens of Nelson felt they were "out of it" and "far removed from Canada's war effort," as the manager of the Vancouver newspaper had suggested. On the contrary, local newspaper articles emphasized Nelson's economic contribution to the war, and clergymen and civic officials alike were calling this "a People's War." There can have been no one in the city that wartime activities did not touch. Young and old sold and bought stamps and bonds; collected or donated on Saturday "tag days;" took part in fundraising events for any number of special causes; tried to "make do" in order to conserve materials for war needs; played host to Commonwealth airmen on leave; baked, sewed, knitted, and collected scrap. They even suffered wet feet that winter when the shortage of rubber meant that supplies of winter rubbers failed to arrive at the shoe stores.

The women of the Auxiliary to the Active Forces sent 856 parcels to servicemen and women overseas in late 1943. Evenings of parcel packing were organized for "navy mothers," "army mothers" and "air force mothers." The auxiliary also made 671 pounds of fruit cake, all butter and sugar having been donated from rations by members and friends. Sugar and fruit shortages had created problems for the Red Cross Jam Committee; even so, 2,256 pounds of cherry and plum jam were prepared and shipped overseas in 1943. In three years the Red Cross branch in Nelson and its auxiliaries "from Robson to Queens Bay" had shipped seven and three-quarter tons of jam.

Children cooperated by collecting Hallowe'en Shellout tickets in place of candy to support the Kinsmen's national Milk for Britain campaign. The chief of police strongly endorsed the Shellout program as a "splendid means of turning the children away from the usual pranks to patriotic purposes." In fact, he issued an edict prohibiting the Hallowe'en customs of "soaping of windows, tampering with automobile tires, and the removal of ashcans, fences and gates." The public bought sheets of Shellout tickets to give to trick-or-treating children instead of scarce candies. Special prizes were given to children who collected the largest number of stamps, and all collectors of stamps got free admission to a special movie matinee (by my memory, probably a Roy Rogers western). Nelson students helped the Kinsmen's campaign also by taking over a two-hour-long section of the *Kinauction of the Air* at CKLN. High- school students performed and elementary school children from each of the three schools, Central, Hume and St. Joseph's Academy, took part in a quiz, sponsored by the IODE. Father Frank Flynn and high-school teacher Walter Elmes acted as quizmasters.

NOTICE
Hallowe'en

Children Must Respect Hallow-
e'en 1942 in its Wartime Aspect

Peanuts, candies, etc., are scarce and
cannot be donated the same as in previous
years.

The soaping of windows is absolutely
prohibited.

Tampering with automobiles, tires, etc.,
can only be treated as an unpatriotic act.

The removal of ash cans, fences, gates,
etc., is more serious an offence than ever
before because of priorities on products of
this type.

All children and parents are invited to
celebrate Hallowe'en at the

Royal Canadian
Naval Band Concert

At the Civic Centre at 7:30

Everyone is asked to cooperate.

Robert Harshaw.
Chief of Police.

KIDS Here is the Plan
for the KINSMEN
MILK FOR BRITAIN

HALLOWE'EN SHELLOUT

1.—Dress up as usual, just as you have always done on Hallowe'en.

2.—Go to the doors of your friends and neighbors and ask them to "Shellout" for the Kids in Britain.

3.—They will give you MILK FOR BRITAIN TICKETS in place of fruits, nuts candies, etc., which are so scarce.

4.—Collect all the tickets you can Keep them and take them home with you.

5.—Count your tickets, place them in an envelope and mark on the envelope the number of tickets enclosed, also your name and address.

ON MONDAY AFTERNOON AT 4 P.M.
Bring Your Envelope to the Free

SHELLOUT MATINEE
AT THE
CIVIC THEATRE

If you have collected sufficient tickets you may win one of the Grand Prizes that are being awarded.

Patriotic Hallowe'en

Hallowe'en was turned into a patriotic exercise for kids during the war. Children were sternly warned against their usual Hallowe'en pranks, and rewarded for collecting "Shellout" stamps instead of candies.

During the winter of 1943–44 the Parent Teachers' Association sponsored a fashion revue, titled "Remake Wrinkles," to illustrate to housewives how to maintain the family wardrobe in wartime. The theme of the revue was the national call to "make it do, wear it out." Held at the Capitol Theatre, the show featured children modelling a "travelling wardrobe" to reveal how "neat and clean clothes for the little ones can be [when] made from adults' castoffs." A booklet, entitled *Remake Wrinkles*, published by the Wartime Prices and Trade Board, was distributed. Not only were patriotic citizens to live conservatively and curtail waste, but also to eat sensibly, following Canada's Food Rules, and thereby conserve their health and strength. The government sponsored the development of a vitamin B-enriched flour "to promote national health and stamina."

The year ended sadly for Nelson residents as they learned of the loss of another two young airmen from the city, Ray Burgess and Russ Clark. On November 16 *Flight Sergeant Raymond Charles Burgess*, age 23, was

National Defence Begins in Your Kitchen

Want to be a red-blooded man?

If you want to be a red-blooded man (or woman)—if you want to enjoy life to the fullest—choose your food carefully. Make sure your blood is getting three nourishing meals every day.

Blood Foods Can Be Divided Into Three Groups

1.—Foods That Make Blood—are Iron and Copper. Good sources of Iron are meat, livers, kidneys. egg yolks, dried beans, beef, and whole grain cereals. Copper is found in bran, liver, mushrooms, whole grain cereals, leafy vegetables, fish, sea foods and prunes.

2.—Foods That Build Blood Cells—are the proteins found in milk beef, lamb, nuts, fish, cheese and eggs.

3.—Foods That Cement Blood Walls — Vitamin C in adequate quantities cements the walls of the blood vessels together—Good sources are tomatoes, citrus fruits, cauliflower, potatoes, bananas. rhubarb, cabbage and watercress.

Bran Flakes, Kelloggs , pkg. 11¢	Milk, tall tins, each ......10¢
Rolled Oats, Ogilvie, carton 22¢	Cheese, Kraft, 1 lb. carton 36¢
Peas, Aylmer No. 5., 2 tins 25¢	Oranges, 2 dozen ....69¢
Butter, Hudsonia, 3 lbs. .$1.23	Grape Fruit, 4 for ....19¢
Coffee, Hostess. lb. ......48¢	Grapes, Tokay, per lb. ....22¢
Tomato Juice, 26 oz., 2 tins 23¢	Bananas, per lb. ....17¢

Hudson's Bay Company.

INCORPORATED 2ND MAY 1670.

Government Ad Promoting Health and Stamina

killed in a flying accident over Lincolnshire, England. He was piloting a Lancaster bomber with RCAF 432 (Leaside) Squadron. One of three survivors of the accident, Flight Sergeant Andy Haggins, has described what happened:

> On the night of Nov. 16, 1943, we were on a cross-country trip at about 18,000 feet when the flight engineer reported engine trouble. Shortly thereafter the two port engines caught fire. The pilot came down to 2,000 feet and, after leveling out, the two starboard engines burst into flames. The pilot came over the intercom, "Abandon Aircraft". The Lancaster started to go into a slow spin. I opened the rear door and the wop/ag, mid upper gunner, and I, bailed out from under 1,000 feet. I landed in a turnip field injuring my ankle. The mid upper gunner and myself spent the night in a nearby hospital. The next morning we received word that the navigator had landed in a duck pond and had spent the night at a farm house. The flight engineer was found in a field, his chute had not opened. The Lancaster had crashed killing the pilot [Ray Burgess] and bomb aimer.[56]

The navigator, Jim Bell, who was to lose his life five months later over occupied France, wrote to Ray's widow of how Ray's action in holding the aircraft steady allowed four crew members to jump clear: "There will be no medals ... but there are four of us who know better than anyone that Ray was a brave man and that he saved our lives by giving his own."[57]

Ray Burgess had lived through 13 operational flights over Germany in his 14 months of overseas duty. Ray and his crew had experienced a previous close call in July 1943 when after a raid on Cologne their Wellington aircraft was coned by searchlights and was either hit by flak (the squadron's official log) or was shot up by a German night fighter (account by one of the crew who bailed out and spent the rest of the war as a prisoner of war.)[58] Despite serious damage to the wings and fuel tank, pilot Burgess had managed to get the aircraft back to England. Being short of fuel and with low cloud and fog hindering their navigation, the crew bailed safely out and the Wellington crashed near Gravesend. This had qualified Ray and his crew for membership in the famed Caterpillar Club, open only to those who have saved their lives by parachute. On another sortie the previous June, the crew had returned early from an attack on Düsseldorf when the pilot's escape hatch blew off. This was the raid in which Harry Warner, also with 432 Squadron, had lost his life.

Pilot Officer Ray Burgess
Photo courtesy of Ray Burgess, Jr.

Born in Liverpool in 1920, Ray immigrated to Canada with his family in 1923 and was raised and educated in Nelson at Hume elementary, junior high and high schools. He was a popular boy, known in the community as an outstanding athlete. Ray was prominent in the Fairview Athletic Club, was outstanding in track and field, and was a member of the rep hockey club that in 1936 won the West Kootenay Junior Hockey Championship for Nelson. He was active also in lacrosse and basketball. Ray worked in the *Nelson Daily News* composing room for four years before he enlisted, and during this period was an enthusiastic motorcyclist and swimmer. He went overseas in September 1942, just six months after his marriage to an equally popular Nelson girl, Geraldine "Deanie" Wallace. Their infant son was named Raymond after his father. Like Peggy (Gibbon) Horswill, Deanie was to lose both a husband and a brother in the war.

Flying Officer Russell Stanley Clark and his crew of six were outward bound in their Lancaster bomber for operations over Berlin on December 16, 1943, when they struck the ground while flying in bad weather and low cloud near Hawnby in Yorkshire. Pilot Clark died from his injuries five days later, on December 21, in the RAF Hospital at Northallerton. Only two of the crew survived. Russ Clark and his crew, members of the RCAF's 408 (Goose) Squadron, had taken part in many of the massive bombing raids of Allied Bomber Command over Berlin, Hamburg and other German industrial centres in mid-to-late 1943. Not long before their fatal accident they had managed a terrifying escape from a German fighter plane when Russ put the bomber into a dive of several thousand feet to shake off the attacker.

Russell Clark's family home was in Erickson, BC in the fertile fruit-growing Creston Valley, but from 1938 to 1942, when he enlisted in the RCAF, he had lived in Nelson and worked at the Imperial Bank of Commerce. He had a Bachelor of Commerce degree from the University of British Columbia. While in Nelson Russ was active in basketball, tennis and badminton. His parents in Erickson received the wire from Ottawa telling of their son's death on Christmas Day. Russ was 25 years old.

1944

CHAPTER FIVE

In January the Russians break the siege of Leningrad and begin to push the Germans back. By May the Germans surrender in the Crimea. US troops land at Anzio, about 30 miles south of Rome, but fail to make rapid headway. In May the 1ˢᵗ Canadian Corps joins other Allied forces to launch a major assault on the Hitler Line through the Liri Valley, allowing the Americans to capture Rome in June. The 1,400-year-old Monte Cassino is destroyed by Allied bombers. On the Pacific front, the Japanese Navy suffers a massive defeat in the Battle of the Philippines Sea, losing more than 400 planes and three carriers. The US Marines go on to defeat the Japanese on Saipan, Guam and other islands of the Marianas. Later in the year the final blow to the Japanese Navy comes with their decisive defeat in the Battle of Leyte Gulf. The US begins its massive bombing of mainland Japanese cities. On June 6 Canadian forces take part in the D-Day invasion of northern France, "Operation Overlord." In total, about 15,000 Canadians land in Normandy. In the weeks that follow the Canadians suffer over a thousand casualties, 359 of them fatal. They face fierce resistance before they finally take Caen and Falaise. In July German military leaders fail in an attempt to assassinate Hitler. In the autumn Allied forces push the Germans back through Northern Italy, and the 1ˢᵗ Canadian Corps breaks through the Gothic Line, the Germans' major defensive barrier in northern Italy. The cost to the Canadians is high: 2,511 casualties. On the Western front, Paris and Antwerp are taken in September and the Allies cross into German territory. Meanwhile, Russian troops enter Prussia in the east. After battling fierce German resistance, Canadian forces clear the Dutch Scheldt and bring food to the starving Dutch people. An ambitious Allied airborne assault on the German-held bridges in the Netherlands, "Operation

Market Garden," results in disaster for the Allies. The Canadian government is forced to send some conscripts overseas, despite its promise to make overseas service voluntary. The Germans launch their secret weapons, the V-1 and V-2 flying bombs, causing the deaths of 14,000 people, mainly in London. On December 16 the Germans begin their final major counterattack through the Ardennes against US troops, in The Battle of the Bulge. By late December the German offensive is halted.

An advertisement for the Victory Loan campaign in August 1944 poignantly described the daily life of a pilot:

PILOT OFFICER

You look at him but you don't know him…he's a lot different somehow. Sure, he jokes about his job, his wings…and he slips into incomprehensible but delightful air lingo once in a while… but he's got that tired, faraway look in his eye.

He's all glamour for the girls, and a great hero to the kids…and everybody's proud he got his commission…but he's a lot different somehow, not the same lad who went off so exuberantly just a year or two ago.

The gang of his own age who are still around look him over goggle-eyed…they ask questions…but he doesn't answer all of them.…

Listen.…

Each day he is living a year. He sleeps with a bunkmate who is on his way home a day or two later…in a coffin…or missing… wandering around in enemy territory.

Some short months and some long minutes have made a pilot of him…wings never come cheap!

He is slammed up against responsibility in the pilot's bucket of a quarter-million dollar bomber…with four or five other lives beside his own…kids in the gun turrets who think he is mighty close to being God…items to check, maps, flight photographs, meteorology, briefing instructions…can't forget a single detail.

Sometimes the return flight is a cinch…after that agonizing age over the target…sometimes it is a bloody nightmare, with dead engines and dying men…sleep comes hard after a mission

...yet he carries on with the cruelest, lousiest job on earth...and comes home in his Sunday best, jokes as gaily as he can and lets you glory in his wings, his commission and rank....

All of it...the ribbons and citations too...doesn't mean much if you are dead tomorrow...they'll just be letters on a cenotaph....

At the end of December 1943, 75 Australian and British airmen from the Commonwealth Air Training Plan arrived in Nelson for a short leave. "There were flying snowballs, laughter and joking as they were paraded along the main street of town, led by local drummers." The men would be wined and dined, as rationing allowed, and were invited to attend, free of charge, all skating sessions at the Civic Centre and the annual New Year's Eve Silver Slipper Ball.

For these young men it was a happy beginning to a year in which some of them would surely lose their lives. For 1944 was a year of attrition for the Allied airmen as the mass bombing of German cities intensified. The statistics are grim. Losses by Bomber Command accounted for one-quarter of all fatalities in Canada's three services. Men in the RCAF were twice as likely to be killed as men in the Canadian Army, and five times as likely as sailors in the navy.[59] Barry Broadfoot wrote:

More than 10,000 RCAF personnel were lost in Bomber Command. More than 10,000 out of 41,000 fatalities for all of Canada's three services. There was never all that much publicity about them. The night-by-night duty of going there and coming back (if you were lucky) did not make especially dramatic reading. But those who were perceptive and could analyze the casualty lists could see that the death toll in Bomber Command was fearful. Through the deadliest flak fire ever thrown up, evading searchlights and the Messerschmidt and Focke-Wulf fighters, night after night the great streams of bombers crossed the Channel and sped deep into Germany; and so many did not come back.[60]

By the middle of 1944, between 1,200 and 1,300 men from Nelson and surrounding communities had joined the armed forces. More than half of the Nelson and district casualties in the war, 38 young men or 55 percent, took place in 1944. For the first half of the year they were mostly airmen, flying missions over occupied Europe and deep into Germany, and soldiers battling their way up the boot of Italy. After the Allied invasion of France in June the number of casualties in the army began to swell. But unlike the country as a whole, Nelson lost more young men in the air force than in the army. According to statistics published by the Canadian War Museum, 55 percent of Canadians killed were in the army, and 40 percent in the air force. Of the 70 casualties from Nelson and district, 40 percent were in the army, and 53 percent were in the air force. Some of the Nelson airmen flew with the RAF in Fighter, Coastal and Bomber Commands. Many of the airmen were with the Bomber Command's No. 6 Group, formed on January 1, 1943, comprised of 15 RCAF squadrons. In 1944 Nelson lost 20 young men in the air force, over Italy, France, Germany, Belgium, Norway and by accident in Canada or the British Isles. Eighteen Nelson men were lost in the army, a few in accidents on British or Canadian soil, but most in combat in Italy, France or Belgium.

The first Nelson casualty of the year was a young airman flying with the RAF's 198 Squadron. He was *Flying Officer Henry Hector MacKenzie*, called Hank or Harry by his friends. During the night of January 3 the Typhoon aircraft he was piloting was shot down between the Forest of Lompeigne and the resort of Le Touquet in the Pas-de-Calais. The 198th was a night fighter-bomber, rocket-equipped squadron that was raiding trains and barges in enemy-occupied territory. Hank MacKenzie had been flying Typhoons since late 1942 when shortly after he arrived overseas he was selected to receive special training in the then-secret aircraft. He had finished his tour of duty and was about to be shipped home when he volunteered to fill in for a missing crew member on the night of January 2/3.

The son of a popular family doctor who had practised in Nelson for many years, Hank received most of his education in Nelson, but attended grade ten in Victoria. His mother later recalled how desperately he had missed his friends in Nelson and pleaded to come home. High-school classmate Dawn Penniket recalls:

> His father and mother sent him to [a boys' school] in Victoria for grade 10 and he raised hell and what for and he joined us for 11 and 12.... He was a great guy, more fun and a lousy dancer but much loved by our gang. He and Bob Crerar owned an old car and it always was in a million pieces spread out on Carbonate Street.[61]

Hank appears to have had an early interest in flying, judging from the verse about him in the 1940 high-school annual: "Girls and boxing and aeroplanes; In which field will he attain fame?"

Hank's parents and brother had moved from Nelson to New Westminster in 1941, the year before Hank went overseas. His cousin, Major Jack Mahony of New Westminster, was to receive the Victoria Cross for heroism at Melfa River in Italy in May 1944, just a few month's after Hank was killed at the age of 23. The name of Flying Officer Henry MacKenzie does not appear on the cenotaph in Nelson, likely because his parents had moved. But surely Nelson was home to Henry.

The same night that Henry MacKenzie was killed, another Nelson airman was shot down with his crew while on a mission over Berlin, and spent the remainder of the war as a prisoner of war. John E. "Jack" Young's Lancaster bomber was among the 27 that failed to return on the night of January 3 when German night fighters attacked the Allied force of some 383 bombers over the target. Flight Lieutenant Young bailed out and landed in a tree, hanging upside down in his tangled parachute. After extricating himself and spending the night in a small barn, he was found in the morning by the German Home Guard and was taken to a hospital just north of Berlin where a German doctor treated his wounds. After miserable days and nights in prisons in Hamburg and Frankfurt, Jack and other captured Allied airmen were moved in cattle trucks and third-class coaches to Stalag Luft 3 at Sagan, the famous camp that staged the Great Escape in March 1944. Jack Young was not among the 76 escapees, 73 of whom were recaptured. Fifty of the recaptured men were executed by the Gestapo; only three managed to reach safety.

For a year Jack was kept at Stalag Luft 3, where the men were "fairly comfortable," doing their own cooking, taking part in all kinds of sports and theatrical entertainments. In January 1945 the Germans, fearful of being overrun by the Russian advance, moved the prisoners on foot some 56 miles to a "decaying prison camp" at Luckenwalde, 31 miles south of Berlin. In telling his story to the Nelson Rotary Club on his return home, Jack described the conditions at the Luckenwalde camp as "terrible." But a fellow prisoner, Pilot Officer Grant McRae, who shared Jack's experiences at Sagan and Luckenwalde, was more graphic in his description of the camp's horrors when he gave an interview to a Toronto journalist:

> Luckenwalde's bunkers were dark and damp, and the odour of feces and urine permeated the wooden walls.... "We were heavily bearded and dirty. We lined up for rations, cabbage and water."

The "outhouses," mere holes atop a craggy hill, were infested with sharp-toothed, hairy rats. "You could hear them below, scurrying around." In the barracks behind...Russian POWs were being treated even worse. "It's something I'll never forget."..."We'd look out the window and see them burying the Russians on a daily basis, just dropping them to the ground and throwing some dirt over them. It wasn't a concentration camp, but it was damn near."[62]

The prisoners were to be liberated by the Russians on April 22, 1945, and eventually Jack Young and the others were returned to Britain and home.

The RAF's 18 Squadron was supporting the Allied advance through Italy when on January 14 one of their Boston aircraft, piloted by **Donald Ernest Gibbon** of Nelson, crashed seven miles northwest of Foggia, just inland from the Adriatic Coast. The crew were on an armed reconnaissance mission over Rome when, on their return flight to base, both engines failed. Warrant Officer Gibbon managed to maintain control of the aircraft long enough for his crew to bail out, but he went down with the plane. He would have turned 21 three weeks later, on February 6. Don had joined the RCAF in 1941 and had been overseas since October 1942, where he took operational training in various parts of the British Isles. Just three months before he was killed he began training as a medium bomber pilot, and with his crew of three was sent to North Africa early in December 1943. In an aerograph to his parents in late December he reported that after two weeks of "looking over Tunis and Algiers" the crew had flown to Italy, arriving there a few days before Christmas.

Don Gibbon was born in Calgary but moved with his family to Nelson in 1925, when he was two years old. He was educated in Nelson schools and took part in many sports, including tennis, baseball and swimming, but was especially known for his hockey prowess. He was a member of the title-winning Panther midget hockey champions in 1938–39, and organized and led the Boy Scouts hockey team. He had been active for several years in Scouts and in the Nelson Boys Band. He left behind his parents, who had moved from Nelson to Trail, a brother, Art, who was later to become managing editor of the *Nelson Daily News*, and three sisters, one of whom was Peggy, the widow of Pilot Officer Syd Horswill.

There were two more tragic losses for Nelson families during that terrible month of January 1944. RCAF warrant officers Teddy Cornfield and Bud Ruppel were killed one day apart during raids on Berlin.

Edward Albert "Teddy" Cornfield was a wireless air gunner with RCAF 429 (Bison) Squadron. He was with a crew of seven flying a Halifax bomber when they failed to return from an attack on Berlin by 673 bombers on the night of January 29. Their bodies were recovered and all are buried in the Berlin 1939–1945 War Cemetery. Teddy was 23 years old at the time of his death. He had attended Nelson High School and was well known by Nelson residents as an employee of Valentine's News Stand on Baker Street, where he was working when he enlisted in 1942. He received his training at Lethbridge and Calgary, and before going overseas in June 1943 was an instructor at Regina and Pearce air training schools. Teddy's brother, James, a wireless specialist with the RCAF, survived the war.

The night after Teddy Cornfield's plane went down, on January 30, *Iverson Frederick "Bud" Ruppel* went missing with his Lancaster bomber crew during operations over Berlin. Bud was a navigator with the RAF's 100 Squadron, which had a Canadian unit. Of the 534 bombers that took part in the raid that night, 33 were lost, mostly to German fighters who followed them on their return flight. Bud's Lancaster bomber crashed in Berlin Stadforst (forest) Spandau. The body of one crew member was later discovered in a nearby grave, but the bodies of Bud and his other crewmates were never found. Their names are inscribed on the Runnymede Memorial.

Bud was another of the Nelson boys with real leadership potential who were lost in the war. He was popular with his classmates, very active in school activities and, according to a classmate, "very bright." The *Mountaineer* annual for 1940 called him "an able mathematician." Bud played the cornet in the Nelson Boys Band for several years, and starred with the high school Blue Bombers basketball and softball teams.

His high-school sweetheart, Dawn Sharp (now Penniket), some 60 years later, echoes the heartache that many young women experienced in those years:

> Iverson (Bud) Ruppel was my high school love and my steady when
> I was in 11 and 12 and I was just devastated when he was declared

MIA [Missing in Action] and later KIA [Killed in Action]. I had a letter from him after he was declared Missing.... I often wonder what he would have chosen for a career if he had come back. We'd have always kept our friendship. I know that for sure.[63]

Bud had turned 22 a month before he was killed. He had been overseas for 14 months.

On February 4 a tragic accident near Port Alice on Vancouver Island took the life of Nelson boy *James John "Jimmy" Eccles*. He was piloting a seaplane when it caught fire and he was forced to crash land. Three other crew members were killed along with Jimmy, who died of severe first- and second-degree burns. The only surviving crew member, Sergeant Ronald Barker, was awarded the British Empire Medal for his valiant attempt to pull Jimmy from the burning plane. Barker's citation tells the tragic story:

Two Close Friends Killed in the War
Airmen Jimmy Eccles (left) and Don Gibbon. *Photo courtesy of* Nelson Daily News

...He rushed into the flames in an endeavour to save the life of the pilot who was stunned by the impact. After his first attempt he was seriously burned and driven back by the flames. His courageous initiative instigated rescue action by the civilian onlookers with the result that the pilot was rescued from burning to death.

According to the Roman Catholic chaplain at the Coal Harbour base, "during the time [Jimmy] was conscious, he was worried about the other victims of the accident much more than about himself, and he said that he was not feeling any pain except for his leg" (he had suffered a compound fracture).[64]

Jimmy was a warrant officer, class II with the RCAF's 120 Squadron which was flying West Coast reconnaissance and antisubmarine duty. He was one of a Nelson trio of boys often called "The Three Musketeers," who had joined the RCAF together in 1941 and had trained together at various schools. The other members of the trio were Flight Sergeant Tommy Griffiths and Warrant Officer Don Gibbon (who had been killed only three weeks earlier). Born in Winnipeg, Jimmy was the only son of parents who moved to Nelson in the mid-1920s. He received most of his schooling at St. Joseph's Academy and was very active in Catholic youth activities. The headline for his obituary in the *Nelson Daily News* called him a "widely popular Nelson boy." He played hockey, basketball and baseball and had won the Kootenay Junior Badminton Championship. Jimmy was an ardent member of the debating team, and a long-time member of the Boy Scouts. His parents had moved to North Vancouver in the summer of 1943. Jimmy is buried in West Vancouver (Capilano View) Cemetery. He was 21 years old.

Only two Canadian men in naval service during World War II were to receive the Victoria Cross. The winners both had strong ties to Nelson: Lieutenant Hampton Gray grew up in Nelson, and Captain Frederick "Fritz" Peters had a sister and mother living in Nelson. The story of Hammy Gray is yet to come in this chronicle.

Captain Frederick Thornton Peters was 53 years old at the time of his death. He was born in Charlottetown, Prince Edward Island. His father had been the first Liberal premier of that province. Young Frederick was educated in private schools in the Maritimes and in Victoria before he left for the Royal Navy and the naval school in England. He had never lived in Nelson.

The citation for his Victoria Cross tells a gallant and terrifying story:
Captain Peters was in the "suicide charge" by two little cutters at Oran. *Walney* and *Hartland* were two ex-American coastguard cutters which were lost in a gallant attempt to force the boom defences in the harbour of Oran during the landings [by U.S. and British troops] on the North African coast. Captain Peters led his force through the boom in the face of point-blank fire from shore batteries, a destroyer and a cruiser—a feat which was described as one of the great episodes of naval history. The *Walney* reached the jetty disabled and ablaze, and went down with her colours flying. Blinded in one eye, Captain Peters was the only survivor of the 17 men on the bridge of the *Walney*. He was taken prisoner but was

later released when Oran was captured. On being liberated from the gaol, he was carried through the streets where the citizens hailed him with flowers.[65]

During World War I, Fritz Peters was the first Canadian to win the Distinguished Service Order, and later was decorated with the Distinguished Service Cross. He lost two younger brothers in that war, John and Gerald, both of whom are remembered on the Menin Gate at Ypres. Following the action that won him the Victoria Cross, Captain Peters was killed on November 8, 1942, when the plane carrying him to England was lost.

In February 1944 a special, private ceremony was held in Nelson at the Stanley Street home of Captain Peters' sister, Mrs. E.E.L. Dewdney, where his mother, Mrs. Fred Peters, who was bedridden as a result of a bad fall, had resided for a number of years. The purpose of the ceremony was to present Mrs. Peters with her son's posthumous US Distinguished Service Cross, the highest award given by the United States government to a foreigner. It was presented on behalf of President Roosevelt by Colonel Ralph Dusenbury of the US Infantry and two other American officers, sent by General Dwight Eisenhower.

Some of the hardest fought battles by Canadian forces during World War II were in Italy, especially in the area of the Moro River and Ortona in the winter of 1943–44. The 1st Canadian Infantry Division battled across the river and eventually took Ortona in house-to-house fighting on December 27, 1943. The next offensive, after a much needed rest, was to move north, along the Adriatic Coast to face the new German defensive "Gothic Line" at Pesaro. The historians Granatstein and Morton write, "The Canadians got their respite, but the winter of 1944 was no Italian holiday. Although the front was largely static, patrolling and limited attacks continued."[66] The weather was bitterly cold and frostbite was common since any farmhouses that might have given shelter had been destroyed. When it wasn't snowing it was raining and the men had to fight the mud as well as the Germans.

It was during this march north along the Adriatic, on February 17, that **Sapper William Percy Woods** died, the first Nelson soldier to be killed in action. He was with the 1st Corps of the Royal Canadian Engineers who supported the Canadian Army through the Italian campaign. He is buried in the Moro River Canadian War Cemetery, with other Canadian soldiers who died during the Ortona battle and in the weeks of fighting before and after it. A native of Saskatchewan, Sapper Woods was working as a miner and living in Nelson when he enlisted. He was 34 years old when he died.

Nelson's sixth air force fatality in the months of January and February 1944 occurred on the night of February 20, when *John Leslie Beattie* and his crew, flying with the RCAF's 419 (Moose) Squadron, failed to return from a night bombing raid on Leipzig. According to reports, the target was cloud-covered and the attack was scattered. The 816 bomber crews on the mission had to contend with strong winds, heavy flak and fierce fighter attacks all the way to the target. John Beattie's was one of 18 RCAF crews, totalling 128 men, who were lost on this raid. Altogether, Bomber Command's losses were 78 aircraft. John was making his sixth operation as a bomb aimer in a Halifax heavy bomber. He had been overseas almost a year and held the rank of warrant officer, class II. His body was never recovered and his name is inscribed on the Runnymede Memorial.

John was the youngest of seven Beattie boys, all well-known in Nelson where the family had resided since 1920. He had four brothers in active service, Bob in the navy, Norman and Donald in the RCAF, and Ronald in the army. Another brother, George, was to join the RCAF later in 1944. About a month before he was killed, John and his brother Don had enjoyed a visit together while on leave in Scotland. John was educated in Nelson schools, but spent his senior matriculation year at Upper Canada College in Toronto. While there he was prominent in sports and was a member of the band and glee club. During his school years in Nelson John played hockey, was a member of the Boy Scouts and the St. Paul's Boys' Choir. He was a popular boy. "Five foot two and eyes of brown, and always tries to act the clown," was how the high school annual for 1940 described him. A school mate recalled that "... a bunch of girls went down to the station to see John Beattie off, and each in turn kissed him good-bye, alone behind the station."[67]

On March 9 *Roscoe "Ross" Armstrong*, a Greyhound bus driver living in Nelson, died of pneumonia while in officer's training with the Royal Canadian Armoured Corps at Camp Borden in Ontario. He was a native of Princeton, BC and had lived in Kamloops as well as a number of

Okanagan communities before moving to Nelson in the early '40s. At the age of 31, Trooper Armstrong left a wife and two young daughters. He is buried in the Kamloops (Pleasant Street) Cemetery.

During these terrible spring months of 1944, the Sixth Victory Loan Drive got underway in March. It is a story of total community commitment to the war effort. A small army of service-club members from the Gyros, Kinsmen and Rotarians was organized into competing teams of canvassers to knock on the doors of all Nelson residents in an effort to sell bonds or collect pledges for the drive. The goal was to raise $500 for each of the 1,300 enlisted men and women from the Nelson district. Mayor Stibbs declared a civic holiday for April 26 so that residents would remain in their homes until the canvassers had called. It was an example of how a community can marshal its resources in times of emergency. The *Nelson Daily News* carried the message:

> Citizens are urged to be prepared to sign on the dotted line in fast order to help speed the salesmen on their way to "Put Victory First." Service club men will canvass the city from top to bottom, from morning to night.

The newspaper reported on April 28 that "Nelson's unique civic holiday sales scheme had paid off in big dividends." Victory Bond sales had been boosted to reach one-third of the quota. Visible rewards for support of the campaign were offered to businesses. There were announcements during the drive of the names of firms that were entitled to proudly fly a three-star pennant, "symbolic of outstanding participation by employees." To qualify, 15 percent of a firm's six-months' payroll had to be invested, and at least 90 percent of the staff must have bought bonds.

The Victory Loan drives were not for adults only. The newspaper reported that "The youngsters are not letting themselves be left behind in the drive to 'put victory first.'" A group of six Hume School pupils subscribed a total of $350 to the Sixth Victory Loan Drive. In May the junior high school's grade nine class supported the drive by staging before a packed house at the Capitol Theatre an "inspiring pageant" based on the "Four Freedoms." The Nelson newspaper described the evening:

> Initiated and prepared by the students themselves, the pageant gave a clear picture of the meaning of the four freedoms.... While biblical and historical scenes unfolded before the audience, two lads in bugle band uniforms stood at the sides of the stage reading

alternately descriptions of man's long fight for freedom.... The audience also saw talking pictures of captured German and Japanese film, and heard addresses by Lieut. Hampton Gray, RCNVR and R.B. Morris on behalf of the Victory Loan Committee. Between scenes Lieut. Gray described experiences he had had in the Fleet Air Arm, detailing the intense training leading up to the first operational flight.... He expressed thanks to the people of Nelson for their help for servicemen, to organizations for the sending of parcels, and expressed pride in the way the people put over the Victory Loan drives.[68]

One of Many Patriotic Rallies
The Capitol Theatre was in constant use during the war years for fundraising concerts and patriotic gatherings.

A visit to Nelson in May near the end of the Sixth Victory Loan campaign by Governor General, the Earl of Athlone and his wife, Princess Alice, who was a granddaughter of Queen Victoria, gave the drive a final boost. An editorial in the *Daily News* on May 12 urged Nelsonites to "go over the top today."

> The Victory Loan Committee is making a big effort this morning to reach the quota by 3 o'clock today so that Mayor Stibbs may greet the Earl of Athlone and Princess Alice with the news on their arrival at Nelson that the people of the city have again done their duty, that they have backed up with their money the more than 1,200 men who have joined the armed forces from the city and suburbs.

By the end of the campaign, sales had reached $853,900—111 percent of its target.

The night of March 24/25, 1944, was a bitter one for Bomber Command. A total of 811 aircraft, including 113 from RCAF squadrons, set out to attack Berlin. Bomber Command lost 72 air crews that night. Among those killed was 27-year-old ***Pilot Officer Maurice Coupland Latornell*** of Nelson, the young man whose death was the inspiration for this book as I set out to discover how he had died. I now know that his Halifax bomber blew up when hit by enemy fire. Maurice is buried in the Kiel War Cemetery, but the bodies of some of his crewmates were never found. Bomber Command's daily diary[69] describes the raid:

> This night became known in Bomber Command as "the night of the strong winds." A powerful wind from the north carried the bombers south at every stage of the flight. Not only was this wind not forecast accurately but it was so strong that the various methods available to warn crews of wind changes during the flight failed to detect the full strength of it. The bomber stream became very scattered, particularly on the homeward flight, and radar-predicted flak batteries at many places were able to score successes. Part of the bomber force even strayed over the Ruhr defences on the return flight. It is believed that approximately 50 of the 72 aircraft lost were destroyed by flak; most of the remainder were victims of night fighters.... This was the last major RAF raid on Berlin during the war, although the city would be bombed many times by small forces of Mosquitos.

Maurice was a navigator with 425 (Alouette) Squadron. He was with the squadron in North Africa in mid-1943, where they flew from a base in Tunisia to attack targets in Sicily and Italy. The squadron had returned to

M. C. Latornell Earns Wings

NELSON AIRMAN ARRIVES OVERSEAS

Sgt.-Navigator Morris C. Latornell, son of Mr. and Mrs. S. C. Latornell of Nelson, who has arrived safely in Britain. His parents received a cable yesterday. Sgt. Latornell, who graduated at No. 2 Air Observer School, Edmonton, Aug. 14, was a member of the Hume School teaching staff before enlistment.

Pilot Officer Maurice Latornell
Photo courtesy of Helen Wood

Nelson Airman in North Africa

Morris C Latornell, R.C.A.F., of Nelson has been in North Africa for the past three months. The former Hume School teacher went overseas as a sergeant-navigator late in 1942. He was a graduate of No. 2 Air Observer School, Edmonton, in August, 1942. The news of his arrival in North Africa was received by his parents, Mr. and Mrs. S. C. Latornell here.

Po. M. Latornell of Nelson Presumed Dead

England to rejoin Bomber Command's No. 6 (RCAF) Group in October or November 1943. Maurice was born in Strome, Alberta, but grew up and was educated in Nelson. He graduated from the University of British Columbia with a Bachelor of Arts degree in 1938 and a teaching certificate a year later. He taught at Hume School in Nelson for two years before enlisting in the RCAF in October 1941. Shortly before he enlisted he had been elected president of the Nelson Figure Skating Club. He was the young man who had taught me to skate four years earlier, and his death brought home to me, more than any of the newsreels or war movies, the reality of the war.

A flying accident on April 24, 1944, claimed the life of *Pilot Officer Richmond Wesley "Richie" Smith*, just three days before his 22nd birthday. The crew of the Halifax aircraft were on a fighter affiliation exercise, a type of operational training, when they crashed two and one-half miles north-east of Topcliffe in Yorkshire. Richie was an air gunner in the same squadron as Maurice Latornell, the 425 heavy bomber squadron. Richie was born in Quebec but spent his boyhood and high-school years in Nelson. He enlisted in September 1942 at the age of 20 and went overseas a year later. He had three brothers in military service, Don and William in the RCAF and Lloyd in the Canadian Army.

The month of April 1944 saw the loss of another Nelson airman, *Harold Arthur Alexander "Harley" Breeze*, who was an air gunner with the RCAF's 434 (Bluenose) Squadron. On the night of April 27/28 Pilot Officer Breeze and his crew joined 143 other bombers and fighters to attack the railway yards at Montzen on the Belgian-German border. The force was intercepted by German fighters and 15 bombers were shot down, ten of them from RCAF squadrons. Harley's plane went down near St. Trond in Belgium. His plane was shot down by Heinz Schnaufer, one of the top Luftwaffe night fighter pilots, who claimed to have shot down a total of 121 Allied bombers.[70] Harley had completed 30 operational flights over the Continent.

Harley was born in Nelson and was educated there. He was a prominent athlete, and played with the Fairview Athletic Club's intermediate hockey team the year it met Vernon in the finals for the provincial title. At the time of his enlistment he was working for Consolidated Mining and Smelting in Trail, and is listed on the Trail Cenotaph, but not the cenotaph in Nelson, his home town. Harley left a wife, Beatrice (Bea) and a young daughter, Dawn. He was 26 years old when he died.

Winning the Battle of the Atlantic was absolutely crucial to the Allies, since they depended so heavily on convoys of men, equipment, food and supplies safely reaching British shores. U-boats were the main menace, but Germany's powerful battleships also threatened to outgun the British fleet. Ever since its launching in 1941, the battleship *Admiral von Tirpitz* was one of the prime targets for the Royal Air Force and the Royal Navy. By April 1944 there had been five attempts to sink her. The first attack to have some success in damaging the ship was made on April 3, 1944, when 93 carrier-based aircraft—Barracudas, Corsairs, Hellcats and Wildcats—attacked her in a Norwegian fjord, scoring 14 hits. Taking part in the raid was Petty Officer Jack Dawson of Nelson, who wrote home to his parents:

> It really was quite an adventure. I was pretty proud of the fact that we took part. It was quite a sight to see all the ships and planes going in for the kill. We fished one of our airmen out of the water when he crashed alongside of us. The poor guy must have been cold for we were nearly frozen and we were all wearing fur Eskimo parkas. We got back with nobody hurt and all excited as the devil. Special congratulations from the King and Winston Churchill.[71]

The *Tirpitz* was not sunk until November, 1944, taking down approximately 1,000 of her crew. But before then and after the April 3 attack, another six attempts were made to sink her. Another Nelson serviceman was mentioned in despatches for his part in a raid on the *Tirpitz* on August 29. He was Lieutenant Hampton Gray, who would later win the Distinguished Service Cross and the Victoria Cross.

On the night of April 29, 1944, the Royal Canadian Navy suffered one of its greatest losses. The destroyer HMCS *Athabaskan,* a heavily armed Tribal class destroyer, was sunk in the English Channel, probably by torpedoes from German torpedo boats. The explosion of the magazine and a boiler on the ship could be seen over 20 miles away. The Navy lost 128 men, including the *Athabaskan's* captain, **Lieutenant Commander John Hamilton Stubbs**, a native of Kaslo, a historic mining community on Kootenay Lake, 40 miles north of Nelson.

John Stubbs was born in Kaslo in 1912, but lived there only until he was ten years old when the family moved to Victoria. At the age of 18

John joined the Royal Canadian Navy and trained with the Royal Navy in Great Britain. Before taking command of the *Athabaskan* he served as navigator on the destroyer *Skeena* and commanding officer of the HMCS *Assiniboine*, a command he assumed in 1943 at the young age of 28. He received the Distinguished Service Order for his "tactical skills" in the *Assiniboine*'s sinking of U-210, and posthumously, the Distinguished Service Cross for his role in the sinking of a German destroyer by the *Athabaskan* and her sister-ship, *Haida,* on April 26, 1944. Historian Michael Whitby described the sinking of the *Athabaskan* three nights later:

> *Athabaskan* and *Haida* were on patrol in mid-Channel when they were ordered to intercept two German destroyers.... *Athabaskan*'s radar soon detected the enemy ships; minutes later, the Tribal opened fire, then altered course towards the enemy to 'comb' possible torpedoes (that is, turn parallel to incoming torpedoes). In spite of this manoeuvre, a torpedo found *Athabaskan*. The hit caused such devastation that Stubbs ordered the crew to stand by in readiness to abandon ship. In the early hours of morning, her decks crowded with men, *Athabaskan*'s 4-inch magazine erupted in a massive blast. Most of those on the port side were killed, and many others were burned by searing oil that rained down on the upper deck. Survivors took to the cold waters of the English Channel as their ship began to sink beneath them. Stubbs is said to have sung to his men while they waited in the freezing water, stanzas from a tune about naval volunteers called "The Wavy Navy" [the nickname of the Royal Canadian Naval Volunteer Reserve—RCNVR—who actually formed about 90 percent of the Royal Canadian Navy]. [The men] were in the water for 30 minutes before *Haida*, having finished off one of the German destroyers, returned to rescue survivors. Although it was near dawn and the enemy coast was only five miles away, *Haida* lay stopped for 18 minutes. According to some witnesses, Stubbs shouted a warning...to the effect "get away *Haida*, get clear".... *Haida* headed back to Plymouth with 42 survivors. Six more of *Athabaskan*'s company made it safely to England in *Haida*'s cutter, while another 85 were picked up by German warships. John Stubbs, badly burned and last seen clinging to a life-raft, was among the 128 who perished.[72]

Signalman John Norris
Photo courtesy of Nelson Museum

Even though he had not lived in the Kootenays for many years, the name of John Stubbs is inscribed on the cenotaph in Nelson. Clearly Nelson claimed him as one of its own.

Among the survivors of the disaster was Signalman John Norris, for whom Nelson was home. He had been a crew member of the *Athabaskan* when it was on convoy escort to the USSR, and also when it came in close contact with the action that sank the German battle-cruiser *Scharnhorst* on Christmas Day, 1943. John suffered severe burns and was invalided home to Nelson. He told his story to the Nelson *Daily News* upon his return:

I was on the flag deck, not sure whether to abandon ship or not, when…a second torpedo caused a violent explosion, blowing the stern almost completely off. Everyone on the flag deck was knocked down by falling debris. I didn't expect to get up, but finally staggered over to the edge, and tumbled into the water, landing on my back. I had on my RCN lifebelt which proved to be perfect…. I could see the others, some had been blinded, and others badly burned. The water was covered with three or four inches of oil. We tried to gather in little groups which seemed to prove more satisfactory. I was about 200 yards from the ship when it turned up on its stern, and with its nose in the air slid out of sight. This was about three minutes after the second explosion. We floated around for about 15 minutes, some of the survivors having put on their little lights, when we saw a large dark form approaching. It was the *Haida*. Our hopes rose high. It was about 300 yards away, and we started to swim toward it, crying out frantically. I didn't get anywhere near it although I swam as hard as possible; the tide was carrying me in the opposite direction.

After the *Haida* left, I felt quite let down, so just let the tide carry me, till I came to another group of men. I then spotted a motor cutter which had been let down by the *Haida*, swam towards it and was picked up. The Captain of the *Haida* had let the cutter down, and asked for volunteers, as he felt that they would have to land on the [German-occupied] French coast. Three of the men volunteered, and we certainly owe our lives to them.[73]

After a terrifying 20 hours in the cutter, with engine trouble and pursued at one point by a German minesweeper, the cutter was spotted by RAF planes and brought to English shores. "My face had become so swollen I could not see," John recounted. "I was blind for about four days. We couldn't wipe the oil off us because of our burns." John eventually recovered from his injuries, earned a teaching certificate, and returned to Nelson to teach at the high school. He later became a published author and historian of the Nelson district.

During the war, feelings ran high in the Nelson district towards the Doukhobor community, in particular the Sons of Freedom, the radical wing of the religious sect. Roughly 7,000 Doukhobors were living in the Nelson area at this time, some 2,000 of them belonging to the Sons of Freedom. Pacifism was a basic tenet of their religion and the community was apprehensive that registration, as required of all persons over the age of 16 by *The National Resources Mobilization Act* in 1940, would be followed by conscription. The Doukhobors had been promised by the Canadian government in 1899, when they emigrated from Russia to Canada, that they would never be required to bear arms. The Victory Loan campaigns, not wanting to forego contributions from Doukhobors, recognized their pacifist beliefs by designing a special sticker for the bonds which stated that "the proceeds received from the sale of the bond will be used by the government of Canada to finance expenditures to alleviate distress or human suffering due to war," and not, by implication, for war materials.

After prolonged negotiations with Ottawa, the Doukhobor community was allowed to register its own people. An elaborate formula had been worked out between National Selective Service officials and Doukhobor leaders for alternative service for Doukhobor conscientious objectors. Some members of the Sons of Freedom still refused to register and were jailed for doing so. In June 1943 a brief prepared by the Nelson Rehabilitation Committee had urged that all young Doukhobors should be subject to National Registration and be treated as conscientious objectors if they refused to enlist in the armed forces. At a public meeting the Reverend H.R. Stovell expressed an attitude held by many Nelsonites at that time:

> [The Doukhobors] are a people...who enjoy freedom of opportunity at the expense of the men and women who have gone out to defend their privileges and freedoms, and yet will not take the responsibility of attempting to repay these men who are giving all.[74]

By February 1944 bitterness had grown on both sides. According to the Nelson newspaper, to protest accusations that "The Doukhobors are staying and making money, while our sons are away fighting," many Sons of Freedom turned in their registration cards, ration books, money and even land title documents. When the issue escalated into nude parade protests and the burning of schools and government property, the Member of Parliament for Kootenay West, W.K. Esling, advocated the deportation of "all members of the Sons of Freedom and any other Doukhobor nationals who violate the laws of Canada."[75] This was an issue that was to leave lingering resentments in the Kootenays.

The situation of the relocated Japanese-Canadians was another issue that developed ugly overtones, on the Coast as well as in the Kootenays, where many families were interned. In the fall of 1943 the Nelson City Council had endorsed a resolution of the Nelson Retail Merchants Association advocating that Japanese-Canadians not be allowed to own real estate or trade licences. The issue by 1944 was what should happen to the internees after the war. The chairman of the Nelson Rehabilitation Committee, H.D. Dawson, argued against the practicality of deporting the internees, many of whom were second- and third-generation Canadians. Others pointed out that many of the Japanese-Canadians held high decorations for their service to Canada in World War I. Dawson urged that they be dispersed throughout Canada, that their skills be recognized and used, that they be prevented from setting up their own communities, and instead be encouraged to share in Canadian customs and laws.

In May 1944 the simmering antagonism directed toward the Japanese-Canadians erupted, when a committee was set up by the Nelson Board of Trade to prepare a brief on "the Japanese menace." W.K. Esling advocated in the House of Commons that the West Kootenay area not be "saddled" with the Japanese after the war. Editorials in the Vancouver and Nelson newspapers argued over where the internees should be re-settled, with the Vancouver papers opposing any large-scale re-settlement at the Coast. An editorial in the *Nelson Daily News* on December 27, 1944, expressed the fear that the Kootenays would suffer economically if the Japanese were allowed to stay in their Kootenay communities:

> Kootenay's position is that the Japanese were accepted on the promise that it would be for the duration only. The fear is that opposition to return to the Coast will be so strong that the Kootenay will be left holding the sack, that some of our most attractive residential and tourist centres will become what the *Sun* calls "Jap-towns." If that should be permitted, the whole district would suffer economically. There would be a bad effect on the labour situation, on retail business and on tourist traffic.

There is no question that war and nationalist fervor can produce both the best and the worst in people.

Among the best was the work carried out in the Red Cross work rooms in Nelson and by hundreds of volunteers from the city and outlying communities, who worked daily to collect, sort and repair donations of clothing, hospital supplies and items needed by the military and by bombing victims overseas. In the four years of the "V Bundles" program, from May 1940 to May 1944, some 22,500 articles, weighing 17,000 pounds, had gone out from Nelson. A detailed account was kept of the articles in each shipment and itemized in the local newspaper. One typical shipment contained the following:

> —Servicemen: 11 pairs seaman's socks, 53 pairs service socks, 12 ribbed helmets, 25 sleeveless sweaters, 3 turtle neck sweaters, 17 steel helmet caps, 3 aero helmets, 5 pairs 2-way mitts, 1 pair minesweeper mitts, 5 pairs broadcast mitts
> —Women's Auxiliary Services: 1 turtle neck sweater, 2 pairs stockings, 5 pairs ankle socks, 3 sleeveless sweaters, 2 pairs knickers
> —Hospital supplies: 11 face cloths, 3 amputation covers (arms), 7 body belts, 6 surgeons' gowns, 12 hospital bedgowns, 6 men's pyjamas, 3 men's pyjama pants, 276 men's handkerchiefs, 24 pneumonia jackets, 30 triangular slings, 48 pillow cases, 12 bath towels, 12 ice bag covers

—Civilians: 22 boys' sweaters, 4 boys' suits (2 piece), 4 infants' sets (3 piece), 1 infants' set (4 piece), 1 pair knee socks, 6 women's nightgowns, 6 women's slips, 6 women's bloomers, 3 women's slacks, 1 child's coat, 12 boys' shirts, 12 boys' pyjamas, 48 infants' nightgowns, 6 children's sleepers, 29 diapers, 12 bandages, 30 crib quilts

During their visit to Nelson in May 1944, the Governor General, Earl of Athlone, and his wife, Princess Alice, attended a tea at the Legion Hall which featured the work of the "V Bundles" program. Some 600 "V Bundle" items were on display, including many items made by the volunteer women. The newspaper reported the event:

Among highlights of the exhibition were lambs made from sweatshirts, dolls made from flour sacks and knitted dolls. Work of Mrs. H. Perdue who had completed 124 pairs of boys' short pants, received special attention. Princess Alice described how the British children had missed having their toys these war years so much that she had seen them cuddling the embroidered figures on their dresses.[76]

CONSUMER'S RATION COUPON CALENDAR				JULY		COUPON VALUES BUTTER - ¼ pound TEA - ¼ pound COFFEE - 1 pound SUGAR - 1 pound CANNING SUGAR - 1 pound	
SUN	MON	TUES	WED	THURSDAY		FRI	SAT
July 1 -- Canned crabapples and canned blueberries go back on the preserves ration.							1
2	3	4	5	6 Sugar Coupons 36, 37 Preserves Coupons 23, 24 Butter Coupons 68, 69 Valid Canning Sugar Coupons F 6, 7, 8, 9, 10		7	8
9	10	11	12	13 Tea-Coffee Coupon T-36 Valid		14	15
16	17	18	19	20 Butter Coupons 70, 71 Valid		21	22
23	24	25	26	27 Tea-Coffee Coupon T-37 Valid		28	29
30	31 Butter Coupons 66, 67, 68, 69 Expire						

Ration Coupon Calendar for July 1944
These calendars appeared regularly in the *Daily News,* reminding citizens of coupon values and expiry dates.

On the night of May 12/13, 1944, Bomber Command sent 120 bombers, all but 12 from RCAF squadrons, to attack the rail yards at Louvain in Belgium. Five of the RCAF bombers did not return, including the Halifax bomber piloted by **Pilot Officer Wilbur Boyd "Wib" Bentz**, who was a graduate of Nelson High School. Wib's plane was shot down on its return flight by Luftwaffe ace Oberleutnant Martin Drewes, flying a Messerschmitt fighter. The plane had crashed in boggy ground near the Dender River, and the bodies of five of the eight-man crew were recovered and buried by the Germans. The body of 23-year-old Wib Bentz was not among them. This had been Wib's fourth operational sortie.

The story of the recovery of the plane and the three missing airmen 53 years later is one of the more dramatic stories of the war. In 1984, after the death of his mother, who was the sister of Wilbur Bentz, Jay Hammond of South Slocan set about looking for information on what had actually happened to his uncle 40 years before. After many years of research, he was able to pinpoint the location of his uncle's downed aircraft, and worked with Karl Kjarsgaard, a Canadian Airlines pilot with experience in aircraft recovery and restoration, to raise the necessary funds to actually recover the Halifax bomber. Funded by the 426 (Thunderbird) Squadron Association and a grant from the Department of Canadian Heritage, the crash site was excavated in September 1997, and the bodies of the three missing crew members were found entombed in the wreckage, 20 feet down in the marshy bog. One of them was Wib Bentz.

An impressive military funeral was held for the three airmen, organized by Veterans Affairs Canada, at the Geraardsbergen Cemetery in Belgium, and they were interred next to the other five crewmen, buried by the Germans in 1944. Jay Hammond described the ceremony to *Calgary Herald* journalist, Duncan Clark:

> When the minister [Veterans' Affairs Minister Fred Mifflin] made his speech and he had such a hard time, that was really touching. That wasn't a politician speaking, that was a man speaking. And I felt honoured that the minister was able to speak that deeply from his heart. And then the salute, the three rounds and the planes coming overhead. It was more than touching…. The full military funeral gave the three airmen the aura of heroism they deserve. Twelve soldiers fired their rifles three times. The piper's lament near the end of the service was joined by four Belgian air

Pilot Officer Wilbur "Wib" Bentz
Photo courtesy of Jay Hammond
and Calgary Herald.

force aircraft, who flew in the missing man formation, where one of the four planes peels off and separates from the others.[77]

An unexpected visitor to the ceremony was Martin Drewes, the German Luftwaffe night fighter pilot who shot down Bentz's bomber. Jay Hammond commented, "He was here today as a man, not as a Luftwaffe pilot." At the memorial service Jay was presented with his uncle's medals and with pieces of the recovered aircraft. The medals included the Belgian Croix du Guerre with Palm in recognition of his contribution to the liberation of Belgium.

Wib Bentz was born in North Bend, BC in 1920 to American parents who had immigrated to Canada. In the mid-1930s the family moved to Nelson, where Wib's father became the chief dispatcher for the CPR. Wib was a tall, muscular lad, who was president of the Gym Club in high school, and was active in most sports, including baseball, hockey, tennis and badminton. He was also an ardent hunter, boatman and fisherman. He was known in high school as "a whizz" at chemistry and math, and according to one of his classmates, was "one super guy." After graduating from Nelson High in 1940, Wib began working as a telegraph operator for the CPR in Penticton. He enlisted in 1941 and went overseas in June '43. His family had moved in 1941 from Nelson to Penticton, and eventually settled in Medicine Hat, Alberta.

The name of Wilbur Bentz is not listed on the Nelson Cenotaph. But before Jay Hammond left for the ceremony in Belgium some of Wib's friends from Nelson High School days gave Jay something of remembrance to take with him: an artificial red rose, tied in a blue and white ribbon bearing the initials NHS, blue and white for the school colours and for the Blue Bombers basketball team on which Wib had starred.

May 23, 1944, was a black day for Nelson. Two of her young soldiers in the Seaforth Highlanders of Canada were killed in Italy when massed Allied infantry, artillery and tank forces attacked the German's defensive "Hitler Line," across the Liri and Melfa Rivers. The Nelson boys were Privates Ray Hall and Jack Wilson. On that same day, in the same battle, two other Nelson men, Major Leigh McBride and Private Bud "Joe" Dyck, suffered wounds and were taken prisoners.

The Seaforth Highlanders of Canada had fought with the 1st Canadian Division in Sicily, through the mountains and valleys of Italy, fighting fierce battles at the Moro River and Ortona. In the attack against the daunting "Hitler Line" the Seaforths formed part of the 2nd Brigade alongside the Princess Patricia's Canadian Light Infantry, the Loyal Edmonton Regiment, and the North Irish Horse tank brigade. The German defences turned out to be much stronger than they had anticipated. Military historian Reginald Roy has described the battle on the 23rd of May:

> ... the Seaforths moved forward crossing the start line at 0607 hours. For a short time the attack went well. Every five minutes the artillery barrage would lift another hundred yards, and between 0600 and 0700 hours the battalion was more than half way to the intermediate objective. But well before this time the enemy retaliatory gun and mortar fire had grown in intensity, and the leading companies were only a few hundred yards beyond the start line before casualties began to start coming back to the Regimental Aid Post.... Some of the tanks began to strike mines. The dust thrown up by the shelling, the smoke from the guns and ground mist cut down visibility to only a few yards. By 0730 hours the tanks reached the barbed wire, but between this point and the objective there were 400 yards of open field.... This open ground was to be a graveyard for the tanks.[78]

By mid-morning three of the four company commanders had been killed or wounded.

Along the three-quarter-mile route of advance were Seaforths— many dead, some dying, and more who were wounded, waiting to be picked up or making their way back painfully on their own amidst fire which the enemy still sent crashing into the fields and orchards.

Through this hell the massed Canadian forces managed to hold on and to eventually break through. Roy quotes the Seaforth's Commanding Officer:

> As it developed, in this battle there was only one possibility of succeeding and that was for each individual to fight forward until he dropped or obtained the objective. Each man did just this and the line was broken…. [Success was gained] by the bravery and sheer guts of men in pride of regiment. I must repeat, this was another ranks battle, "their finest hour."

The Canadian forces suffered a thousand casualties in this battle, and for the Seaforth Highlanders it was the hardest won battle of any the battalion experienced in the entire war. They suffered 210 casualties, including 52 killed, 106 wounded and 52 taken prisoner.

Raymond Edmund Hall, a private with the Seaforths, was one of those killed. He had grown up and attended school in Nelson. His father, Lee, was a motorman with the Nelson Street Railway. After leaving school, Ray worked as a miner at the Sheep Creek gold mine. He was 21 years old when he died.

The other fatal casualty from Nelson that day was *Private John Woodrow "Jack" Wilson*, who was born and raised in the city. After leaving Nelson High, Jack was working in Trail when he enlisted. He had been wounded in the battle around Ortona at Christmas time, and the cable reporting his death was the first news his mother received that he had gone back into action. Like Ray Hall, Jack was 21 years old.

Both Ray Hall and Jack Wilson were eventually buried in the Cassino War Cemetery in the Liri Valley, where their bodies were moved from the 2nd Canadian Infantry Brigade Cemetery at Pignataro. A member of the North Irish Horse has described the original burial ceremony on May 25:

> After spending most of the day getting tanks ready again for battle, we paraded for a Service of Consecration, in the early evening, to say farewell to…the many Canadians who had lost their lives two days previously. The service, conducted by Padre Elwyn Hughes and his counterpart from Seaforth Highlanders of Canada, was held at the foot of a narrow strip of land, bounded on three sides by trees. (Regrettably, in my opinion, the dead were later removed

from this hallowed ground to be re-interred in the Cassino War Cemetery.) As the Service progressed, a mist started to fall on the upper reaches of the cemetery. As the two padres gave their final blessings upon those assembled, the sounds of a bagpipe could be heard. Then, down the slope and out of the mist, came bearded Pipe-Major Edmund Esson, MBE, of the Seaforth Highlanders, playing the *Scottish Lament*, tearing many an eye. We learnt later that the Pipe-Major headed the team that recovered the bodies of the killed, of both Regiments, from the field of battle.[79]

Two other Nelson men were victims of this battle, both wounded and taken prisoner on May 23. Leigh McBride was acting major with the Seaforth Highlanders, and was commanding one of the four attacking companies on that day. Their situation became desperate as they faced poor visibility and tremendous fire from hidden German guns, all compounded by poor wireless communication. Major McBride later described his experience:

Taking the small group of company headquarters that was still intact, I started to pick my way very carefully through enemy wire.... Suddenly there was a tremendous explosion and I woke up on the ground back in front of the wire, but Pte. H.J. Johnson had been killed instantly as had L/Cpl. J.V. Warner.... The young radio operator had a bad gash in his cheek and I...patched him up temporarily with a field dressing. That eliminated all of company headquarters except myself and trying to locate the three platoons I came across a private from the Pats and we went on together.... Suddenly we came under machine-gun fire and hit the dirt. Every time we moved in the deep hay it showed up and we got another blast for our trouble. I am not sure what happened next...but whatever it was hit me in the left eye and when I more or less came to it was to find several Germans looking down on me. They put a bandage on my eye and when it started to get dark they put me in an ambulance and we no sooner got underway when a large shell went off beneath the vehicle and some unfortunate Jerry who had a bunk below me in the ambulance got almost the full brunt of the explosion.[80]

Leigh's next memory was coming to in a German operating room in Rome. He had suffered shrapnel wounds and was to lose one eye.

Leigh remained in hospital in Italy for two months before he was moved to POW camps, eventually Oflag 7B, a camp for 2,750 Commonwealth officers near Eichstatt, 50 miles north of Munich. There he met most of the army officers taken prisoner at Dieppe in 1942. He later described his experience as a POW and the wide range of activities in the camp, including sports, theatricals, music, handicrafts, and "the mart," where a barter system was in full sway. In February he became the first Nelson POW to be freed by the Germans in a prisoner exchange, and he arrived back in Nelson at the end of the month, accompanied by his mother who had met him at the Coast. Four months after his capture, Leigh was to lose a younger brother in the war, Captain Ken McBride, also in the Seaforth Highlanders in Italy. Leigh had graduated in law from the University of Alberta before enlisting, and after the war he practised law in Nelson and Trail.

While he was in Oflag 7B, Leigh had received a message from the other Nelson soldier who was captured on May 23, Joe "Bud" Dyck, who was in a nearby camp. Private Dyck, with the North Irish Horse, was manning a Bren gun in the line when the German barrage began about 6:00 a.m. Before long only two of the North Irish Horse's 54 tanks were left, and only 70 men from the battalion were not killed or wounded. They held the line all day until late afternoon when the Germans counterattacked. Bud (sometimes called "Jo-Jo") has described how he, a sergeant-major and seven other men remained in position until 9:00 p.m., when they decided to try to get back to the Canadian line. "We came out of our hole and in front of us were the Germans, with their big guns and their tanks. I thought every Jerry in Germany was there." They were taken prisoner, several with wounds, including Bud Dyck, who had a shrapnel injury on his hand. According to Bud's account to a journalist from the New Westminster *British Columbian* they received no medical care for days, and only a little black bread to eat on the second day of their capture.[81] They were placed in boxcars, 60 to a car, and for five days, while the Allied planes strafed the tracks, the men suffered extreme heat, thirst and dysentery. They were taken to Stalag 7A near Munich, where their daily diet consisted of black bread, a pint of soup and sometimes potatoes. "We would have starved without the Red Cross [parcels]. The Russians didn't have anything."

Bud Dyck had a flair for languages, including German, so he was the interpreter for his group in the camp. He learned from the guards of their great fear of the Russians and their amazement that Canada had gone to war against Germany. He described how his facility with German almost got him into deep trouble when he was caught imitating one of Hitler's speeches; he barely escaped being reported to the harsh, disciplinarian captain of the camp. Bud's camp was liberated by the Americans on April 13 and he was flown to England, where he took part in V-E Day celebrations.

There is a striking difference in the description of POW camps for officers and camps for the enlisted men. Bud Dyck's experience of working in labour gangs on the railways and on farms, and of drastically meagre food rations, contrasts sharply with Leigh McBride's description of basketball and tennis courts, a hockey rink, exhibitions of art work, a 30-piece symphony orchestra, "a splendid library," and educational courses in accounting, law and languages. However, the food was never enough no matter which prison camp, and as Germany was collapsing, life for all the prisoners became even more miserable.

For many Nelson families it must have been a huge relief to be informed that their loved one who had been "missing in action" was found to be a prisoner of war. It was common for families to suffer the agony of not knowing for some months. In many cases, especially for those in the air force or the navy, death was never confirmed, only "presumed." Among the Nelson families who heard the good news about their loved ones were those of airmen Allan Harper, Sigurd Mathisen and Alfred Limacher.

Allan Harper, a graduate of Nelson High and a flying officer/air bomber in the RCAF, went missing on March 25, 1944, on the same night, and possibly the same raid, in which Maurice Latornell was killed. He eventually became a prisoner in Stalag Luft I at Barth on the coast northeast of Hamburg, along with some 6,000 other Allied air force officers. Accounts of Stalag Luft I tell of extreme overcrowding and scant rations, although, being a camp for officers, it also had some of the better facilities and equipment for sports, theatricals and other pastimes.

Treatment of POWs by their German captors seems to have been a matter of chance as well as a matter of rank. Some, such as Acting Major Leigh McBride, received relatively prompt medical attention by the Germans for their serious wounds. Other prisoners were not so fortunate, such as Lieutenant Sigurd Mathisen, a Nelson resident with the US Army Air Force, who went untreated for some time for his serious burns, resulting in long-term pain and permanent damage.

Nineteen-year-old Alfred Limacher was a flight sergeant and top-turret gunner with the RCAF 425 Squadron when on the night of November 4, 1944, his Halifax aircraft, part of a raid by 749 bombers, was shot down over their target of the steelworks at Bochum. Al bailed out after the plane was hit by flak and a few hours later found himself a prisoner of war. Much later Al told his story to his boyhood friend, author Ken Morrow:[82]

> ...some German soldiers captured him and took him to the mayor of a nearby town. From there they moved him to a German interrogation center near Welstar, and questioned him about the details of the new H2S radar equipment on his plane. Al said, "I was amazed at how much they knew about this new radar, and that they knew all of my crew members by name." His torture consisted of alternating his cell temperature, hour by hour, from very hot to very cold. Despite this ordeal, Al refused to answer their questions, and gave them only his name, rank, and serial number. They threatened to treat him as a spy because he was out of uniform, having left all of his identification in the plane. Later he was moved to several different prisoner-of-war camps.

Like fellow Nelsonite Jack Young, Al took part in a murderous forced march to the terrible, dilapidated camp at Luckenwalde.

> As the Russian Army advanced into Germany, he was part of a forced march further into Germany, beginning January 19, 1945. The prisoners walked 155 miles in blizzard conditions, and were threatened with being shot if they fell out of the column. Al and his friend Jim Gale, even though they were both weak and sick, by physically and mentally helping each other, were among the 900 out of 1,200 who arrived at Luckenwalde 21 days later. This overcrowded camp held 30,000 prisoners of many different nationalities. Their morale was low because almost all of them were starving and had dysentery.... Even with some Red Cross food parcels, food was very scarce, and he weighed less than a hundred pounds when the Russians finally liberated the camp two months later.

Their liberation at first was a mixed blessing. The liberating Russians were unable to provide food for the prisoners, and even when the Americans arrived, the Russians insisted on keeping the prisoners under their control, forcing them to unload transports. When Al was finally returned to England he was a guest at the king's tea party at Buckingham Palace, and was able to speak to the king and queen and the princesses.

Unlike the men in the German camps, the prisoners in Japanese camps were most often unable to receive the parcels from home. In Nelson the Red Cross Society coordinated the collection of goods for parcels to be sent to the prisoners, and Red Cross member Mrs. E.D. Rutherglen handled enquiries from district families about POWs. The parcels sent to the men were called "capture parcels," and they were assembled and sent to a prisoner as soon as word of his capture was received by the Red Cross. Included in the parcels was a complete outfit of clothes, and "many comforts and necessities." Red Cross workers created "housewives" to add to the parcels, consisting of a long strip of material with several compartments or pockets to hold needles, thread, bootlaces, trouser buttons, safety pins, and other such "necessities."

The war was the centrepiece of everyday life at home during 1944. The front page of Nelson's daily newspaper was almost exclusively war coverage, and the inside pages were peppered with stories and pictures of local servicemen and women in training, receiving their commissions, going overseas, or home on leave. The war also dominated the syndicated columns carried by the Nelson paper. One such daily column was *Interpreting the War News* by Pulitzer Prize winner and Associated Press war analyst, Kirke L. Simpson. Another regular feature was the syndicated *Today's Victory-Garden-Graph* by Dean Halliday, offering illustrated advice on the cultivation of garden vegetables in the effort to encourage Victory Gardens.

Social gatherings often included crowding around the piano to sing the war tunes that most everyone knew: *The White Cliffs of Dover, When the Lights Go On Again* or *Praise the Lord and Pass the Ammunition*. In 1943 *Comin' In on a Wing and a Prayer* had been on the radio hit parade for 21 weeks; in 1944 the big hit was *I'll Walk Alone*. The sports-minded might be playing softball for either the *Spitfires* or the *Boeings*, or maybe bowling for the *Zombies*, the *Cruisers* or the *Clippers*. It was not possible to escape the war by going to the movies either. The bill at the Civic Theatre included these war features just in the two months of May and June, 1944: *Salute to the Marines, First Comes Courage, Passage to Marseilles, Thousands Cheer, Sahara, Song of Russia* and *We Dive at Dawn*. The movie poster for the un-warlike title *In the Meantime Darling* summarized the plot: *They had a GI Honeymoon…In a second-rate hotel…but they wouldn't trade their memories for all the water in Niagara.*

The biggest event of 1944, and one that Allied and occupied countries had been anxiously waiting for, was D-Day on June 6 when Allied armies, including some 14,000 Canadians, stormed the beaches of Normandy. In those first few days of the invasion, people of the Allied nations, Canadians in particular, held their breath in the hope that it would not turn out to be another and much bigger Dieppe. There were no fatal casualties among Nelson servicemen on D-Day itself, but there certainly were Nelson boys who took part in the massive landing. Ronald Cox was among the men of the Canadian Scottish Regiment who stormed Juno Beach. Petty Officer Jack Dawson was serving on the destroyer HMCS *Algonquin,* which took part in the shelling of the French coast, and Dewett McCuaig was a naval motor mechanic who helped man a landing craft which took the first troops to their landing points on the invasion beaches.

A soldier who lived across the street from my family on Mill Street, Lance Bombardier David Ferguson, wrote to his parents a letter he entitled "My War in Eight Days:"

Well, to begin with, the first big and exciting thing that happened to me on D-Day was that our craft hit a mine just as we were making our final run in on the beaches. Before that they had been machine-gunning us but never hit us. When we hit the mine the whole front was blown off, killing about six of the fellows sitting there. When it started to go down, I went over the side, and started for shore. I don't know how far it was but I was in the water about two hours before I crawled out on the shore. Honest, I was so weak I couldn't even wade ashore, but lay down and let the waves carry me in until I could crawl out. I landed about a mile farther down the beach from where everyone else was going ashore, so I headed their way, life enough coming back into my legs to start walking. I got a couple of drinks and a bit to eat, then I went aboard a beached craft and had a sleep for a couple of hours.… When I awoke I could manage okay, so I started out to find my outfit. After a couple hours of walking and thumbing lifts, I did meet them, but boy! did I have the shakes, and my chest was so sore from drinking salt water, all I did after getting there was roll into some blankets and sleep. You know, until that morning I had never seen a dead person, but I sure made up for it all at once.[83]

David went on to tell his parents about the next several days as the army consolidated its forces and supplies and began to move forward, under sporadic machine gun fire. On the eighth day of the invasion David was wounded by a German mortar shell, and was evacuated to England.

Only four days after D-Day another Nelson boy, 20-year-old Bob Morrow, had a narrow escape at sea. Able Seaman Morrow was a crew member of HMCS *Teme*, one of the frigates assigned to protect allied shipping from U-boats in the Bay of Biscay and the English Channel. At about 2:00 a.m. on the morning of June 10 the *Teme* detected a U-boat in the vicinity of the British aircraft carrier HMS *Tracker* and was ordered to give the carrier full protection. At "full speed ahead" the *Teme* readied to attack the submarine and signalled the *Tracker* to turn hard to port. The *Tracker* mistakenly turned to starboard instead, putting it on a collision course with the *Teme*. It resulted in the *Teme* being almost split in two. Bob Morrow has described the action:

> In a matter of minutes, an order came from the bridge—"stand by to ram." On that order each man was to lay flat on his stomach or back. Since I didn't have my life jacket on, I ran to get it—but at that moment *Tracker* struck *Teme* amidships. It hit with such force, I was catapulted off the gun deck and on the way down hit the outer wire railing of the deck below, and was then again catapulted off that wire into the wild waters below. After the carrier hit the *Teme*, our twin propellers continued to function for a short time. The suction from the propellers dragged me down and my body was tossed furiously around under water like a cork. Since I must have been down a long distance, it also must have taken some time to come back to the top. I began to think that I wasn't going to make it. I just couldn't hold my breath any longer. Then, suddenly, the force of it all shot me out to the surface behind our ship.... Eventually, I figured out where I was in relation to the ship and immediately started to holler for help. Moments later I saw some of my mates throwing me a heaving line. I attempted to catch it as it hit the water, but was unable to do so.[84]

Bob was finally pulled onto a "carly float," a cork life raft from the ship, only to find himself slipping through a hole in the middle, and once again nearly drowning. But he made his way back to the float. The

Tracker eventually spotted the float in the water and lowered a Jacobs Ladder. Bob had a third close call while climbing the long ladder to the ship's deck. Sick from all the oil he had swallowed and covered with diesel oil (he had shed his clothes in the water), at the top of the ladder he slipped from the grasp of the rescuing sailors on the carrier and almost fell a long way back into the sea, but he managed to grab a hand hold long enough for a blanket to be wrapped around him so he could be pulled on board. Bob returned with the *Tracker* to Belfast, Ireland, and was transferred to the naval hospital in Greenock, Scotland, to recover from the ingested oil. The RCN frigate HMCS *Outremont* managed to tow the *Teme* 200 miles to Cardiff, Wales, where she was repaired and eventually returned to convoy duty.

Bob credits his survival to his boyhood in Nelson when he and his friends would swim off the assembled boathouses on the lake. They would practice holding their breath under water and regularly fought the current to swim across the arm of the lake and back.

Flight Lieutenant Bob Andrew
Photo courtesy of Ann Rolph

The summer months of 1944 were deadly for Nelson servicemen. Three Nelson district men were lost in June, seven in July and seven in August, 17 in all. On June 24 two Nelson airmen were killed in separate air operations. ***Flight Lieutenant Eric Morrow "Bob" Andrew*** was a navigator with the RAF's 7 Squadron, a pathfinder force which at that time was focusing its raids on flying-bomb sites in France and Belgium. His Lancaster bomber went down near Dunkirk, on the border with Belgium. The only RCAF officer in his crew, he was buried in the Esquelbecq Military Cemetery in France.

Bob was born to Robert and Amy Vivian Morrow (no relation to Bob

Morrow above), and had been adopted by Robert and Emma Andrew, close friends of his father, when he was three months old. His mother had died at the age of 24, leaving the infant Bob and his older sister with their father, who had no family in Canada and was unable to manage on his own. Bob's mother was a member of the Horswill family, and Bob was a cousin of Syd Horswill who was killed in 1942. Bob attended Nelson High School, and "was a livewire in sports, particularly track and field." He also played on the Blue Bombers basketball team. He enlisted in October 1941 and after training went overseas in the fall of 1943. His best friend was Ray Burgess, who had been killed seven months earlier. So many of the boys his age (born in 1920) were lost in the war. Bob's widow, Audrey (now Heustis), recalls:

> Mr. and Mrs. Andrew (my first in-laws) were more like parents to me (having lost their only child). Their upstairs was the central gathering place for all his [Bob's] friends. Mom Andrew remarked once that after school at least six or seven boys would troop up the back stairs to play pool. Both she and Dad were glad they came home instead of going uptown to Gelinas's Pool Room. Five of those boys never returned from overseas.[85]

Audrey remembers anxiously watching the telegraph girl each day pass her residence on Nelson Avenue, and thinking "Thank goodness. Another day." When Bob was killed his parents gave his piano to his music teacher, Amy Ferguson, with a memorial note slipped into the piano's interior. Bob had turned 24 two months before he died.

On the same day that Bob Andrew went missing, one of his classmates at Nelson High, *Wilfred Clark "Jerry" Wallace*, was killed with his nine-man crew on a return flight from a night antisubmarine patrol. Jerry was a wireless air gunner with the rank of warrant officer, class I. They were flying in Coastal Command with the RAF's 59 Squadron when they crashed on Benevenagh Mountain in Ireland. Their Liberator aircraft struck the mountain 50 feet below the 1,280-foot summit. It was near their home base at Ballykelly in County Londonderry, and there the crew was buried with full Royal Air Force honours. The squadron made a record number of 98 sorties during 1944 and lost three Liberators, all of them in June. Jerry was born in Cranbrook and later moved with his family to Nelson where he attended high school. At the time of his enlistment he was working for the *Nelson Daily News*. His sister, Deanie, was the widow of Pilot Officer Ray Burgess, another classmate of Jerry's at Nelson High. Jerry Wallace, Ray Burgess, and Bob Andrew had all been born in the first four months of 1920 and likely shared the same home room for some of their school years.

When **Barrington Farr "Barry" Cleeton** was commissioned at Saskatoon in 1942 he became the RCAF's youngest pilot officer, at the age of 19. A year later he was overseas flying with a Mustang fighter squadron, and early in 1944 he transferred to the RAF and was flying Spitfires with the Royal Navy Air Service. On June 25 he was spotting in his Spitfire for a naval bombardment of the French coast when his plane went down over Cherbourg in enemy territory. The body of Flight Lieutenant Cleeton was found in April 1946, and was re-interred in the war cemetery at Bayeux. Barry's death certificate lists Brilliant as his residence, the site of a dam on the Kootenay River near Castlegar. His father was the station agent there for the CPR, and the family had previously lived in Trail, Rossland and the Grand Forks area, so was well known in the Kootenay-Boundary district. Barry had attended school in both Grand Forks and Rossland. He was 21 years old when he was killed.

Private Matthew Aylmer from Queens Bay was the first Nelson district soldier to be killed in France. He was serving with the Canadian Scottish Regiment, which landed in France on D-Day and fought its way to Caen. While a platoon from the Canadian Scottish was preparing to lay a minefield as an antitank defence near the Carpiquet airstrip, which Canadian forces had wrested from the Germans, a crate of mines exploded on handling, killing eight men. One of them was Matthew Aylmer, who died from his multiple injuries. He lies buried in the Beny-Sur-Mer Canadian War Cemetery among some 2,000 other Canadians who were killed in the early days of the Normandy campaign.

Matt was the only son of Lord Basil and Lady Aylmer, both of whom were first-contingent veterans of the First World War. The family was Anglo-Irish gentry from County Meath in Ireland, where they had held land since pre-Tudor times. It was a family with a strong military tradition, both in naval and army service. Matthew was named after his grandfather, Lord Aylmer, the 8th Baron of Balrath, who had a long career in the Canadian Army and served for a time as inspector general of the

Canadian forces. Young Matthew, 27 at the time of his death, was in line to become the 10th Baron of Balrath, succeeding his uncle John, who had no children.[86]

Matt was born in Victoria in 1917 but spent most of his youth at Queens Bay. He attended school there and in Balfour before moving to Nelson, where he boarded with a family while attending high school. After high school he worked for the Canadian Bank of Commerce in branches in Nelson, Trail, Fernie and Oliver before enlisting in February 1942 in the Canadian Infantry Corps. He first served at Vernon in Quartermaster's Stores, and later trained in England with the Calgary Highlanders before transferring to the Canadian Scottish Regiment. One of Matt's closest friends from boyhood days was Henry "Hank" Hartridge of Balfour, who had been one of the first casualties of the war from the Nelson district. Like his friend Hank, Matt was to have a mountain in the area named in his memory. Aylmer Mountain rises behind Sunshine Bay on the narrow arm of Kootenay Lake, very near Hartridge Mountain.

A week later, on July 7, another Nelson district soldier, *Private Hugh McKean*, also with the Canadian Scottish Regiment, was killed during the push to Caen. The final assault through surrounding villages lasted for three days, July 7 to 9, before the Canadian and British forces drove the Germans from the city. The cost to the Canadians was high, as historian Reginald Roy has recounted:

> During this assault on Caen the Canadian forces as a whole had lost more men than they had on D-Day. This held true of the Canadian Scottish also. During the battle for Cussy the battalion suffered a total of 40 killed and 80 wounded. There was little compensation in the thought that the 12th SS Panzer Division had been very badly mauled. A comparison of such grim statistics probably brought unsmiling satisfaction to the staff planners at Corps and Army Headquarters. But within a battalion each figure on the casualty list was a friend or comrade lost, one whose offer of life or limb was ripped from him as the price of victory.[87]

Hugh McKean's family home was in Winlaw in the Slocan Valley, but he attended Nelson High School. He is buried in the Bretteville-Sur-Laize Canadian War Cemetery on the main road from Caen to Falaise. He was the same age as Matthew Aylmer, 27 years old.

Once Caen was secured, *Operation Goodwood* got underway. Commencing on July 18, it was a joint British-Canadian operation to clear the Germans out of the suburbs of Caen. The next day, after massive air and artillery bombardments, soldiers from the Black Watch, Royal Highland Regiment of Canada crossed the Orne River and advanced toward Verrières Ridge, a strategically important 250-foot hill on the road south from Caen.

> In heavy rain the Germans counterattacked, and in their first ten minutes on the battlefield, six out of ten men in the Fusiliers Mont-Royal were killed or wounded, and two companies were virtually wiped out…. By the evening of July 20, some degree of order had been restored. However, during the next day, while the rain continued, the finger-hold on the ridge began to slip. The Black Watch was ordered to try to restore the situation. The barrage began at 6 p.m. and the Black Watch leaned into it, moving up the hill in a "text-book operation." Tanks remained at the crossroads until the battalions' anti-tank guns were in position. The Canadians held a line that stretched along the road from Saint-André-sur-Orne to the Caen-Falaise highway, but they were still on the lower slope and Verrières Ridge loomed ahead. Casualties had been very heavy. Second Div. lost 1,349 men, including 249 killed and 200 evacuated for battle exhaustion. The scale of the losses was not fully understood at the time and many men who fought fierce engagements and bested the enemy believed that the division had done very well in its first battle.[88]

One of the casualties in that battle was 21-year-old ***Private Michael Thomas Patrick "Mickey" Prestley***, a native of Nelson. He died on July 22 from "injuries sustained in action." He is buried in the Beny-Sur-Mer Canadian War Cemetery. The *Daily News* called Mickey a "Nelson hockey star and youth leader" and "a flashy forward on the Nelson Juniors." He took part in nearly all sports available to him, including lacrosse, basketball and baseball. Mickey was a member of the Catholic Youth Organization's (CYO) basketball team that won the local championship for three years running, with its line of Gagnon-Eccles-Prestley. The others were Louis Gagnon and Jimmy Eccles. Mickey received his schooling at St. Joseph's Academy in Nelson. He was an all-round student with many interests and talents. He was an active debater and represented the Nelson CYO on a number of debating teams in competitions with other Kootenay communities. He was a senior soloist in the choir of the Cathedral of Mary Immaculate and was a member of the Nelson Boys Band. A boyhood friend, Bob Morrow, remembers how pleased Mickey was when a poem he wrote won a contest in support of a referendum to build a new civic auditorium, the Civic Centre. After leaving school, Mickey worked for the Nelson Transfer Company. He enlisted in November 1942 and went overseas just before the D-Day invasion.

A plane crash on July 18 took the life of *Lieutenant Colonel Charles Wellington Steele*, the son of pioneer residents of Nelson. He was with the Canadian Army Dental Corps and was the chief dental officer of Western Air Command. At the time of the accident he was making an inspection tour of coastal units. The RCAF transport plane, nicknamed "The Northern Witch," crashed while taking off and burst into flames when it struck the ground, killing the pilot and five of the nine passengers. Charles Steele grew up and was educated in Nelson. He served overseas with the Canadian Field Artillery in World War I, afterwards graduating from the Dental College at the University of Toronto. He practised dentistry in Lethbridge and Weyburn, Saskatchewan before enlisting in the Dental Corps on the outbreak of war in 1939. He was 50 years old when he was killed.

One of three Nelson district airmen lost in the month of July 1944 was 29-year-old *Flying Officer Ambrose Bain*, who was with the 630 RAF Squadron. His Lancaster bomber with a crew of seven was one of four that failed to return from an attack on the railway yards at Givors, a suburb of Lyons. Ambrose's family home was Castor, Alberta, but he had been working as a labourer in Nelson prior to his enlistment in the RCAF.

A double tragedy for Nelson families that July was the loss of *Warrant Officer First Class John "Pro" Dingwall* and *Flying Officer Clarence Francis "Clare" McDougall*, air gunners in the same Halifax bomber that was shot down on the night of July 29. They were flying with the RCAF's 408 (Goose) Squadron when their plane went down two miles from Heide, Germany after an attack on Hamburg. On the homeward flight from the raid, German fighters attacked and shot down 32 of the 307 bombers. Twenty-two of them were from RCAF squadrons. On this mission Bomber Command's No. 6 Group (all RCAF squadrons) suffered their greatest losses in the war to date. John Dingwall and Clarence McDougall and their five crewmates were buried in a field bordering the road to Meldorf, Germany, in a common grave, marked by a white cross with the inscription, "ici reposent sept aviateurs Canadiens bombes dans la nuit, au le 29 Juillet 1944." Their bodies were later exhumed and re-buried in the Kiel War Cemetery.

Pro Dingwall grew up in Nelson and attended Nelson High, where he was known as a "natural athlete." He played lacrosse in the West Kootenay Boxla League and, alongside Syd Horswill and Hank MacKenzie, was a member of the Nelson junior lacrosse team which won the BC Interior championship for 1937. In the South Kootenay Hockey League Pro was judged the most valuable player for 1939–40. He enlisted in the RCAF in May 1941 and went overseas shortly after graduating as an air gunner from the Bombing and Gunnery School at Lethbridge in late 1942. He was 24 years old when he died.

Like Pro Dingwall, Clare McDougall was well known in Nelson as an all-round athlete. In team sports he was active in hockey, softball and basketball and he held several local championships in tennis. He had attended both St. Joseph's Academy and Nelson High School. When he graduated in the summer of 1943 as a wireless air gunner at Mont Joli, Quebec, he won a bracelet for top honours in his RCAF class. Clare was 30 years old.

Operation Totalize, from August 7/8 to 10, was an attempt by Canadian and Polish troops to break through German defences and take Falaise, 18 miles south of Caen. The German defenders included well-seasoned troops, the fierce 12th SS Panzer ("Hitler Youth") Division, and punishing heavy artillery. Bombardier Peter "Pete" Pearce of Nelson was with the 6th Field Regiment in support of the Cameron Highlanders of Canada, who on August 8 were attacking Fontenay Le Marmion, six miles south of Caen. When the captain of the regiment was wounded a second time and unable to carry on, his assistant, Pete Pearce, took his wireless set to another building, and throughout the day directed artillery fire against the Germans, with "a high degree of accuracy, sending back the only picture that was available, as it was still impossible to make contact by road in any direction."[89] His heroic action on that day won him the

Distinguished Conduct Medal, one of the army's highest decorations. His citation reads:

> Gnr. Pearce was acting as Observation Post [OP] assistant during the attack by Camerons of Canada on Fontenay le Marmion.... His officer was wounded but was able to carry on until hit a second time at about 1100 hours. From then until relieved about eight hours later, Gnr. Pearce took command of the Observation Post and maintained communication with the guns, engaged many hostile targets, kept contact with the infantry and throughout kept his regimental commander informed of the tactical situation. These duties of an OP officer were performed by Gnr. Pearce under heavy and continuous machine gun and mortar fire. Often under direct observation by the enemy. For several hours the position of Camerons of Canada was completely surrounded, and all their means of communication had been put out of action. The fact that Gnr. Pearce remained at his post and kept contact with his regimental commander was the sole means by which the Brigade Commander was enabled to learn of the desperate situation and plan necessary steps to restore it. The performance of Gnr. Pearce was an outstanding example of the greatest courage, presence of mind and ability to take responsibility in a most critical and dangerous situation. It was in keeping with the highest traditions of the service, and earned the admiration and gratitude from those whose ultimate safety he was largely responsible.[90]

Peter Pearce was the son of Frank B. Pearce, principal of Central School, one of Nelson's two elementary public schools. Pete enlisted on September 2, 1939, before war was declared, and had been overseas since August 1940. He survived the war and returned to England, his birthplace, where he died a few years ago.

Operation Totalize was not a success story for the Canadian Army, which gained only half the distance to its objective. It would take another major assault to capture Falaise. Many Canadian lives were lost in the three days of *Totalize*, including three from Nelson. The day that Peter Pearce was desperately directing artillery fire under constant bombardment, **Lieutenant James Esmond Clark** was to lose his life in the same battle. He was serving with the Royal Canadian Artillery when he died from wounds received in action on August 8. James Clark was born in Victoria but grew up and was educated in Penticton. He joined the staff of the Bank of Commerce in Penticton in 1936 and later transferred to the Nelson branch, where he was employed as a ledger-keeper before signing up with the 111th. He went overseas with the rank of sergeant in 1940, but returned to Canada to obtain his commission. He returned to overseas duty in December 1943 with the rank of lieutenant. James was awarded a Certificate of Merit in July 1944, just weeks before his death at the age of 25. The certificate was accompanied by a letter from Field Marshal Montgomery:

> It has been brought to my notice that you have performed outstanding good service, and shown great devotion to duty during the campaign in France. I award you this certificate, as a token of my appreciation, and I have given instructions that this shall be noted in your Record of Service.[91]

Trooper William Swift was with the tank corps, the 28th Armoured Regiment (Duke of Connaught's Own British Columbia Regiment), when they joined the assault of *Operation Totalize* in the early hours of August 9. They were to join the Algonquin Regiment in taking Hill 195, about five miles north of Falaise. Douglas Harker, historian of the British Columbia Regiment, described the battle:

> By dawn the leading squadron was in the area of the hill, but slightly to the east. The other squadrons were moving up fast. The thrust had carried the regiment to within 2,000 yards of the headquarters of the 21st Panzer Division. Then the Germans struck. Masses of enemy guns from the area around the Hill opened up on the Canadian tanks. Enemy tanks appeared and Tigers and Panthers blasted at the attackers. Hill 195 was the plug in the bottleneck leading to Falaise and here the Germans made their most desperate stand in the battle for Falaise. They hurled everything they had at the DCORs and the Algonquins and they had the whole area covered with fire. On one section of ground along the Hill there were 24 enemy 99 mm. guns.... From dawn to 8 p.m. the battle raged with a fury that had no precedent, even in the earlier beachhead fighting and the struggle for Caen. The German artillery and tanks systematically wiped out strip after strip of the Canadian square and hammered the other squadron near Quesnay Wood. One tank after another was hit, its crew

bailing out to dig in with the Algonquin infantry who had slit trenches among the tanks. The crews lugged machine guns from their tanks with which to continue the fight.... "After fourteen hours of heroic resistance in the face of overwhelming enemy fire, the regiment was practically destroyed," records the official history of the Fourth Armoured Brigade. It would be impossible and invidious to pay individual tribute to the cool courage and determination shown that day by the men on the Hill.[92]

Harker calls it "the fiercest and bloodiest of the regiment's encounters during the Second World War." The 28th Armoured Regiment was virtually annihilated by German tank forces and artillery, losing 48 out of 52 tanks. "Its personnel casualties on August 9 totalled, as closely as they can be calculated, 112, of which 40 officers and men were killed or died of wounds and 34 became prisoners."[93] Near the town of Soignolles in Normandy is a memorial which reads:

SACRED AREA
To Those Who Fell
August 9 1944
28th Armoured Regiment
4th Can. Division
British Columbia Regiment
Algonquin Regiment of Ontario

William Swift was 39 years old when he was killed in this battle, older than most of the men he served with. He was a native of Vernon, BC, but was homesteading in Blewett, six miles west of Nelson, at the time he enlisted. He left Nelson on August 3, 1940, along with 17 other recruits, one of whom was Oscar Dorval who had lost his life in 1943.

Another victim of *Operation Totalize* was **John Clarence Harlow**, who, like James Clark, was with the 6th Field Regiment, Royal Canadian Artillery, with the rank of warrant officer, second class. He died of wounds on August 10, the last full day of the operation. John Harlow was born in Medicine Hat, Alberta but spent his boyhood in Crawford Bay, on the east shore of Kootenay Lake, and in Nelson. He was a noted boxer and was a fireman with the Nelson Fire Department when he enlisted. He left Nelson with the 111th Battery in the first year of the war. John was 33 years old.

On August 15 during a second push to reach Falaise, another Nelson soldier was to lose his life. He was 32-year-old *Edward George "Ed" Shardelow*, a private in the Canadian Scottish Regiment. On that day the regiment fought one of its fiercest battles to reach Hill 168, just two miles from Falaise. Ed Shardelow was one of 34 men in the regiment who were killed that day. The unit's war diary described how few prisoners were taken. Suicidal remnants of the 12th SS Panzer Division, which the Canadians had pushed back the day before, "preferred to die rather than give in." Reginald Roy wrote of the battle:

> Many things had gone wrong during the battle. The absence of close armoured support, the shelling by our own artillery, communications breaking down, and other incidents made it a strictly infantry battle. What the Canadian Scottish had won they won by themselves. It was a personal victory for the battalion, a tribute to the leadership of the officers and NCOs as well as to the spirit and aggressiveness of the men.[94]

Ed Shardelow was born, raised and educated in Nelson. He was an outdoorsman and ardent fisherman. After leaving school he worked for the CPR from 1929 to 1932, when he bought and operated Shardelow Auto Camp and gas station on Nelson Avenue, near Lakeside Park. Ed joined the Army in August 1942 and went overseas in December '43. He had many relatives in England and had written home to his sister, his only immediate family member, of his visits with them just before going to France.

After the capture of Falaise, the Canadian Army struck out for the Seine and crossed with little resistance. En route to the city of Rouen the leading edge of the attack entered a hilly, forested area called the Fôret de la Londe. General Crerar and the commanding officers expected little resistance from the Germans, and the Canadian troops were advised that this would "probably be a non-tactical move and no, or very few enemy would be encountered."[95] When the troops entered the forest on August 27 they came under heavy fire from German mortar and artillery posted on a ridge called the "Chalk Pits." The next day Major General Foulkes, despite the misgivings of company commanders about intelligence reports that indicated enemy strength was slight, ordered an assault, led by the South Saskatchewan Regiment. Forty-three men of the Regiment were ambushed and killed, and another 145 wounded. Among the dead was 34-year-old Corporal *William Stanley "Stan" Smith* of Nelson.

Stan was born and raised in Nelson and attended Nelson High School in the late '20s. He was active in baseball and in a United Church youth group, the Tuxis Rangers. He also played the clarinet in the Nelson City Band. Stan was employed as a fireman for the CPR for several years before taking a job at the Trail smelter in 1934. While there he was an active member of the International Union of Mine, Mill and Smelter Workers, and also played in the Trail band. He enlisted in June 1940 and became a staff sergeant in the Princess Patricia's before he transferred to the South Saskatchewan Regiment. Stan's father, W.S. Smith, was a city alderman at the time of his son's death.

August 1944 also saw the deaths of two more Nelson district airmen, one in a flying accident, and the other in a mine-laying mission. Twenty-one-year-old *Flying Officer Ronald Greavison* of Slocan Park was navigator in a Wellington bomber that was on a 30-mile cross-country night training flight when the plane crashed in the sea off Lossiemouth, Scotland. He was with the RCAF's #20 Operational Training Unit. A creek on his family's property at Slocan Park has been named in his memory.

On August 27 *Flying Officer Gustaf "Gus" Flegel* was an air gunner in a Lancaster aircraft that failed to return from a night mission to lay mines in Danzig Bay. Five of the 30 Lancasters on the mission were lost that night. Twenty-three-year-old Gus Flegel was buried in Mandal Churchyard in Norway. Gus was a member of the Flegel family which had emigrated from Austria in 1901 and settled eventually in the Kootenays. Gus was working at the smelter in Trail at the time of his enlistment in January 1943. His name is inscribed on both the Trail and Nelson cenotaphs.

In the fall of 1944, while the Allied armies were fighting their way through France and Belgium and into Holland, the Canadian Army in Italy continued its battle northward along the Adriatic coast to face the next major German hurdle, the Gothic Line at the northern extremity of the Italian boot. The fiercest fighting since the Canadians broke through the Adolf Hitler Line took place in mid-September. In the thick of the fight were the Seaforth Highlanders of Canada, who were ordered to occupy the town of San Martino. The German forces were reeling from a major defeat at Coriano, so when the Seaforths advanced towards San Martino in the afternoon of September 16, they were surprised to find that the German paratroopers had regained the town and "were fighting in the best tradition of their service."[96] The battle raged for three days, with heavy losses to both sides.

Kenneth Gilbert McBride of Nelson lost his life in that battle on September 16. He was advancing near the front line when the carrier in which he was riding struck a mine, killing both Ken and his driver. Ken was a widely known and popular young man who was already a captain with the Seaforth Highlanders of Canada at the age of 24. Ken and his older brother, Leigh, were both officers with the Seaforths during the terrible battle for Ortona the previous Christmas. Ken had written home to his parents on New Year's Day 1944 about his meeting with his brother there:

> Well, I never will spend another Xmas like my 1943 one—what a nightmare. You will have read about it in the papers by now, but Leigh and I were in the middle of it. I'd call it Stalingrad No. 2. Only time I saw Leigh was on Christmas night—his platoon took over my platoon position so we could pull out and have Christmas dinner. We wished each other a Merry Xmas—he gave me a cigar and I gave him the dope on the enemy so he'd know where to expect the Germans in the morning. Leigh said he got a thrill when orders were issued from C. Coy, HQ "McBride to relieve McBride."... And here's wishing my Mother and Dad a wonderful New Year, and keep your chins up—Leigh and I will look after ourselves."[97]

Four months later Leigh was to lose an eye in battle and be taken prisoner for the duration of the war. He was on the "missing in action" list for four months. His parents learned he was a prisoner just two days before they were notified that their son, Ken, had been killed. Their father wrote to a friend:

> We had two happy days. On Sept. 20 we received a wire from Ottawa saying that Leigh was a prisoner of war in Germany. On Sept. 22 we received another wire from the director of records, saying that dear old Ken had been killed in action on Sept. 16. The distressing news almost stunned us. We had been worrying a

The McBride Brothers
Leigh (left) and Kenneth were officers in the Seaforth Highlanders.
Photo courtesy of Deedee and Sam McBride

great deal about both boys—Leigh being missing, and Ken in the thick of the fighting around Rimini. But during those two days, we were so completely happy that we forgot, for the time being, the danger that might occur to Ken.... Ken wrote us three lovely letters dated Sept. 4-6-10 which we received on the day that we heard Leigh was safe. He told us about being through two heavy weeks previously. He was happy and told of going in swimming and the big yellow moon, and of the German night raider that kept circling overhead. He wrote more letters which arrived after we heard the very sad news.... Ken and Leigh never let us down. How they wrote us as often as they did is more than we can figure out. They were both good soldiers—and they did their part.[98]

Ken McBride was born and raised in Nelson. He was a natural athlete, excelling at badminton, basketball and softball, but especially at golf. A verse about him in the Nelson High's *Mountaineer* for 1939 speaks of his popularity and athletic abilities:

Ken is the dark-haired class Romeo
For amongst our gals he is not so slow!
He's also NHS's great badminton ace
And in golf he is always sure to set the pace

After attending the University of Alberta for one year, Ken moved on to UBC, and while there enlisted in the army. It seems likely that he would have made a name for himself as a golfer. He won many championships in the Kootenays and also while he attended university, winning the UBC championship in both 1940 and 1941. In his last year there he captained a UBC team that toured Washington, Oregon and California, "competing against the best golfers on the Pacific Coast." In 1946 the cup for the Nelson Invitational Open Golf Championship was named the Kenneth McBride Memorial Trophy, in honour of the hometown boy whose promising golfing career was cut so short.

By the fall of 1944 the heavy losses of men in Italy and Normandy were creating severe shortages of manpower for the army. The many advertisements urging conscripts to "wear the GS badge" that signified the choice of "General Service on any battle front, anywhere in the world," were not producing the desired number of volunteers.

I signed up to fight—to go overseas—to do the work of a real soldier! That's why I'll wear the GS badge on my arm. It's a decoration—something any man can be proud to wear—because only those willing to do their *full share of service* are permitted to wear it.

"You're on the *wrong* beach fella!" headlined another ad that pictured soldiers storming a beach while a young man sat idly sunbathing. Canadian soldiers at the front, after having survived so many bloody battles and

Ad Promoting Overseas Service

Conscripts were urged to volunteer for overseas service, allowing them to wear the "GS" badge. Until late in the war, Canada's overseas forces were all voluntary.

being so long away from home, were showing some impatience with the war, and in particular with men who had been drafted under the *National Resources Mobilization Act* (*NRMA*) but had not volunteered for overseas service. These home-service conscripts were popularly given the derogatory name of "zombies." One gunner on the Italian front, complaining about the lack of conscription for overseas service, told a war correspondent, "…what we would like is a policy for getting us home, five years overseas is a damn long time."

The MacKenzie King government had promised "conscription if necessary, but not necessarily conscription" for overseas service. But in November 1944 the government decided that "necessity" had come. Anti-conscription demonstrations broke out in late November at six BC centres: Vernon, Chilliwack, Nanaimo, Courtenay, Prince George and Terrace. There was a sit-down strike by Home Defence soldiers at Terrace, and nearly 1,000 soldiers from the Vernon Military Camp paraded through the streets shouting "Down with Conscription!" According to statistics of the Department of National Defence, 4,029 "zombies" were residents of BC; only 36 of them were from Nelson.[99] In the fall of 1944 the hunt was on in earnest for "draft dodgers," men who had failed to answer their military call-up notices. But there turned out to be very few actual draft dodgers, only 36 in all of British Columbia. The *Daily News* reported the findings:

> It was found in many cases that the men had not received their notices, that they already were in the services, or that they were dead. In one case a man reported to be delinquent, had lost a leg at Dieppe and was sitting in a wheel-chair at home when the RCMP arrived with his call-up notice.[100]

The British Columbia Regiment (Duke of Connaught's Own), nicknamed "The Duke's," had landed in Normandy in the third week of July 1944. It was part of the Canadian Army that fought its way through Caen and the Falaise Gap and across the Seine to Belgium. Nelson native Maxwell Carne served in the 28th Armoured Regiment (BCR) and survived bloody battles through France, Belgium, the Netherlands and into Germany. He was the only member of his original tank crew that was not killed or taken prisoner, and was the driver of the tank in which Lieutenant Colonel Donald Worthington was killed in the disastrous tank battle for Hill 195 between Caen and Falaise in early August 1944, in which 48 of the regiment's 52 tanks were knocked out.

Among the casualties of the 28th Armoured Regiment was ***Trooper Evander Donaldson Rogers*** of Slocan City. Maxwell Carne remembers him as the driver of a water truck for the regiment, killed by a sniper's bullet in Belgium on September 26, 1944. One of the soldiers in the regiment was so incensed at the killing that he insisted on staying behind when the regiment moved on, in order to dispatch the sniper, which, according to Maxwell Carne, he did. The name of Trooper Rogers is among those inscribed on the Nelson Cenotaph. He was 35 years old.

The South Saskatchewan Regiment was with the Canadian Army liberating the Channel ports, including Dieppe on September 1, 1944, where they had been part of the disastrous raid two years earlier. They battled through Belgium and into the flooded polders and knee-deep mud of Holland, crossing canals and taking heavy casualties. *Private Stanley Frederick Castle* of Nelson was with the regiment when on October 29 he was killed as they crossed the canal at Gravenpolder, just into the Netherlands from Belgium. Stan Castle had been a member of the 111th (Nelson) Field Battery before the outbreak of war. His father, Fred, a veteran of the First World War, was quarter-master sergeant for the battery and together father and son were among the first contingent to leave Nelson for training in Edmonton in October 1939. Stan went overseas during the winter of 1940–41. He grew up in Nelson, where his father operated Van de Camp's Bakery. John Norris, survivor of the HMCS *Athabaskan,* was a boyhood friend and neighbour of Stan's and recalls the pink buns Fred Castle used to make for the kids. John had also been a sparring partner with Stan, who built quite a reputation as an amateur boxer. Stan was 23 when he was killed.

Many Nelson servicemen had interesting stories to tell about their experiences: near-misses, lucky escapes or special assignments. Flying Officer Gib Goucher of Nelson piloted a Stirling aircraft which was towing a glider during *Operation Market Garden,* the massive landing of an airborne army in Holland in mid-September 1944. An RCAF press release described his terrifying brush with death:

> Just after taking off [the aircraft] twisted to port and started down in a spiral dive. A glider which apparently had hit the slipstream and gone out of control, dragged the tow ship's tail and made it momentarily uncontrollable. Goucher…stood up at the controls in an effort to bring the Stirling out of the spiral which started 2,500 feet from the ground. He finally controlled it only a few hundred feet above the ground. Meanwhile the glider's tow rope broke and the glider pilot landed in a corn field nearby.[101]

After 572 flying hours as an air gunner, Pilot Officer Peter Melneczuk, who grew up in Nelson, had a near-miss on the very last mission of his second operational tour. A RCAF press release told his story:

> Peril pursued PO Peter Melneczuk of Nelson, BC, Bluenose Squadron gunner, right up to the end of his second operational tour. His last target was Hamburg, a daylight raid. Clouds concealed the enemy town so well that it was decided to return to Britain without dropping the bombs. Over England disaster caught up with his aircraft. Both starboard propellers flew off. The bomb-burdened aircraft slanted toward earth and the skipper ordered the crew to "hit the silk." There was no question of jettisoning the bombs; the pilot could only try to land and he didn't want his crewmates to share the risk. Melneczuk headed into space about 5,000 feet up, floated safely down, manipulating the cords of his chute so as to fall in a river. He landed in the soft mud on its bank, unhurt as were the other flyers. Meanwhile the pilot attempted to belly-land in a field, the petrol exploded and he was killed.[102]

H.W.R. "Bert" Ramsden, a pilot with the RCAF's 404 (Buffalo) Squadron, survived one of the fiercest air battles of the war. One of the squadron's jobs, as part of Coastal Command, was to attack enemy shipping in the North Sea along the Norwegian coastline. Bert and his squadron were part of an attack over the icy waters of Forde Fjord on February 9, 1945, when rocket-firing Allied planes seriously damaged German shipping and tangled with a dozen Focke-Wulf 190 German fighters. Nine Allied aircraft were lost in the raid, which was labelled "Black Friday" by their home base at Dallachy, Scotland. Bert told me how his small stature possibly had saved his life earlier in the war. When his air crew was assigned to larger bombers, Bert found that his feet could not easily reach the rudder controls, so he transferred to smaller aircraft. His crew was taken over by a pilot, Frank Morrow, who had worked with Bert for a short time at the Bank of Commerce in Nelson. In June 1944 Frank and Bert's old crewmates went down over Germany; three were killed and four were taken prisoners.

Sub-Lieutenant Victor I. "Vic" Graves of Nelson was a survivor of the sinking of the minesweeper, HMCS *Clayoquot,* a victim of U-806 off Halifax harbour on Christmas Eve day, 1944. The minesweeper was on convoy escort duty when the torpedo struck in mid-afternoon of December 24. The crew was praised for its orderliness and "cool behaviour" in abandoning ship. All of the 73 men who managed to get off the ship were rescued by a corvette after about a half hour in the icy water. "Their teeth were chattering but they were still bravely singing *Oh, Come All Ye Faithful.*" The *Clayoquot* was the first Canadian warship to be built in Prince Rupert, and the twentieth to be lost in the war.

In the summer and fall of 1944 the first V-1 flying bombs, popularly known as "doodle-bugs," "buzz-bombs" or "robot bombs," had begun bombarding London. Some Nelson servicemen, on leave in Britain, experienced them first-hand. Leading Aircraftman Jim Coleman required hospital treatment for injuries he received from a V-1 in September. Signalman John McGinn wrote home of his experience:

> We heard one coming over. The motor quit and we went on to the floor under the table. The windows just folded up and the splinters flew in all directions. None of the pieces hit any of us, however.... The blast of one of them is terrific. You'd almost think someone was pushing you around.[103]

There were Nelson men among the engineers and skilled technicians who played an important role in the war. Sapper S. Jorgenson of Nelson was among the Royal Canadian Engineers honoured by Canadian Army Commander, Lieutenant-General A.G.L. McNaughton, for the work the company did in Gibraltar by tunnelling out great sections of "The Rock" for gun emplacements, underground water systems and a hospital.

Private George "Scotty" Williams of Blewett, who left Nelson with the 111th Field Battery in 1939, was part of a Light Aid Detachment in Italy that repaired shot-up artillery pieces, tanks and motor vehicles, often in the thick of battle. An article in *The Maple Leaf* magazine in May 1944 featured Scotty:

> "Scotty" is no spring chicken, but he hops around the big guns in the midst of engagements, repairing, balancing gears, charging them with air and oil, and considers it "just an ordinary job."...
> [He] is officially a gun fitter but to the boys he's a "gun doctor."

Flying Officer Ian Carne, brother of Maxwell Carne, had the novel assignment of flying copies of *SEAC*, the daily service newspaper of South East Asia Command published in Calcutta, to men in the forward lines, scattered over a 700-mile front. A feature article on the airmen in an issue of *SEAC* told how they often had to face worse enemies than the Japanese:

Flying through the jungles in all kinds of weather, including the monsoons which cause great damage, they also have to battle the hawks for whom the aircraft seems to have a special fascination.[104]

Private Fred Thompson was with the Royal Canadian Army Medical Corps, serving in casualty clearing stations and sometimes as a stretcher bearer, first in the Mediterranean, then in North Africa, Sicily, Italy and after D-Day in France, Belgium and Holland. Corporal Tudor Rutherglen served overseas with the British Columbia Regiment (DCO) as a mail clerk, collecting and distributing mail for over a thousand men.

Two Nelson men were on the personal staff of General Harry Crerar, who commanded the First Canadian Army in 1944. Major John Weir, who had spent his boyhood in Nelson, was personal assistant to General Crerar in Ottawa and in Europe; and one of General Crerar's personal drivers in Europe was Eddie Leeming, who was a meatcutter in my father's butcher shop in Nelson.

On the homefront throughout 1944, Nelson citizens, young and old, continued their enthusiastic support for the war effort, and in both civic and school activities the war was central. The junior high and high school cadet corps distinguished themselves, not only in British Columbia, but nationally. In December the high school cadet corps won the Earl Grey Challenge Trophy, awarded to the corps achieving the highest general proficiency in Canada. In one of their inspection manoeuvres, two attacking sections of the cadets had seized Gyro Heights, part of a popular Nelson park, while another section defended it. A First Aid team and a Signals Squad were also in the action. Inspecting District Cadet Officer, Major W.R. Critchley, spoke highly of the citizens of Nelson for their "noticeable and outstanding" support of their youth. He pointed out that there was no other corps in BC with as many efficiency chevrons. The girls' corps was also highly praised. And in the spring the junior-high corps had been called "the best in British Columbia" by inspecting officers.

The war hung heavily over young people despite their patriotic zeal, having seen so many of their older friends, brothers and neighbours go off to battle, and expecting that they would be next. It was the sobering theme of the Nelson High valedictory address by Bruce Arneson in 1944:

With the war going into its fifth year, the things we have begun to learn in school must be carried on with greater force outside. We must be able to sacrifice many forms of pleasure. We must have courage, especially those who are going to be leaving easy forms of living to take up harder tasks in our country's service....[105]

The students, of course, were aware of how they were being rushed into adulthood. A letter to the editor of the *Daily News* on October 9, 1944, signed "A Student," raised an important question:

Sir – Perhaps some reader could explain to me why Canadian youths are not allowed to vote until they become 21, yet these same youths are accepted to fight for the defence of Canada when they are 18? If 18-year-olds are old enough to fight for their country, why should they not be old enough to share in the governing of their country?

The pressure on school children to contribute even more was relentless. In November 1944, Nelson schools were visited by the director of School War Savings for the BC-Yukon district, who had a chastising message for Nelson's youth. Their per-student purchase of War Savings Stamps ranked only fourteenth in the province, while the record of students in another Kootenay centre, Cranbrook, ranked third. Once again, the traditional Hallowe'en "trick-or-treating" that October had been turned into a fundraiser for the Kinsmen's Milk for Britain campaign. The children not only collected the Hallowe'en Shellout tickets instead of candies, they also had helped in the sale of tickets to householders. The proceeds "turned their Hallowe'en fun into an estimated 8,000 quarts of milk for their cousins in Britain." Children also played a large part in the numerous paper drives that took place in 1944. Under adult supervision, they worked in teams to collect paper from homes throughout the city, and helped in the loading of the paper into city street cars that picked up the bundles on their route. Two railway boxcars of paper were sent to Vancouver in the summer of 1944, each carrying over 20 tons of paper.

On October 23, 1944 the 7th Victory Loan Campaign got underway with the blowing of whistles, fire and police sirens for one minute, and a parade, with bands and decorated floats, through the centre of town. The Victory Loan flag-raising ceremony took place during a concert featuring the 44-piece CWAC (Canadian Women's Army Corps) Military Band before an "overflowing crowd of 700" in the Capitol Theatre. The effort that went into organizing and coordinating the Victory Loan drives is impressive. Once again, a civic holiday was proclaimed so that canvassers would find residents at home when they called. Fifteen teams of service-club members, divided into three competing groups, acted as salesmen who set out to visit every home in the city. Team members could win prizes for the largest sales, and the winning group members would be guests at a banquet, with the second-place group serving the tables, and the third-place group providing the food.

On October 16 a military convoy had toured the Kootenays in support of the coming drive, parading through Nelson and stopping at the schools, to the thrill of "swarms of Nelson school children who scribbled their names all over the vehicles." According to the *Daily News*:

> All day long the kids swarmed in and out of the armored reconnaissance cars and squeezed themselves into the turret tops to handle the Bren guns. Imitating the chatter of the Bren gun, they "potted" scores of watchers. Others handled rifles and were shown how to operate them by the troopers who seemed to be enjoying themselves hugely.

In the afternoon the convoy toured the North Shore as far as Balfour.

Nelson businesses took out many ads in the local newspaper, urging support for the Drive. "Feed the Guns" was one advertising theme:

> ...We at home cannot fire the guns—but we can feed them—we must feed them. Not with hundreds—or with thousands—but with millions of shells.... Thousands of our Canadian guns fire as many as 700 shells in an 8-hour attack! *How many shells are you planning to buy?*

Individuals, too, used the local newspaper to urge support for the campaign. One instance was a letter to the editor from Frances Carne, mother of Maxwell and Ian who were serving overseas:

> I have only two boys to represent me in this war, Max who is 24 today, being with a tank regiment in Belgium, and Ian, with the RCAF in India.... I am very proud of my corporal and my lieutenant and they are doing their work every bit as well as the lowest or highest in rank in all the services, but their part in life is to come back home as soon as possible and get into a normal stride.... Cannot those of you who are holding back, come and give in an application at any bank or with a canvasser from the loan committee, so that we can get these boys home?[106]

The Nelson district's campaign collected over one million dollars in the Seventh Drive, 32 percent over its quota. H.A. Matthews, a provincial organizer, commented:

Nelson district's response has in every way been a creditable one. Not only did it meet its biggest war loan assignment, but, as far as we can ascertain, it has set a record in Canada by receiving 14 honour pennants for over-subscription in its various sub-units.[107]

In 1944 the WA to the Active Forces sent out 980 Christmas parcels; they went to every fighting front as well as to POWs and Nelson servicemen and women across Canada, in the United States and Great Britain. On December 29 the *Daily News* reported the typical parcel contents, and how much appreciated they were:

Best known Nelson address overseas is, undoubtedly, 1023 Front Street. To the home of Secretary Mrs. A.D. Oliver have come hundreds of letters of thanks to the auxiliary from appreciative men in strange lands. Into each man's parcel went: a cake, sox, cigarettes, hankie, shoe laces, comb, razor blades, chocolate bars, powdered chocolate, pencil, tooth powder, gum and a Christmas card. A waxed maple leaf, Canadian symbol, was a well-received addition to the service women's parcel, each of which included: a cake, a box of paper tissues, comb, chocolate bars, gum, cigarettes, hair net, powder puff, tooth powder, talcum, shoulder straps, bobby pins, pencil and a Christmas card.

Individuals could purchase pre-packaged parcels from The Hudson's Bay, with four different prices from which to choose. A box for $3.36 contained mentholatum, shaving cream, shoe polish, tooth paste, a pocket mirror, a sewing kit, a writing kit, a pencil, a novel, a half pound of cheese, and a tin of Prem. The Bay offered a personal shopping service to customize the gift boxes with additional items such as sweaters, shirts, wallets and "air force diaries." Thank-you letters from the servicemen and women provided "perhaps the most welcome Christmas present" for many Nelson families and the committee in charge of sending the parcels. One Nelson soldier wrote his thanks through the newspaper:

From France to Nelson seems a long way, but when one received such remembrances as your box it makes us feel we are very close to home. I've seen an awful lot of France, and a great amount of Belgium, but none of it can compare to our Kootenays.

Overseas Christmas Gifts
The Women's Auxiliary to the Active Forces mailed out hundreds of Christmas parcels each year to men and women overseas, but families could also purchase gift packages for their loved ones.

The Red Cross work rooms, the Women's Institute and the IODE continued to ship out an enormous number of items for "V" Bundles to go overseas. The women took pride in the congratulatory messages they received about the high quality of knitting that came from Nelson. R.L. McBride reported that on his visit to the Vancouver headquarters of the Red Cross he found that Nelson was known as "the knitting city." In 1944 the Red Cross had also shipped out 36,656 pounds of jam, plus money collected for the Jam for Britain Project. Eighty-four "nursery bags" for British children were sent out, and "ditty bags" for sailors. These were being assembled and sent out from City Hall by various organizations and individual volunteers. The newspaper reported how the ditty bags "fill a real need in the lives of Canada's fighting sailors, as well as being a remembrance from the folks at home." They contained "the little necessities from the corner drug store, the tobacco shop, the variety store or the book store, necessities that cannot be obtained on shipboard."

In September 1944 the IODE began collecting items for bridal trousseaus to be sent to Britain for Canadian war brides. The brides had already begun to arrive in Canada, many with young children. The first war bride to arrive in Nelson was Mrs. David Matthews, who was presented with a bouquet of flowers from the soldiers' wives of Nelson and the City when she arrived at the CPR station in March 1944. In November a Welcome Home Service Organization was formed by the Legion, Red Cross, IODE and the WA to the Active Forces. Their plan was to greet war brides as well as returning servicemen and women at the train station. An information desk was set up and light refreshments were offered, as well as taxi service if needed.

There was more tragic news to come for Nelson residents at the end of 1944. Another young man of great promise, *Flying Officer Norman Holmes Boss*, was killed in a flying accident in England on the night of November 15. Norman was the navigator in a Halifax bomber on a routine cross-country flight when it was in a mid-air collision with another aircraft. They crashed five miles southeast of Winkleigh, Devon. The crew was part of #1661 Heavy Conversion Unit, converting from two- to four-engine aircraft. Norman was born and raised in Nelson. He was an outstanding student and from high school won a scholarship to Queen's University, where he studied forest engineering. He transferred to UBC and was a bursary winner in his fifth year of studies. Immediately after graduating with an Honours B.Sc. in 1942, Norman joined the RCAF. He was engaged to be married to a Grand Forks girl who was in nurses' training in Vancouver. Norman was 25 years old.

The last Nelson man to lose his life on the Italian front was *Private William Allen*, who was with the Westminster Regiment (Motor), nicknamed "the Westies." They were part of the attack on the Gothic Line in northern Italy, where tanks, vehicles and men battled the Germans through roads and fields of mud. From September 1 the fighting went on unabated for almost two months in the flood plains of the Foglia River in the push toward Ravenna, which was finally taken in early December. It was in this attack that 29-year-old Private Allen was killed on November 18. Not much is known about William Allen's life before the war. As a child he spent some time in an orphanage in Victoria, then travelled for a time with his father, who worked for a circus.[107] He was working as a cook in Nelson when he enlisted in the army.

The British forestry industry was unable on its own to supply the huge amount of wood needed to support the war. It was estimated that every soldier consumed five trees: one for living quarters; one for crates to ship food, ammunition, and war machines; and three for explosives, gun stocks, ships and factories.[109] As they had in World War I, the Canadian and British governments cooperatively established the Canadian Forestry Corps (CFC) in May 1940. The main areas of operation were in Scotland, where CFC camps were constructed from scratch, and logging operations provided the timber for the building of barracks, roads, bridges, ships, power plants and some 130 rafts to support the Normandy invasion. The CFC operations cleared an estimated 230,000 acres of forest in Scotland.

Recruitment to the Forestry Corps was heaviest, as one would expect, in areas of the country where the forest industry was thriving; many men from the Nelson district signed up. Among them was *Lieutenant James Robert "Jim" Hughes*, who was the only Nelson member of the corps to lose his life in the war. He died in Scotland on December 3, 1944, from multiple injuries he suffered when the vehicle he was driving overturned. He was 28 years old.

Jim's family had lived in various parts of BC and Alberta. He attended elementary school in Kelowna, and had moved with his family to the

Kootenays in 1928, residing in Queens Bay and Boswell. He attended high school in Calgary. In Nelson he worked as a truck and tractor driver and later as a salesman. He was well known in the city for his singing abilities and was often a guest soloist at Trinity United Church. Jim also was a sports enthusiast and was active in badminton, tennis, soccer and hockey. While overseas he had married a Scottish girl; she came out to Canada after the war but later returned to Scotland.

By the fall of 1944, with the Germans retreating on all fronts, victory seemed inevitable. Kirke L. Simpson's daily column, *Interpreting the War News*, was increasingly optimistic. But the major offensive by the Germans through the Ardennes, beginning on December 16, brought it home that the killing and the misery were a long way from over. The Christmas Day editorial in the *Nelson Daily News* reflected that mood:

> Our Christmas of 1944 is clouded by our fears for our boys in the services, our deep desire for their return home…but it is brightened by the solid grounds for hoping that within a year victory will have crowned the gallantry and endurance and self-sacrifice of the armies, the navies and the air forces of the United Nations…. We can extend Christmas greetings with that knowledge and with full confidence that, while some of the hardest battles of the war have yet to be fought and that there must be ever more vigorous endeavour and self-denial by all of us at home to support with munitions and reinforcements our warriors in all the services, the cause of Democracy will be triumphant, that our freedom and our liberties will be preserved.

The loss over Christmas of 25-year-old ***Patrick Henry George*** was the final blow of 1944. Pat was a technical sergeant with the US Army Air Force, and was a top-turret gunner in a B-24 bomber that went down on Christmas Eve in a raid on the transportation and communication centre of Euskirchen, Germany, during the Battle of the Bulge. Pat was flying with the 714th Squadron of the 448th Bombardment Group (8th Army Air Force) out of Seething Airfield in Norfolk. After completing high school in Washington State, he had joined the Air Force in January 1941 and graduated from training as a technical engineer. He had served for a year with the 10th Air Force in the China-Burma-India theatre of war, but contracted polio and was returned to the United States for hospitalization. After his recovery, Pat trained for service in Liberator bombers and returned to active service in England in September 1944 with the 448th.

Pat was born in Nelson and spent most of his boyhood there. He left after junior high school for Anacortes, Washington to reside with his sister; he attended high school there. In November 1945 Pat was to receive a Purple Heart, and in January 1946 a special ceremony was held in the Nelson City Council chambers. US Colonel J.H. Harrington presented Pat's mother with the US Air Medal, with two oak-leaf clusters. The citation for the Air Medal reads:

> For meritorious achievement in accomplishing with distinction, several aerial operations missions over enemy occupied Continental Europe. The courage, coolness, and skill, displayed by this individual in the face of determined opposition, materially aided in the successful completion of these missions. His actions reflect great credit upon himself and the armed forces of the United States.[110]

In May 1949 when his body was returned to the city for burial, citizens of Nelson paid him special tribute. A procession wound its way through town at the slow march, along Baker Street to St. Saviour's Anglican Pro-Cathedral, where Reverend T.L. Leadbeater conducted the funeral service. Members of the Canadian Legion, various service clubs and cadets, and city council members attended, along with family and friends.

Mrs. Paddy George, Pat's mother, was the widow of a Nelson pioneer who had located the Molly Gibson Mine at the head of Kokanee Creek. She had two other sons in the service: Lawrence, with the Canadian Scottish Regiment; and Dennis, a paratrooper with the Special Service Corps. Sergeant Dennis George was wounded three times in battle, twice in Italy and once in France. He was a member of the First Special Service Force, composed of hand-picked American and Canadian soldiers, popularly known as "The Black Devils" and largely misrepresented in the Hollywood movie *The Devil's Brigade*. They carried out dangerous commando raids behind enemy lines, were the leading force in the invasion of the south of France, and were the first Allied troops to enter Rome.

1945

CHAPTER SIX

The final year of the war opens with Soviet forces capturing Warsaw. They liberate Auschwitz and Birkenau and the world discovers the horrors of the Nazi concentration camps. The Allies continue their bombardment of German cities, including the firebombing of Dresden, which results in 135,000 casualties. Shortly after, the Americans begin their firebombing of Japanese cities. US Marines take the islands of Iwo Jima and Okinawa, the first of the Japanese home islands to be reached, but suffer terrible losses. In March the Allies capture the bridge over the Rhine at Remagen and advance to take the city of Cologne. At the same time the Canadians are given the job of holding the line along the Nijmegen Salient and they push into the Rhineland. By March 10 German resistance west of the Rhine is eliminated. The cost to the Canadians is 5,304 killed, wounded or missing. Mussolini is captured and executed by Italian anti-fascists. On April 12 President Roosevelt dies of a cerebral hemorrhage, and is succeeded by Harry S. Truman. Soviet troops capture Vienna and move on to Berlin. Hitler commits suicide in his Berlin bunker on April 30; Admiral Karl Dönitz is named his successor. Germany surrenders unconditionally on May 7 and the next day is declared V-E Day—Victory in Europe. Clement Atlee replaces Winston Churchill as prime minister. At the Potsdam Conference the US, Britain and China issue a declaration giving an ultimatum to Japan to surrender unconditionally or face "prompt and utter destruction." On August 6 a US B-29 drops an atomic bomb on Hiroshima, resulting in the death of 140,000 people by the end of the year. Three days later an atomic bomb takes the lives of 70,000 people in Nagasaki. On August 14 Japan finally agrees to unconditional surrender; the next day is declared V-J Day—Victory over Japan.

There were some 53,000 Canadian servicemen wounded in World War II, some of them shipped back home permanently, but many treated in hospitals overseas and sent back into action. If the ratio of wounded to fatal casualties for the country as a whole holds true for Nelson and district, we could expect that between 85 and 90 Nelson servicemen received serious wounds during the war.[111]

One of those severely wounded in Germany was Lieutenant Lyall Hawkins of Nelson, a 28-year-old with the Algonquin Regiment, who was invalided home as the war was drawing to a close. He had been awarded the Military Cross for his action in February 1945 when the First Canadian Army was preparing to cross the River Maas from Holland into Germany. The citation for the medal describes the action in detail:

> On February 5, 1945, a fighting patrol from Algonquin Regiment crossed the River Maas, west of Heusden, with a task of capturing a prisoner to provide identification, which patrols for a week prior to this time had been unable to obtain. Lt. Hawkins was in command of the patrol with orders to investigate a machine gun post. At point of crossing, the river was some 300 yards wide and subject to strong tidal currents. Despite these difficulties and intense fire from enemy machine guns on the flanks of the crossing, the patrol reached the far shore and scaled the icy bank, without casualties. To reach the objective it was necessary to proceed under continuous fire across some 400 yards of open ground. By skillful control of his artillery support, Lt. Hawkins manoeuvred his platoon into position to assault the enemy defences, and 8 men led by Lt. Hawkins attacked the post at close quarters. Four of the enemy were killed, two wounded and two taken prisoner. This task completed, Lt. Hawkins ordered the patrol to withdraw. During the withdrawal one of the prisoners was killed by enemy fire. So skillfully did Lt. Hawkins direct his men that the entire party reached safety on the south bank without a casualty. There can be no doubt that the success achieved by the model patrol can be attributed to Lt. Hawkins, who led his men with such skill and dash that they succeeded in obtaining information which previous attempts had failed to produce. The courage and complete disregard for personal safety shown by this officer was

an inspiration to all ranks under the command and a magnificent example for the remainder of his regiment.[112]

The unexpected massed attack of German forces through the Ardennes in December 1944, the deadly V-1 and V-2 attacks on England, and the fierce defence the Germans were mounting in the Low Countries, all were an indication that victory was not imminent. Yet as early as September 1944 plans were being made for a victory celebration in Nelson. As they sensed that victory was not too far distant, the Legion, WA to the Active Forces and Veterans Guard, together with schools, churches and other bodies, had begun to plan a victory parade and ceremonies of thanksgiving.

The Nelson IODE, among many other local service clubs and organizations, continued their vigorous fundraising and other activities in support of the forces, led by the tireless Mrs. E.C. Wragge, who was their War Work convenor. In January 1945 the IODE mounted a major campaign nationally in support of libraries for servicemen and women. The IODE had been collecting books to support libraries throughout the war, to provide "a respite from the weight of boring routine or long hours of danger which form the life of those in the services." This particular campaign late in the war was given the official support of the federal government and was to raise some $300,000. The Nelson IODE had also sponsored a second ship, the HMCS *Kootenay*, a destroyer that had been transferred from the Royal Navy to the Royal Canadian Navy in April 1943. In February 1945 the local IODE presented its crew with a new washing machine, and many smaller items to make the crew's life aboard more comfortable: cribbage boards, playing cards, darts, checkers, phonograph records and thermos bottles. At the same time the chapter donated a film projector to their other adopted ship, the HMCS *Kokanee*.

Servicemen were already returning home: airmen who had completed their tours of duty, and some of the wounded. But there were to be another 11 fatalities from the Nelson district before the war came to an end.

The first of 1945 was a naval tragedy that took the lives of two young men who were natives of Nelson, **Able Seaman David Charles Motley** and **Petty Officer John Meredith Routh**. They were both with the RCN Volunteer Reserve in His Majesty's Canadian 29th Motor Torpedo Boat

(MTB) flotilla, which suffered a disaster on February 14 in the Belgian harbour of Ostend. Boats of the 29th flotilla were berthed at the harbour for maintenance before carrying out a planned sweep of the coast for mine-laying German E-Boats. Naval historians Darlington and McKee have described the terrible accident:

> At 1630 on 14 February some 100-octane gasoline had been vented into the restricted calm water of the harbour from one of the boats when pumping out a fuel tank contaminated with water. An accidental spark, possibly even a cigarette, ignited the gasoline floating on the surface and in moments the whole basin was aflame with a roar. The wooden boats, themselves impregnated to some extent with oil and the floating gas, caught fire almost at once. The on-deck torpedoes and depth charges exploded with thunderous crashes, heard as far away as England, and boat after boat was swept up in the conflagration.[113]

The explosions continued for about two hours. Seven British and five Canadian MTBs were destroyed and 60 men were killed, 26 of them with the 29th Canadian MTB flotilla. Since five of the eight boats in the flotilla were destroyed, the 29th ceased to exist. It had played an active part in the D-Day landings and was said to have seen more constant fighting service than any branch of the Canadian Navy.

David Motley was born in Nelson in 1921 and lived with his family at Bonnington. He was 18 when he enlisted in the Royal Canadian Naval Volunteer Reserve at Esquimalt on the outbreak of war in 1939. He graduated as a naval radio-telegraph operator first class, and served for a time on corvette duty on the Pacific coast. He later transferred to the torpedo gunnery service, graduated at the Halifax Naval School, and served in the Atlantic. He survived the sinking of two of the ships on which he served as a torpedo gunner. David was with MTB 462 in the 29th flotilla as it carried out constant raids on German shipping and enemy ports, and in the action on D-Day. He was commended for bravery and attention to duty. He left behind a wife and young son in Victoria.

John Routh was born in Nelson in 1916. He had been a mechanic for Canadian Pacific Airlines in Vancouver before the war. He was serving as a motor mechanic with the 29th flotilla when the accident at Ostend took his life. Only nine months before, John's younger brother, Corporal Patrick Routh, serving with the Princess Patricia's Light Infantry, had been killed in Italy. John left a wife in Vancouver; he was 28 years old.

The Crew of MTB 462

Able Seaman David Motley of Bonnington stands second from the right in the middle row. *Photo attributed to Gilbert Alexander Milne. Library and Archives Canada, PA 176741*

The battle for the Rhineland began at Nijmegen in the Netherlands, close to the German border. A web site of Veterans Affairs Canada describes the month-long battle:

> The Allied assault started on February 8, 1945, first against the German troops occupying the Reichswald Forest. Thawing ground and rain hampered tank traffic and turned the ground into such a quagmire that it has been likened to the conditions at Passchendaele. It took five days to drive the Germans from the forest and into open ground. Then came the most difficult task, clearing the enemy from the Hochwald and Balberger heights guarding Germany. It was attack and counter-attack over appalling ground. It took until March 4 for victory to be declared. Some 5,500 Canadians were casualties of the month of fighting.[114]

Two young Nelson soldiers were to lose their lives in this battle. The first was **Private Robert Gordon Ludlow**, who was killed on February 20. He was with the Canadian Scottish Regiment as it fought to clear the Germans from Moyland Wood near Cleve, just west of the Rhine, and faced the freshly-arrived German 6th Parachute Division. Bob Ludlow was born in Lethbridge but had moved with his family to Nelson when he was five weeks old. He attended school in Nelson and was active in hockey. Bob was working for CPR Telegraphs in Nelson and later in a shipyard in Vancouver before he enlisted in the Royal Canadian Artillery in October 1943. After his arrival overseas in July1944 he was transferred from the artillery to the infantry. Bob would have turned 20 in April.

The second Nelson casualty in the battle for the Rhineland was another young man of great promise, **Private James Earl "Jim" Hoover**, with the Calgary Highlanders who were in the battle for the Hochwald Forest, just south of Moyland Wood. He was killed in action on March 4, less than a month after he arrived at the front. He had volunteered to revert from corporal to private in order to go into action. He was 20 years old.

Jim attended junior high and high schools in Nelson after moving there with his family from Medicine Hat in 1938. He was a leader in high-school activities, especially in the army cadet corps, where he rose to the rank of colonel. He was minister of finance in the high-school cabinet (the school used the parliamentary system for its student government), played soccer and loved to hunt and fish. Jim was also a scholar, winning a scholarship in his senior matriculation year for achieving the highest marks in the Kootenays in the provincial examinations. The military was a major interest of Jim and his family: his father was a lieutenant-colonel and veteran of the First World War, and his brother, George, took Jim's place at the head of the Nelson High School Cadet Corps. Jim was a member of the Rocky Mountain Rangers during his year of senior matriculation and, upon graduation, enlisted in the army in June 1943. He had won a scholarship to UBC, but opted instead to study at Queen's University under an army-sponsored program in science and engineering. There he passed his examinations with honours, and took advanced training at Yarmouth and Aldershot, Nova Scotia, before going overseas in November 1944. He acted as an instructor in the infantry in England before he volunteered for active service with the Calgary Highlanders.

As the 3rd Canadian Infantry Division was fighting the last German resistance west of the Rhine, another Nelson soldier, *Lance Sergeant Stuart Alan Spiers*, lost his life in an accidental mine explosion on March 16. He had been with the 6th Field Company of the Royal Canadian Engineers when they suffered heavy losses on D-Day as they fought alongside the Royal Winnipeg Rifles. Stuart was working as a carpenter with the CPR bridge crew before he enlisted in January 1941 and went overseas in June of that year. Along with Bob Ludlow and Jim Hoover, he is buried in the Groesbeek Canadian War Cemetery near Nijmegen in Holland. He was 28 when he died.

One other Nelson soldier was to die on German soil before hostilities ceased on May 8. The death of *Captain Agner Emile Dalgas* on April 29, just nine days before the war in Europe ended, must have been a shock to the people of Nelson. It was Captain Dalgas who had promoted the military in Nelson and commanded, with the rank of major, the 111th (Nelson) Field Battery. He was killed at the age of 57 as the Canadian 2nd Corps advanced into northern Germany when the vehicle in which he was riding ran over a mine. His wife learned of her husband's death the same day she had received a letter from him, dated April 23, in which he told her he was "way past the Rhine."

Agner was born and raised in Denmark, where he graduated from Officers' Training School at the age of 19. He had served in the Danish army for five years before he immigrated to Canada with his family in 1910 and settled in Crescent Valley in the Slocan district. Agner worked at the Coast as a civil engineer until World War I broke out. He went overseas with a Canadian unit, later transferring to the Royal Engineers of London. He served with them throughout the war and was decorated with the Military Cross and the Italian Silver Medal for valour in the field. After the war he settled with his wife in Nelson and worked as an engineer with the BC Department of Public Works.

Agner accompanied the 111th Battery to Edmonton and was assigned to instruction and training duties, but he was determined to go overseas. So he waived rank and enlisted as a gunner with a Montreal battery that was heading to England. He regained the rank of captain but once again found himself placed in the educational branch of the Royal Canadian Artillery. Finally, in early April 1945 he managed to get to the front, about three weeks before he was killed. Agner was very popular with the

Agner Dalgas in the Field
Agner Dalgas (centre, pointing) in the field with Major-General A.G.L. McNaughton, Commander of the 1st Canadian Division, to his right. *Photo courtesy of Corinne Dalgas*

young men who had served under him in the 111ᵗʰ Battery. One of them wrote home after visiting him while on leave in Britain:

> Dalgas is now a captain, you will be glad to hear…. There never was a finer man than he, and I am filled with admiration for his indomitable spirit and moral courage and determination.

He added the hope that Captain Dalgas would return to Nelson with his old rank of major.

There were to be three more Nelson district airmen lost in Bomber Command before the European conflict was ended. *Pilot Officer John Richard "Jack" Kubin* was the only member of his Lancaster crew to be killed during an attack on Dortmund on February 21, 1945. He was a flight engineer with RCAF 424 (Tiger) Squadron. His pilot, Flight Sergeant William Cozens, received the Distinguished Flying Medal for his part in the action, which is described in a RCAF chronicle:

The Ruhr's famed defences were active, with many searchlights probing the sky and night fighters harrying the bomber stream during the whole of the flight over enemy territory.... Despite the activity of enemy fighters all the Canadian losses on the Dortmund raid were apparently due to flak.... The DFM was awarded to Flight Sergeant W.J.G. Cozens of the Tigers for this sortie. During the bomber run his Lanc was hit by anti-aircraft fire and afterwards attacked by a fighter. Both starboard engines were put out of action, the hydraulic system was damaged and the bomb doors could not be closed. The bomber lost height so rapidly that as soon as the lines were crossed Cozens ordered his crew to abandon aircraft. After five had jumped the Lanc was too low to permit the pilot and his one remaining comrade to bale out. With skill and coolness he made a successful crash landing north of Aachen. Four of the crew were safe in Allied hands, but Sergeants A.T. Skett and J. Butler drifted down on the enemy side of the lines and were captured. The seventh member of the crew, Sgt. J.R. Kubin, was missing, presumed dead.[115]

Jack Kubin, who had graduated from St. Joseph's Academy in Nelson, was 11 days shy of his 20th birthday. His name is inscribed on the Runnymede Memorial.

Two Nelson district airmen were members of the same bomber crew that was lost on a raid against the Deurag oil refinery at Misburg, on the outskirts of Hanover, on the night of March 15. *Pilot Officer Richard Barron "Dick" Jones* of Ymir was bomb aimer, and *Pilot Officer Francis John "Jack" Miller* was an air gunner on the Lancaster, flying with RCAF 405 (Vancouver) Squadron, the only RCAF pathfinder squadron. The crew had previously flown together in a Halifax bomber with the renowned 408 (Goose) Squadron and had completed a tour of duty with the 408 before they were reassigned to 405 Squadron. In the transfer they opted to stay together as a crew. They are buried in the Hanover War Cemetery.

Born and raised in Ymir, Dick Jones was known in the district for his athletic abilities, especially in baseball. He had worked as a miner in Ymir, at Britannia Mines and in Yellowknife. Before enlisting in September 1942 he was employed in Nelson by the CPR and by the McDonald Jam Company. His wife, Gwen, was an officer in the CWAC, stationed

Pilot Officer Jack Miller
Photo courtesy of Dawn Nelson

in Toronto. Dick was 31 years old when he was killed.

Jack Miller was born and raised in Grand Forks, where his father operated a hardware store. He moved to Nelson in 1933 and became a member of the sales staff of the Nelson Transfer Company, where he worked until he joined the RCAF in July 1943. He was known throughout the Kootenays as a sportsman, especially as a marksman. He headed the skeet and traps section of the Nelson Rod and Gun Club and was described by members as a "twenty-fiver," meaning a deadly shot. Jack was a popular and respected member of the squadron. Air Vice Marshal Curtis wrote to his widow, "It is most lamentable that a promising career should thus be terminated. His loss is greatly deplored by all those with whom he was serving."

Jack spent his last leave in England with Geoff Hartridge and his war bride, Florence, at her family home. Geoff was also with the RCAF and was the brother of Henry Hartridge, who had been killed early in the war. Jack's daughter, Dawn (now Dawn Nelson), was 11 when her father was killed. She recalls coming home for lunch from Hume School to find her mother surrounded by women, all of them in tears. "No one wanted to tell me what had happened," she recalls. But eventually she was told and was sent back to school for the afternoon. Her father was 37 years old.

Four weeks before the war in Europe came to an end, Mayor Stibbs kicked off the Eighth Victory Loan Campaign with a flag-raising ceremony at the corner of Ward and Baker Streets in the centre of town. Many Nelson servicemen now home from the war were in attendance, along with the school bands. Nelson's objective in the campaign was set at $604,000, about $500 for each of the 1,300 men and women from the city and district still overseas. In fact, the campaign raised over a million dollars. There was to be no let-up, even though it now seemed certain that the end of the war was very near at hand. A ninth campaign was to be launched in the fall of 1945, to cover the country's borrowing needs, to bring the servicemen home and help them resettle into civilian life.

Stop! Look! Listen!

The Mayor has proclaimed Monday, April 23rd, to be a civic holiday to enable everyone to take part in the

Eighth Victory Loan

If you are not one of those who, as volunteer salesmen, will be going from house to house canvassing for subscriptions to the loan, you are asked, as a patriotic duty, to stay at home and receive the salesman who will be calling on you. Have your mind made up and help him on his way as he has many calls to make. Remember, he too is doing this job for you. He gets nothing for it, except the satisfaction of knowing he is helping to hurry up the day when the boys will return.

Sponsored by

Wood, Vallance Hardware Co. Ltd.

NELSON, B.C.

Victory Loan Civic Holiday
Mayor Stibbs often declared a civic holiday to ensure that residents would be home when Victory Loan canvassers called.

When on May 7 the announcement came of Germany's unconditional surrender, to be formalized the following day, the news was received quietly in Nelson. But the local newspaper reported "an undercurrent of excitement" as "merchants and householders quickly had flags flying," and in the afternoon "when children released early from school thronged the streets." In the evening thanksgiving services were held in all the city's churches. On the following day, the actual day of surrender, commemoration and celebration burst forth. A parade "more than three blocks long was cheered by crowds who lined the sidewalks the full length of the parade route" as it wound its way through town to the cenotaph on Vernon Street. Taking part in the parade were veterans and recently discharged servicemen and women, cadets and school bands, city and provincial police, the mayor and council, members of the IODE, the WA to the Active Forces, Boy Scouts, Girl Guides, Cubs and Brownies. The parade marshal was Captain George Wallach, a veteran of the ill-fated raid on Dieppe. Wreaths were laid at the cenotaph and the half-hour service was climaxed by the victory speech of King George VI, played over a public address system. In the evening, dances were held at the Legion, Eagles Hall and Playmor.

The following Sunday, Mother's Day, the churches again dedicated their services to thanksgiving and remembrance of those who did not come home. The *Daily News* reported the service at Trinity United Church:

Miss Margaret McCosham and Miss Dolores Smith read the names of those serving in the Armed Forces as recorded in the Remembrance Book.... A period of silence was observed in memory of those from the congregation who had made the supreme sacrifice: Norman Boss, Raymond Hall, Jim Hoover, and Kenneth McBride.... Minister Rev. Boothroyd paid tribute to the "noble record of mothers throughout more than five and one-half years of war" who required long-term resources of patience, bravery and faith.

But, of course, the war was not over. It raged on against the Japanese in the Pacific for another three months, ending finally a few days after the dropping of atomic bombs at Hiroshima and Nagasaki on August 6 and 9. A witness to the bombing of Nagasaki was Ward Redshaw, who had attended high school in Nelson and was then a corporal in the US Army. He had been taken prisoner by the Japanese during the battle for Corregidor early in the war, and was in a POW camp in Japan at the end of the war. Without realizing at the time what he was witnessing, Ward described the dramatic explosion he saw from across the bay from Nagasaki, some 25 miles away.

I saw a cloud. It was a beautiful rose-pink and it went higher and higher. It smelled—well, peculiar. The smell made me think the Nagasaki chemical plant had exploded.[116]

Two hours before the bomb was dropped on Nagasaki on August 9 **Lieutenant Robert Hampton "Hammy" Gray** led a flight of Corsair fighters into an attack on Japanese warships at Onagawa Bay in northeastern Japan. He was with the 1841 Squadron of the Royal Navy Air Arm, flying from the carrier HMS *Formidable*. Historian Spencer Dunmore has written a dramatic account of the action:[117]

Gray, leading the second flight of 1841 Squadron, had been briefed to attack airfields. Just before take-off, a petty officer, Dick Sweet, rushed to his aircraft, threading his perilous way between spinning propellers on the deck. He jumped onto Gray's wing. A convoy had been spotted in Onagawa Bay, he told Gray; he was to attack the convoy instead of the airfields. Gray acknowledged the message and took off, with two 500-pound bombs on exterior racks beneath the distinctive inverted gull wings of his Corsair.... Intense flak greeted them. Darting, twinkling lights peppered the sky. The Corsair pilots could hear the thud of cannon fire and the kettledrum rat-a-tat of machine guns. The bomb-carrying Corsairs headed for their drops, flying low over the water, lining up on their targets, readying themselves for skip-bombing, literally bouncing their bombs on the surface of the bay and into the sides of their targets. It was an effective method, but perilous for the attackers, because they had to fly straight and level in the face of murderous flak.... Gray lined up to attack an escort destroyer, *Amakusa*, skimming low over the water. Amid a storm of defensive fire from several ships Gray released his remaining bomb. At the same instant his aircraft staggered, hit again and again. The first flickers of flame could be seen coming from the lower part of his engine. Now Gray roared over his target, trailing a plume of black smoke. His bomb struck home just below a gun platform on the *Amakusa* ... the bomb burst into the ship's engine rooms and killed some 40 sailors before blowing up the magazine.... She capsized and sank in minutes, taking more than 70 sailors with her. Gray's Corsair headed for the open sea. In vain. The fire became an inferno. The Corsair rolled abruptly to starboard and, inverted, went straight into the bay, vanishing in an explosion of spray.

**Sub-Lieutenant Hampton Gray in December 1941
while he was stationed at Yeovilton in England.**
Photo by John Stewart, courtesy of Phyllis Gautschi

Hammy was to win the Victoria Cross for his action that morning, but he lost his life, the last Canadian serviceman to be killed in action during the war. He was also posthumously awarded the Distinguished Service Cross for sinking a destroyer in a low-level attack against the naval base at Maisuru, north of Kyoto, in July 1945. He had been mentioned in despatches a year earlier for his action against the German battleship *Tirpitz*, lying in Norwegian waters. Dunmore also describes this action:

> Gray had gone for his targets with his customary elan, boring in so close that his combat photos showed only the muzzle flashes of enemy guns. Most of his rudder disappeared, shot away by the intense flak. Gray managed to control his Corsair, however, and landed safely on the carrier.

It was little wonder that Hammy was considered by his colleagues as "fearless, [the] perfect pilot."

Hampton was born in Trail in 1916 and moved to Nelson with his family at the age of eight. In high school he was a quiet, studious boy, "the scholarly type" his mother called him, with interests in literature and international affairs. He was also a hockey enthusiast, was widely popular for his easygoing, friendly nature and "wonderful sense of humour." He showed early signs of the leadership qualities that would come to the fore during wartime. A fellow officer on the *Formidable* said of Hammy's death:

> The bottom fell out on board after it happened and the victory, when it came, seemed hollow somehow. He was so well loved by us all.[118]

One of his high school teachers remembered another side of Hammy:

> Hammy was a good student, always pleasant and courteous, quiet-spoken, and with a fine spirit of cooperation. He was rather fond of an argument, and I recall at election time the trio of Peter Dewdney, Stan Horswill and Hampton Gray were always eager to waylay me in spare moments, and to good naturedly boost their political parties.[119]

Hammy spent two years at the University of Alberta before transferring to a pre-med program at UBC. He was active in campus life, was associate editor of *The Totem* yearbook, and house manager for his fraternity. Initially he was a supporter of the Student Peace Movement but changed his mind as the Nazi blitzkrieg scored victory after victory. In the summer of 1940, between his third and fourth year of university, he was working at the HB Mine at Sheep Creek, near Salmo, when he decided to enlist. His father remembered the late night when Hammy and his two close buddies, Peter Dewdney of Nelson and Jack Diamond from Trail, "The Three Musketeers" as the boys were called, wakened him to borrow the car in order to drive all night to Calgary to join the navy. Hammy and Jack enlisted in a program to supply officer candidates to the Royal Navy, and sailed for England in September. A couple of months into training Hammy and Jack Diamond opted to join the Fleet Air Arm. Peter Dewdney, meanwhile, took a four-month course at the naval college, HMCS Royal Roads on Vancouver Island, before being assigned to a ship. Hammy was back in Canada taking additional training when he wrote to his parents in the summer of 1941:

> I am beginning to realize that longing for things [one] cannot have becomes rather unimportant. This thing is too gigantic. It is no longer a struggle between two countries wanting what the other has, but rather a struggle on England's part and Russia and China on the others to prevent the loss of precious freedom. It is getting bigger and bigger and everything else becomes pretty insignificant. What happens to us or any number of individuals doesn't matter anymore. If we should lose it certainly would not matter, if we win there is a chance (maybe only a slim one, but still a chance if we are wise) that the world will emerge a little better....[120]

During his career he flew many different fighter aircraft with various squadrons and in many different theatres of the war. He flew Albacores, Sea Hurricanes, Swordfishes and Walruses out of South Africa, and Fulmars, Martlets and Hurricanes out of Kenya and Tanganyika, before he was assigned to the HMS *Formidable* in August 1944, just a few weeks before its Corsairs attacked the *Tirpitz* off Norway. The *Formidable* joined the British Pacific Fleet in April 1945, which together with the US Navy was attacking the last remnants of the Japanese Navy. It was from this carrier that Hammy led the fighters of 1841 Squadron in his final, fatal attack.

In a letter home, dated July 15, 1945, Hammy had written about a certain impatience to return home to his family and his beloved Nelson:

> Things must be drawing to a close very soon now. Everybody is going on doing their job, but in the back of their minds (and mine) is the big question "when will we get home?" I don't really mind

staying out here. I have, as a Canadian, been treated very well really and there are many people in my squadron who have had only two or three weeks at home since they started five years ago, while I have had three months altogether. So, when I complain, I do not feel right about it.... You will undoubtedly be hearing about us on the news. I will be with those who are mentioned, but do not worry please, I really think that I will be home before the end of this year, and I hope to stay at home when I come next.[121]

When it was announced on November 13, 1945, that Hammy was to be awarded the Victoria Cross, the Nelson newspaper featured many tributes. Mayor Stibbs spoke of the pride Nelson citizens felt:

The honor he has brought to this community will place his name alongside that of one of the Empire's outstanding naval heroes, whose name our city bears with pride. Along with this pride comes realization that this act of heroism that has just been signally honored was just what one would expect from a boy who showed such leadership in his school days....

Lieutenant Peter Dewdney spoke warmly of his close friend:

Wherever Hammy went, he made friends, not only because of his high good fellowship and his wonderful sense of humour, but because he was unselfish and honest and was never known to do anyone a bad turn.... Hammy's death has been a keen loss to me, but his heroic deeds have brought glory to the Kootenays and to Canada.

While Hammy was the last Canadian to die in action in the war, his younger brother Jack had been the first casualty from the city of Nelson. Hammy's posthumous Victoria Cross was presented to his parents on February 27, 1946, four years to the day that their son Jack had been killed. The boys' sister, Phyllis, recalled how the family did not hear of Hammy's death until after V-J Day:

We thought the war was over and he'll be coming home, then we got the news a few days later. The last time he was home was in 1944, and then the telegram came. He was just an ordinary, really good guy and suddenly he was gone. My parents were very proud of him for serving but it was very hard on them to lose both their sons.[122]

Every year (since 1950) the Royal Canadian Legion selects a Silver Cross mother to represent all mothers of Canada at the Remembrance Day ceremony in Ottawa. Jack and Hammy's mother, Wilhelmina Gray, was selected for this honour in 1969.

Nelson's Silver Cross Mother, 1969
Mrs. Wilhelmina Gray lays the wreath from "The Mothers of Canada" at the Ottawa Remembrance Day ceremony. She lost two sons in the war. *Photo courtesy of Phyllis Gautschi*

Much has been written about Hampton Gray as one of Canada's military heroes. There are many memorials to him, and one near home that is a memorial to both Hammy and his brother. Grays Peak in Kokanee Glacier Provincial Park is named in honour of them both. In Nelson the Post Office is named for Hammy, plaques in his honour sit on the bridge at Nelson's Gyro Park and on the Canadian Legion building, and a mural by artist L.X. Forde depicting Hammy's action in Onagawa Bay hangs inside the Legion Hall. Farther from home there is a school named for Hammy in Dartmouth, Nova Scotia, and also a community centre in Shearwater, Nova Scotia. Gray Lake near Edmonton bears his name; and in Elgin, Scotland, home base of the Fleet Air Arm, Gray's Walk is named for him. A memorial to Hampton, dedicated in 1989, overlooks Onagawa Bay where he was killed.

Hammy is to be part of a major memorial to Canada's wartime heroes planned for Ottawa, called the "Valiant Group." He is one of only 16 men and women chosen from the length of Canadian history whose statues will line Elgin Street to the War Memorial and the Tomb of the Unknown Soldier.

Of the "Three Musketeers," Hammy Gray, Jack Diamond and Peter Dewdney, only Peter survived the war. Lieutenant Jack Diamond was killed in 1942 in action with the Fleet Air Arm, flying an Albacore over the North Sea. Peter Dewdney, a lieutenant in the Royal Canadian Naval Volunteer Reserve, captained a number of Fairmiles, motor launches that played a vital role as convoy escorts, patrol and rescue boats, in the North Atlantic and in the Caribbean. Over five years he saw much action, but did not lose a single boat. Canada's only two naval Victoria Crosses in the war were awarded to men very close to Peter: his uncle, Frederick Peters, and his boyhood friend, Hammy Gray.

Nelsonites welcomed the long-awaited news of the Japanese surrender with "the blaring of horns, shouts and showers of confetti." People crowded the downtown streets cheering and waving flags. The *Daily News* reported the excitement on August 15:

> An announcement of a Victory Ball to be held at the Civic Centre interrupted the celebrations, but they resumed again as soon as the touring car with the loud-speaker left the main streets.... Cars wildly decorated with flags of all nations and sizes paraded the streets, drivers and passengers shouting and singing and honking. The CPR whistles, fire sirens and bells and the Brewery horns added to the noise. Flags appeared on the streets, and stores and offices closed.

The liquor store had a rush. Firecrackers were set off on the main street. Youngsters blew horns and decorated bicycles in preparation for the V-J Day parade to be held the next day. The CPR stopped work at 4:30.

Amid the celebrating there were many moments of sadness and reflection. The newspaper reported one such moment:

> There was one girl with the gay smile and the hurt brown eyes, cheering and laughing, her hair blowing like a victory banner. "Your boyfriend will be home now," someone said to her, pausing for a moment from blowing a striped horn. Her gay smile spread, the head raised proudly. "Yes, yes," she replied, "I don't know when but he will be back—soon." The smile faded and her eyes looked bravely into a liberated world. "But my brother won't."

Next moment she was as gay as the rest, her hair blowing like a
Victory Banner.

On April 13, 1945, the day of a special flag-raising ceremony in
Nelson to celebrate victory in Europe, a *Daily News* editorial note had
summarized, with considerable pride, the city's contribution to the war
effort:

> Men and women from Nelson entered all branches of the
> services for World War II. Many lost their lives; many received
> decorations. At home, Nelsonites served in the home militia,
> raised funds through the Victory Loan Drives, hosted airmen
> training with the Commonwealth Air Training Plan, and worked
> in the war industry projects in Nelson. Children saved for War
> Savings Certificates, and helped with collecting war materials, the
> "recycling" of the day. Servicemen and women were sent parcels
> with everything from socks to cigarettes to cake. Assistance went
> to war orphans, prisoners, and those in hospital. Nelson adopted
> a ship and her men. And all the while they kept praying for the
> safety of their loved ones on the sea, on the land and in the air.

Each year, as part of the Remembrance Day service, the Nelson Pilots
Association salutes the war dead with a fly-past. Several aircraft fly in loose
formation over the cenotaph as the ceremony on the ground is ending.
There are still relatives and townspeople who gather at the cenotaph each
November 11th who knew some of the men and boys whose names are
recorded there. They remember them as vibrant young men, most of
them fine athletes, some with talents for music or scholarship, many of
them leaders among their peers. Most of us know only their names. We
honour the sacrifice they made for our sake, and the sacrifice their loved
ones made as well. And we grieve the lost years, the further contributions
they might have made. Now, through these pages, we can at least know
them a little better—what they accomplished in their short lives, and
how they died.

SOME WHO CAME HOME

CHAPTER SEVEN

Telling the story of the Nelson men, most of them mere boys, who were lost in this war, fills one with an overwhelming sense of loss, even after all these years. Lives barely lived, promises unfulfilled, families forever changed. The nephew and namesake of one of the Nelson casualties, Stan Smith, has described the traumatic effect his uncle's death had on his family:

> My uncle's death was a dark, brooding theme in my family life, one that ebbed and flowed sporadically through time but always came up, even if not spoken about, certainly on Remembrance Day. My father and my grandfather almost never talked about it and when they did it was with few words, hushed tones and great sadness and regret. When I was a child it was as though we had entered a church whenever the memory of his death visited us. I swear the light in the house changed to somber tones when this topic came up. It was as though something deeply unfair had been done to them and there was no redress.[123]

The loss was felt by the community itself. Robert Smillie, who was on the staff of Nelson High School from 1918 to 1942, taught so many of them. In 1945 he described for the *Daily News* sentiments that were shared in the community by other residents who had watched these boys grow up and go off to war:

> Teachers of the Nelson schools have been called upon often in the last few years to suffer hard blows when the news would tick off the wires—"missing or killed in action." No one, I'm sure, can realize the loss to our district and country more than these teachers for they learned to know these boys well, both at work

and at play. Nelson High School gave to the services a host of grand boys, but it seems a hard fate that so many of the boys lost were the very cream of the high quality group …[124]

Of course, most of the boys who fought in the war did come home, many of them as heroes whose feats of bravery and stoic endurance won them medals. The Distinguished Flying Cross, one of the high awards made to air force officers, was won by several Nelson men who survived the war. The *Daily News* reported that Flight Lieutenant Harry Sandgren was the first city boy to win a decoration in service with the RCAF. He was awarded the DFC in October 1943 for "the determination with which he has pressed home his attacks in the face of intense opposition."

Many who won the DFC flew an unimaginable number of sorties, some of them only a day or two apart. Their citations speak of outstanding ability, cool courage, fortitude and leadership. Pilot Officer Ted Rutherglen completed almost two tours, a total of nearly 60 sorties, as a wireless air gunner. He suffered shrapnel injuries to his face which he carried for the rest of his life. He was to become "one of the finest game wardens in the business" and was to have a lake, situated below Kokanee Glacier, named for him: Ol' Tedi Lake.

The Emmott brothers, Flight Lieutenant Alan and Flying Officer Norman, both DFC winners, each flew well over 30 missions as navigators with Bomber Command, Alan in a RAF pathfinder squadron, and Norman with 433 (Porcupine) Squadron. Norman flew in the same raid against Hamburg in which Nelson boys John Dingwall and Clarence MacDougall were killed in July 1944. After the war Alan was to serve as reeve, later mayor, of Burnaby for 12 years in the 1950s and '60s.

Flying Officer Lewis Rees was a gunner, observer and bomb aimer who took part in 30 operational flights, most of them against the most heavily defended targets in Germany. A letter home read, "We only got hit twice, and that's pretty good," a testament to his "calm and quiet manner," which his DFC citation praised. It credits him with being "largely responsible for the high standard of morale and efficiency attained by his crew." He took part in the same operation in which Nelson's Bud Ruppel was killed in January 1944.

Flight Lieutenant Stan Horswill, awarded a DFC in October 1944, was the brother of Syd Horswill who was killed in a flying accident early in the war. Stan completed 36 sorties as a navigator with the RCAF's 424 (Tiger) Squadron, during which he survived a fighter attack over

Schweinfurt, was coned twice by searchlights in a raid over Berlin, and took part in a low-level raid at 1,000 feet over Bonnetot. The brother of another RCAF casualty was to win the DFC: Flight Lieutenant Ralph Flynn from the Slocan Valley, the older brother of Larry who was killed in 1942. Ralph had been in action from mid-1942 until 1945, first in North Africa, and later with the 420 (Snowy Owls) Squadron over such heavily defended targets as Mannheim, Cologne, Hamburg and Essen. He flew a total of 46 sorties.

Gordon Smith was only 19 when he won his wings and commission in 1942. Flight Lieutenant Smith flew Spitfires with the RCAF's 421 and 411 Squadrons, and was credited with destroying at least three enemy aircraft and destroying or damaging 65 mechanical vehicles.

Flying Officer L.P. Horace Lapointe, who made his home in both Nelson and Trail, flew with the RAF's 101 Squadron. His DFC citation calls him "a navigator of outstanding ability," and refers to his "outstanding cheerfulness in the face of danger" which was "an excellent example to his crew." In the five-month period between December 1944 and April 1945 he flew a total of 32 sorties.

Norman MacLeod was a well-known Nelson athlete and lifeguard at Lakeside Park before he joined the RCAF in the spring of 1940. He was a pilot with 431 (Iroquois) Squadron in over 30 attacks on enemy targets. His DFC citation records one attack over Arras on June 12, 1944, when his bomber was attacked by an enemy fighter, just prior to the target run. "By excellent evasive action, this captain evaded the attacker and carried on to the target." Flight Lieutenant MacLeod married Syd Horswill's widow, Peggy, in England in 1945, and after the war had a chiropractic practice in Nelson.

Another prominent Nelson all-round athlete, Joe Gallicano, was nicknamed "Joe The Tiger" when he played and coached lacrosse with the Sheep Creek Bombers before he was recruited by the New Westminster Salmonbellies in the Coast Intercity League. To play in this league was Joe's boyhood dream, but it was short-lived when the war intervened and he enlisted during his rookie year. He completed 34 operational flights over Germany and occupied countries as a flying officer with the RAF's 514 Squadron. His DFC citation tells of an attack on Osterfeld in February 1945 when the starboard outer engine of his Lancaster was hit and set on fire. He managed to extinguish the fire and successfully complete the mission.

There are other stories of harrowing experiences by DFC winners. Flying Officer Walter Nisbet, son of a Nelson judge, was a pilot with the RAF's 226 Squadron in February 1945 in an attack against a strongly defended railroad bridge at Deventer, Holland. When his aircraft was hit by anti-aircraft fire he received shrapnel wounds in his leg, but managed to maintain his position in the formation and release his bombs on schedule. His citation records the flight home:

> Without informing his crew of his injury, Flying Officer Nisbet, unaided, flew the aircraft back to the nearest available airfield and executed a safe landing. His wound was so severe and the loss of blood so great that Flying Officer Nisbet was given a blood transfusion before he was lifted from the aircraft.

After the war Walter became a lawyer and Queen's Counsel.

Nelson native Flying Officer Ed Matheson was navigator on a Canso Flying Boat with 162 Squadron, doing antisubmarine and convoy patrol out of Iceland and Northern Scotland. On June 14, 1944, they successfully attacked and sank U-1225, but anti-aircraft fire from the U-boat downed the Canso. The pilot, Flight Lieutenant David Hornell, managed to bring the flaming plane down in a "gale-lashed" sea, and to bring it to the water's surface, enabling the crew to climb into their dinghy. They landed on waves 12 feet high. The dinghy blew up while crew members were attempting to scramble aboard, leaving room for only five of the eight in the dinghy. The men took turns in the dinghy and in the water, and after five hours they were sighted by an aircraft that stayed with them for the next 15 hours until they could be rescued. Altogether they spent 21 hours in the water. Three of the crew died, including the pilot Hornell, who was later awarded the Victoria Cross. The citation for Ed Matheson's Distinguished Flying Cross reads, in part:

> During the run in to attack a U-boat, in face of devastating anti-aircraft fire and at a time when the aircraft was being hit repeatedly, the starboard engine out of action and on fire, [Ed Matheson] coolly and courageously stood to his post and operated a hand-held camera, because the automatic camera had been wrecked by flak.… During the subsequent 21 hours in the water, this officer did all in his power to assist the others, to such an extent that due to over-exertion he was himself receiving artificial respiration when a high speed launch arrived.

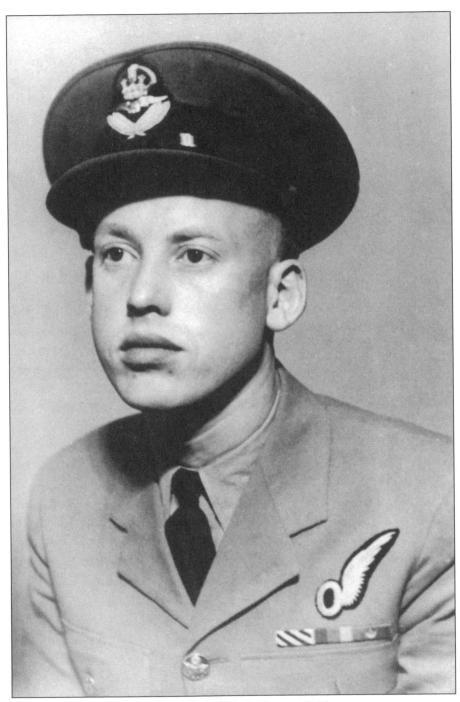

Flying Officer Ed Matheson, DFC
Photo courtesy of Nelson Museum

Several Nelson district men were recipients of other high honours. Major Gordon (Gary) Bowell, a graduate of Nelson High School, Queen's University and a Rhodes Scholar, was made a member of the Most Excellent Order of the British Empire (MBE) for his war service. Lance Corporal E.P. Hogan was cited for distinguished conduct for his part in repairing the bulkheads of a ship which had been in a collision while crossing the Atlantic, "with full knowledge that there was small chance of escape should the bulkheads give way or the ship be sunk by enemy action." Lieutenant W.D. "Doug" Elsdon, a native of Nelson and graduate of Nelson High, was awarded the George Medal for "great bravery in rescue work during an ammunition explosion in Holland" in May 1945. Ignoring personal safety, he had rushed into the inferno and carried seriously wounded men to safety. It was not reported at the time that the men he saved were German prisoners of war.[125]

A number of award recipients were Nelson boys serving in the US armed forces. Among them was Second Lieutenant Paul Brook, a Nelson High graduate, who had joined the US Army Air Force while a student at the University of Washington. He was awarded the Air Medal "for exceptionally meritorious achievement while serving as the navigator of a B-17 Flying Fortress on a number of sustained bomber combat missions over Germany and German-occupied countries." Another graduate of Nelson High School, Machinist's Mate Second Class Ralph Johnson, served with the US Naval Reserve and participated in eight invasions, including Iwo Jima, Guam, Lingayen Gulf and Bougainville. He received a citation for gallant performance of his duties.

Many of the men who returned came home with brides. Among them was Fred Castle, father of Stan Castle who was killed in October 1944 in Holland. Fred's brother had married an English girl during World War I but had died shortly after from the gassing he received in the war. When Fred went overseas he called on his brother's widow and subsequently they were married. By the fall of 1945 over 20 war brides had arrived in the Nelson district.

We are indebted to the boys who survived the war, and came home changed men, some with scars and memories too terrible to share. So many families lived through years of anxiety, of hoping the telegraph boy or girl would pass them by. So many families had two, three or four loved ones overseas, among them the following: Rutherglen, Breeze, Winlaw, Beattie, Read, Brook, McCuaig, Harper, George, Horswill, Jarrett,

Limacher, Dalgas, Matheson, Gallicano, Dyck, Campbell, Noakes, Burgess, Cox, Grant, Norris, Ruppel, Spiers, Gray, McBride, Flegel, Hartridge, Mitchell, Stout, Carne, Fleming, Flynn, Smith, Jackman, Forbes, Barwis, Gibbon, Cornfield, Leno and van Ruyskenvelde.

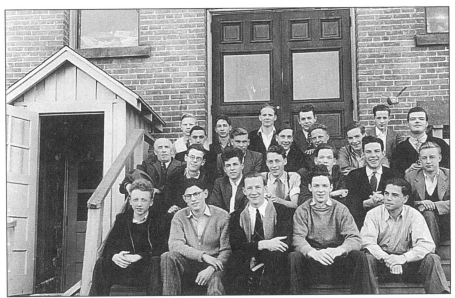

A Nelson High School Class in 1939
Many boys in the NHS classes of '39 and '40 went off to war. Among many who did not return are three who are seen here with teacher "Pop" Smillie, on the front steps of the high school: Iverson "Bud" Ruppel 2nd row, middle), Jack Gray (to his left), and Wilbur "Wib" Bentz (back row, 2nd from the right). *Photo courtesy of H.W.R. "Bert" Ramsden (back row, far right).*

The story of Nelson during those dark years, of a community that came together in a united effort to face an imminent danger, is the story of towns and cities across the country. But there is something special about this community, in times of peace or war—its "sense of family," its pride of place, the "atmosphere" and "personality"—that Bruce Hutchison wrote about in 1940, and that remains to this day.

EPILOGUE

Two of the men listed among the World War II casualties on the Nelson Cenotaph were killed after the war ended, both in accidents. *Private Austin James Brennan* died on October 30, 1945 from multiple injuries he received in a road accident in Holland. He had gone through four years of fighting in Italy and Holland with the Hastings and Prince Edward Regiment. Austin was born and raised in Nelson. He was a popular baseball player from a well-known baseball family. In 1941 he had coached the Nelson junior team. He was working as a meatcutter with the Union Packing Company before he enlisted. Austin left behind a wife and young daughter. He was 27 years old.

Another name on the cenotaph, listed among the World War II casualties, is that of **Lieutenant George Armstrong Greenwood**, who was killed at the age of 24 in a flying accident on October 17, 1946, more than a year after the war ended. He was flying with the Royal Canadian Navy Fleet Air Arm when his Tiger Moth collided with an Oxford aircraft over England. George saw action during the war in Sicily, Italy and Norway, and had volunteered for service in the Pacific after the war in Europe ended. He had grown up in Vancouver, but was married to a Nelson girl, Bernice Dickson, which likely accounts for his name being on the cenotaph in Nelson.

The research for this book centred originally on the names inscribed on the Nelson Cenotaph. I was able to find informative obituaries in the *Nelson Daily News* for most of the men, but in a few cases only sparse information, because their connection with Nelson was very brief. I was surprised to learn that there is no uniformity as to what names are included on the cenotaph of a city, town or village. I posed the question of how names are selected to the Dominion Command of the Royal Canadian Legion, who replied that the information comes exclusively from local registrars and municipal records. In most cases, as in the case of Nelson, the local cenotaph was erected by a branch of the Canadian Legion, with support of the local city council. But there is no uniformity in this regard either. A historical account of cenotaphs in British Columbia indicates that some were funded by public subscription, others by local organizations such as the Women's Institute, the IODE, seniors' organizations, or other local service clubs. In Rossland the cenotaph was paid for from commissions paid to Victory Bond salesmen.[126]

Since we are a nation on the move, a serviceman's name may appear on more than one cenotaph. Seven of the men listed on the Nelson Cenotaph, for instance, are listed also on the cenotaph in Trail, in most cases because they were employed at the Trail smelter at the time they enlisted. But there is one name on the Trail Cenotaph that is missing from the Nelson monument, and might well be there: **Harold Breeze**, who was born and raised in Nelson. In some instances, the parents of young men who spent much of their boyhood in Nelson had moved from the city during the war. This likely explains the absence of names that one feels should be on the Nelson monument: **Wilbur Bentz** and **Henry MacKenzie**. The name of Nelson native **Pat George** is not there, perhaps because he did not serve in the Canadian forces. Pat was in the US Army Air Force but is buried in Nelson Memorial Park.

In the course of collecting information for this book I have talked to so many people who are part of the story of Nelson at war. One of the more satisfying experiences was reuniting two veterans who had been boyhood neighbours and friends, one of whom believed the other had died in the war. I was also able to help the son of a lost airman, who was an infant when his father was killed and had never known him, locate one of his father's crewmates and close buddies. Another satisfaction was in discovering that the film in which Jack Gray had taken part in 1941, *Target For Tonight*, has been issued as a video and is in the collection of a public library in North Vancouver. After 62 years, Jack's sister, Phyllis Gautschi, was able to see her brother in the film for the first time; she had missed the showing in 1941.

There is another story concerning the Gray family that has to be told in this epilogue. The memorial to Hampton Gray that overlooks Onagawa Bay in Japan was supported by the local Japanese townspeople and by one veteran in particular, Yoshi Kanda, who wanted to celebrate the peaceful relations that now exist between Canada and Japan. The monument was unveiled by Hampton's sister, Phyllis Gautschi, who with her family was warmly welcomed by the local people. In the mid-1990s Phyllis's granddaughter, Marcia George, was on an exchange program to a Japanese town nearby. She also was welcomed by the people of Onagawa Bay, and became friends with Yoshi Kanda's three grandchildren, so much so that they came from Japan to West Vancouver to attend Marcia's wedding in 2003. Two generations later, the children of old enemies were celebrating together.

Geographical Memorials to Nelson and District World War II Casualties

Cenotaphs are not the only memorials to our fallen servicemen. Twenty-eight of the men from the Nelson District who died in World War II (and also Frederick Peters, whose mother resided in Nelson, and John Stubbs, originally from Kaslo) are remembered by mountains or other geographical features in BC, named in their honour. Most are located in the Kootenay Land District, as the table below indicates. These are towering and everlasting memorials.

Serviceman	Geographical Feature/Map	Location	Coordinates
Pte. Matthew Aylmer	Mount Aylmer Map 82F/10	S. of Fraser Narrows, West Arm of Kootenay Lake	Lat. 49°34'00" Long. 116°59'00"
WO John Beattie	Mount Beattie Map 82F/6	W. side of Five Mile Creek, in West Arm Provincial Park	Lat. 49°28'25" Long. 117°09'10"
PO Wilbur Bentz	Bentz Peak Map 82F/5	NW of Krestova, N. of Castlegar	Lat. 49°29'10" Long. 117°43'45"
PO Harold Breeze	Breeze Peak Map 94C/2	W. of junction of Omineca and Osilinka Rivers, N. of Germansen Landing	Lat. 56°02'45" Long. 124°40'20"
PO Raymond Burgess	Burgess Point Map 82F/10	W. shore of Kootenay Lake, S.W. of mouth of Crawford Bay	Lat. 49°32'35" Long. 116°50'15"
WO Edward Cornfield	Mount Cornfield Map 82F/11	Head of Sitkum Creek on W. side of Kokanee Glacier Prov. Park	Lat. 49°41'00" Long. 117°16'00"

Serviceman	Geographical Feature/Map	Location	Coordinates
Tpr. Oscar Dorval	Mount Dorval Map 82F/13	Head of Hail and Ice Creeks, SE of Burton on E. side of Lower Arrow Lake	Lat. 49°52'06" Long. 117°45'02"
WO James Eccles	Mount Eccles Map 82F/11	Headwaters of Trozzo Creek, NW of Nelson	Lat. 49°36'00" Long. 117°26'00"
FO Gustaf Flegel	Flegel Creek Map 94C/2	Flows N. into Osilinka River below Wasi Creek, N. of Germansen Landing	Lat. 56°07'35" Long. 124°49'25"
PO F. Larry Flynn	Mount Flynn Map 82F/12	N. of junction of Cougar and Koch Creeks, SW of Slocan	Lat. 49°40'00" Long. 117°49'00"
F/Sgt. John Gray and Lieut. R. Hampton Gray	Grays Peak Map 82F/11	Between headwaters of Kokanee and Coffee Creeks, S. end of Kokanee Glacier Prov. Park	Lat. 49°44'00" Long. 117°07'00"
FO Ronald Greavison	Greavison Creek Map 82F/12	Flows NE into Slocan River opposite Slocan Park	Lat. 49°31'00" Long. 117°37'00"
WO John Harlow	Mount Harlow Map 82F/13	W. of Hoder Creek, W. of Slocan	Lat. 49°46'00" Long. 117°49'00"
Sgt. Henry Hartridge	Mount Hartridge Map 82F/10	S. of entrance to West Arm of Kootenay Lake	Lat. 49°34'00" Long. 116°56'00"
Pte. James Hoover	Mount Hoover Map 82F/11	Head of South Lemon Creek, NW of Nelson	Lat. 49°38'00" Long. 117°24'00"
Lieut. James Hughes	Mount Hughes Map 82N/6	Just W. of Golden	Lat. 51°19'00" Long. 117°06'00"
PO John Kubin	Mount Kubin Map 82F/11	W. of Mount Grohman at head of Baldface Creek, N. of Nelson	Lat. 49°37'00" Long. 117°21'00"

Serviceman	Geographical Feature/Map	Location	Coordinates
Pte. Charles Lequereux	Mount Lequereux Map 82F/13	W. of upper Koch Creek, W. of Slocan	Lat. 49°48'00" Long. 117°53'00"
Pte. Robert Ludlow	Mount Ludlow Map 82F/12	Between Hoder and Koch Creeks, W. of Slocan	Lat. 49°44'00" Long. 117°49'00"
Capt. Kenneth McBride	Mount McBride Map 82F/13	Head of Heart Creek in the Valkyr Range, E. side of Lower Arrow Lake	Lat. 49°50'00" Long. 117°56'00"
Pte. Hugh McKean	Mount McKean Map 82F/13	Between heads of Hoder and Koch Creeks, just W. of Valhalla Prov. Park	Lat. 49°48'00" Long. 117°48'00"
Capt. Frederick Peters	Mount Peters Map 82F/11	NW of Nelson	Lat. 49°33'10" Long. 117°23'00"
Pte. Michael Prestley	Mount Prestley Map 82F/13	SE side of Valhalla Lake in Valhalla Prov. Park	Lat. 49°46'00" Long. 117°41'00"
Pte. Terence Rowley	Mount Rowley Map 82N/11	SE of Blackwater Mountain, at SE side of Kinbasket Lake, NW of Golden	Lat. 51°39'00" Long. 117°19'00"
Petty Off. John Routh	Routh Islet Map 92F/9	In Blind Bay, E. side of Strait of Georgia at S. side of entrance to Jervis Inlet	Lat. 49°43'15" Long. 124°10'55"
WO Iverson Ruppel	Mount Ruppel Map 82F/11	W. boundary of Kokanee Glacier Prov. Park	Lat. 49°44'50" Long. 117°16'50"
Pte. Edward Shardelow	Mount Shardelow Map 82F/13	SW of head of Koch Creek, E. of Lower Arrow Lake	Lat. 49°46'25" Long. 117°57'15"
L/Sgt. Stuart Spiers	Mount Spiers Map 82F/12	Between heads of Grizzly and Russel Creeks, W. of Little Slocan River	Lat. 49°33'00" Long. 117°53'00"
Lieut. Comm. John Stubbs	Mount Stubbs Map 82K/3	E. of Wilson Creek	Lat. 50°10'00" Long. 117°14'00"

Source: BC Ministry of Sustainable Resource Management, *BC Geographical Names*, 2001. <http://srmwww.gov.bc.ca/bvnames/> (May 3, 2004).

MOUNT BEATTIE

NAMED IN HONOUR OF

WARRANT OFFICER
JOHN L. BEATTIE

1921 - 1944

R.C.A.F. 419 SQUADRON (MOOSE)

The plaque on Mount Beattie, named in memory of Warrant Officer John Beattie, one of 28 geographical features in BC named after men from the Nelson district who died in the war. *Photo courtesy of Don Beattie*

Nelson and District World War II Casualties: Date of Death and Place of Burial or Memorial

Pte. William **Allen**
Westminster Regiment (Motor), RCIC
November 18, 1944
Ravenna War Cemetery (Italy)

F/Lt. Eric Morrow **Andrew**
RAF 7 Squadron, RCAF
June 24, 1944
Esquelbecq Military Cemetery (France)

Trp. Roscoe **Armstrong**
Royal Canadian Armoured Corps
March 9, 1944
Kamloops (Pleasant St.) Cemetery

Pte. Matthew **Aylmer**
Canadian Scottish Regiment, RCIC
July 1, 1944
Beny-Sur-Mer Canadian War Cemetery (France)

FO Ambrose **Bain**
RAF 630 Squadron, RCAF
July 27, 1944
Clermont-Ferrant (Des Carme Dechaux) Communal Cemetery (France)

AB William Donald **Barwis**
RCN Volunteer Reserve, HMCS *St. Croix*
September 20, 1943
RCN Memorial (Halifax)

WO2 John Leslie **Beattie**
419 Squadron, RCAF
February 20, 1944
RCAF Memorial (Runnymede)

*Pte Theodore Benjamin **Beninger**
Veterans Guard of Canada
July 17, 1943
Nelson Memorial Park

*PO Wilbur Boyd **Bentz**
426 Squadron, RCAF
May 13, 1944
Geraardsbergen (Grammont) *Communal Cemetery (Belgium)*

FO Norman Holmes **Boss**
#1661 Heavy Conversion Unit, RCAF
November 15, 1944
Brookwood Military Cemetery (England)

* indicates not listed on the Nelson Cenotaph

*PO Harold Arthur
Alexander **Breeze**
434 Squadron, RCAF
April 28, 1944
Heverlee War Cemetery (Belgium)

Pte. Austin James **Brennan**
Hastings & Prince Edward
Regiment, RCIC
October 30, 1945
*Groesbeek Canadian War Cemetery
(Netherlands)*

*Cpl. William **Brown**
Veterans Guard of Canada
September 18, 1943
Nelson Memorial Park

PO Raymond Charles **Burgess**
432 Squadron, RCAF
November 16, 1943
*Cambridge City Cemetery
(England)*

FO John Alexander **Campbell**
87 Squadron, RAF
May 12, 1940
*Maastricht General Cemetery
(Netherlands)*

Pte. Stanley Frederick **Castle**
South Saskatchewan Regiment,
RCIC
October 29, 1944
*Bergen-Op-Zoom Canadian War
Cemetery (Netherlands)*

Lieut. James Esmond **Clark**
Royal Canadian Artillery
August 8, 1944
*Bretteville-Sur-Laize Canadian War
Cemetery (France)*

FO Russell Stanley **Clark**
408 Squadron, RCAF
December 21, 1943
*Harrogate (Stonefall) Cemetery
(England)*

F/Lt. Barrington Farr **Cleeton**
RAF 63 Squadron, RCAF
June 25, 1944
Bayeux War Cemetery (France)

WO2 Edward Albert **Cornfield**
January 29, 1944
*Berlin 1939-1945 War Cemetery
(Germany)*

Lieut. **Robert Clifton Craufurd**
18th Field Company,
Royal Canadian Engineers
July 9, 1942
*Brookwood Military Cemetery
(England)*

Capt. Agner Emile **Dalgas**
Canadian Army – General List
April 29, 1945
*Holten Canadian War Cemetery
(Netherlands)*

WO1 John **Dingwall**
408 Squadron, RCAF
July 29, 1944
Kiel War Cemetery (Germany)

Trp. Oscar Anthony **Dorval**
3rd Army Tank Brigade,
Royal Canadian Armoured Corps
July 3, 1943
*Brookwood Military Cemetery
(England)*

WO2 James John **Eccles**
120 Squadron, RCAF
February 4, 1944
*West Vancouver (Capilano View)
Cemetery*

FO Gustaf **Flegel**
RAF 166 Squadron, RCAF
August 27, 1944
Mandal Churchyard (Norway)

PO Francis Larry **Flynn**
#1651 Conversion Unit, RCAF
June 26, 1942
RCAF Memorial (Runnymede)

*T. Sgt. Patrick Henry **George**
448th Squadron,
US Army Air Force
December 24, 1944
Nelson Memorial Park

WO1 Donald Ernest **Gibbon**
RAF 18 Squadron,
RCAF
January 14, 1944
Bari War Cemetery (Italy)

FO John William **Grant**
#52 Operational Training Unit,
RCAF
June 11, 1943
*Shawbury (St. Mary) Churchyard
(England)*

F/Sgt. John Balfour **Gray**, Jr.
RAF 144 Squadron,
RCAF
February 27, 1942
*Bessacarr Doncaster (Rose Hill)
Cemetery (England)*

Lieut. Robert Hampton **Gray**
RN Fleet Air Arm,
RCN Volunteer Reserve,
HMS *Formidable*
August 9, 1945
RCN Memorial (Halifax)

FO Ronald **Greavison**
#20 Operational Training Unit,
RCAF
August 23, 1944
Lossiemouth Burial Ground (Scotland)

Lieut. George
Armstrong **Greenwood**
RCN Fleet Air Arm
October 17, 1946
*Brookwood Military Cemetery
(England)*

WO George Evelyn **Greenwood**
407 Squadron, RCAF
May 31, 1943
*Cherbourg Old Communal
Cemetery (France)*

Pte. Raymond Edmund **Hall**
Seaforth Highlanders of Canada,
RCIC
May 23, 1944
Cassino War Cemetery (Italy)

WO2 John Clarence **Harlow**
6th Field Regiment,
Royal Canadian Artillery
August 10, 1944
*Beny-Sur-Mer Canadian War
Cemetery (France)*

Sgt. Henry Percival **Hartridge**
RAF 21 Squadron, RCAF
July 23, 1941
*Flushing (Vlissingen) Northern
Cemetery (Netherlands)*

Pte. James Earl **Hoover**
Calgary Highlanders,
RCIC
March 4, 1945
*Groesbeek Canadian War Cemetery
(Netherlands)*

PO Richard Sydney **Horswill**
#14 Advanced Flying School,
RCAF
July 2, 1942
Ollerton Cemetery (England)

Lieut. James Robert **Hughes**
Canadian Forestry Corps
December 3, 1944
*Kilmorack New Parish Churchyard
(Scotland)*

PO Robert Stewart **Jardine**
RCAF
April 22, 1943
RCAF Memorial (Ottawa)

PO Richard Barron **Jones**
405 Squadron, RCAF
March 15, 1945
Hanover War Cemetery (Germany)

PO John Richard **Kubin**
424 Squadron, RCAF
February 21, 1945
RCAF Memorial (Runnymede)

PO Maurice Coupland **Latornell**
425 Squadron,
RCAF
March 25, 1944
Kiel War Cemetery (Germany)

Pte. Charles Henry **Lequereux**
Veterans Guard of Canada
October 30, 1942
Nelson Memorial Park

Pte. Robert Gordon **Ludlow**
Canadian Scottish Regiment,
RCIC
February 20, 1945
*Groesbeek Canadian War Cemetery
(Netherlands)*

Capt. Kenneth Gilbert **McBride**
Seaforth Highlanders of Canada,
RCIC
September 16, 1944
*Coriano Ridge War Cemetery
(Italy)*

FO Clarence Francis **McDougall**
408 Squadron, RCAF
July 29, 1944
Kiel War Cemetery (Germany)

Pte. Hugh **McKean**
Canadian Scottish Regiment,
RCIC
July 7, 1944
*Bretteville-Sur-Laize Canadian
War Cemetery (France)*

*FO Henry Hector **MacKenzie**
RAF 198 Squadron, RCAF
January 3, 1944
*Marissel French National Cemetery
(France)*

AC2 Robert Lindsay **Main**
RCAF
June 11, 1943
Nelson Memorial Park

PO Francis John **Miller**
405 Squadron, RCAF
March 15, 1945
Hanover War Cemetery (Germany)

AB David Charles **Motley**
HMC 29th MTB Flotilla, RCN
Volunteer Reserve
February 14, 1945
RCN Memorial (Halifax)

Pte. Michael Thomas
Patrick **Prestley**
Black Watch (Royal Highlanders),
RCIC
July 22, 1944
*Beny-Sur-Mer Canadian War
Cemetery (France)*

OS George Henry
Trevelyan **Rasmussen**
RN, HMS *Woolwich*
December 9, 1939
*Haslar Royal Navy Cemetery
(England)*

Trp. Evander Donaldson **Rogers**
28th Armoured
Regiment (BCR)
September 26, 1944
*Adegem Canadian War Cemetery
(Belgium)*

Petty Off. John Meredith **Routh**
HMC 29th MTB Flotilla
RCN Volunteer Reserve
February 14, 1945
RCN Memorial (Halifax)

Pte. Terence Butler **Rowley**
Canadian Scottish Regiment,
RCIC
October 4, 1940
Esquimalt Veterans Cemetery

WO2 Iverson Frederick **Ruppel**
RAF 100 Squadron, RCAF
January 30, 1944
RCAF Memorial (Runnymede)

Pte. Edward George **Shardelow**
Canadian Scottish Regiment,
RCIC
August 15, 1944
*Bretteville Sur-Laize Canadian
War Cemetery (France)*

PO Richmond Wesley **Smith**
425 Squadron, RCAF
April 24, 1944
*Harrogate (Stonefall) Cemetery
(England)*

Cpl. William Stanley **Smith**
South Saskatchewan Regiment,
RCIC
August 28, 1944
*Bretteville-Sur-Laize Canadian
War Cemetery (France)*

L/Sgt. Stuart Alan **Spiers**
6th Field Company,
Royal Canadian Engineers
March 16, 1945
*Groesbeek Canadian War Cemetery
(Netherlands)*

Lieut. Charles Wellington **Steele**
Army Dental Corps
July 18, 1944
Vancouver (Mountain View)
Cemetery

FO Leonard James **Stewart**
RAF 7 Squadron, RCAF
April 9, 1943
RCAF Memorial (Runnymede)

Lieut. Comm. John
Hamilton **Stubbs**
RCN, HMCS *Athabaskan*
April 29, 1944
*Plouescat Communal Cemetery
(France)*

Trp. William **Swift**
British Columbia Regiment,
RCAC
August 9, 1944
*Bretteville-Sur-Laize Canadian War
Cemetery (France)*

Sgt. Thomas **Wallace**
#111 Operational Training Unit,
RCAF
June 28, 1943
RCAF Memorial (Ottawa)

WO1 Wilfred Clark **Wallace**
RAF 59 Squadron, RCAF
June 24, 1944
*Tamlaght Finlagen Church of
Ireland Churchyard (Northern
Ireland)*

PO Harry Dale **Warner**
432 Squadron, RCAF
June 12, 1943
RCAF Runnymede Memorial

Pte. John Woodrow **Wilson**
Seaforth Highlanders of Canada,
RCIC
May 23, 1944
Cassino War Cemetery (Italy)

Spr. William Percy **Woods**
Royal Canadian Engineers
February 17, 1944
*Moro River Canadian Cemetery
(Italy)*

Military Units of Nelson and District Casualties

NAVY

Royal Navy
  George Rasmussen (HMS *Woolwich*)

Royal Canadian Navy
  John Stubbs (HMCS *Athabaskan*)

Royal Canadian Naval Volunteer Reserve
  William Barwis (HMCS *St. Croix*)
  Hampton Gray (Fleet Air Arm)
  David Motley (HMC MTB 29th Flotilla)
  John Routh (HMC MTB 29th Flotilla)

ARMY REGIMENTS

Black Watch (Royal Highland Regiment) of Canada, RCIC
  Michael Prestley

British Columbia Regiment, Royal Canadian Armoured Corps
  Roscoe Armstrong
  Oscar Dorval
  Evander Rogers (28th Armoured Regiment)
  William Swift (28th Armoured Regiment)

Calgary Highlanders, RCIC
  James Hoover

Canadian Army Dental Corps
  Charles Steele

Canadian Forestry Corps
  James Hughes

Canadian Army – General List
>   Agner Dalgas

Canadian Scottish Regiment, RCIC
>   Matthew Aylmer
>   Robert Ludlow
>   Hugh McKean
>   Terence "Harry" Rowley
>   Edward Shardelow

Hastings and Prince Edward Regiment, RCIC
>   Austin Brennan

Royal Canadian Artillery
>   James Clark
>   John Harlow (6th Field Regiment)

Royal Canadian Engineers
>   Robert "Cliff" Craufurd (18th Field Company)
>   Stuart Spiers (6th Field Company)
>   William Woods (1st Corps Troops)

Seaforth Highlanders of Canada, RCIC
>   Raymond Hall
>   Kenneth McBride
>   John Wilson

South Saskatchewan Regiment, RCIC
>   Stanley Castle
>   William "Stan" Smith

Veterans Guard of Canada
>   Benjamin Beninger
>   William Brown
>   Charles Lequereux

Westminster Regiment (Motor), RCIC
>   William Allen

AIR FORCE SQUADRONS

RCAF

120 Squadron – Bomber Reconnaissance
James Eccles

405 Squadron (Vancouver) – Heavy Bomber Sqn – Pathfinder – 6 Group
Richard Jones
Francis "Jack" Miller

407 Squadron – Coastal Sqn
George "Chub" Greenwood

408 Squadron (Goose) – Heavy Bomber Sqn – 6 Group
Russell Clark
John Dingwall
Clarence McDougall

419 Squadron (Moose) – Heavy Bomber Sqn – 6 Group
John Beattie

424 Squadron (Tiger) – Heavy Bomber Sqn (flew N. Africa, Italy)
John Kubin

425 Squadron (Alouette) – Heavy Bomber Sqn – 6 Group
Maurice Latornell
Richmond Smith

426 Squadron (Thunderbird) – Heavy Bomber Sqn – 6 Group
Wilbur Bentz

429 Squadron (Bison) – Heavy Bomber Sqn – 6 Group
Edward "Teddy" Cornfield

432 Squadron (Leaside) – Heavy Bomber Sqn – 6 Group
Raymond Burgess
Harry Warner

434 Squadron (Bluenose) – Heavy Bomber Sqn – 6 Group
Harold "Harley" Breeze

RCAF – Unassigned
Robert "Bert" Jardine (lost at sea en route to Great Britain)
Robert Main (died while in training in Canada)

RAF

7 Squadron – Bomber Command
Eric "Bob" Andrew
Leonard Stewart

18 Squadron – Bomber Command
Donald Gibbon

21 Squadron – Coastal Command
Henry Hartridge

59 Squadron – Coastal Command
Wilfred "Jerry" Wallace

63 Squadron – Bomber Command
Barrington Cleeton

87 Squadron – Fighter Command
John Campbell

100 Squadron – Bomber Command
Iverson "Bud" Ruppel

144 Squadron – Bomber Command
John Gray

166 Squadron – Bomber Command
Gus Flegel

198 Squadron – Fighter Command
Henry MacKenzie

630 Squadron – Bomber Command
Ambrose Bain

#14 Advanced Flying School
Richard "Syd" Horswill

#20 Operational Training Unit – Bomber Command
Ronald Greavison

#52 Operational Training Unit – Fighter Command
John Grant

#111 Operational Training Unit – Reconnaissance
Thomas Wallace

#1651 Conversion Unit – Bomber Command
Francis "Larry" Flynn

#1661 Conversion Unit – Bomber Command
Norman Boss

US ARMY AIR FORCE

8th Army Air Force - 448th Bombardment Group – 714th Squadron
Patrick George

HOME ADDRESSES OF NELSON AND DISTRICT CASUALTIES

NELSON:

General Delivery — William Allen
William Woods

613 Second St. — Stan Smith
616 Second St. — Jack Miller

508 Fourth St. — Bert Jardine

308½ Baker St. — Agner Dalgas
350 Baker St. — Jack Wilson
415 Baker St. — Jim Clark
815 Baker St. — Jack Gray
Hammy Gray

304 Carbonate St. — Jack Kubin
504 Carbonate St. — Henry MacKenzie
711 Carbonate St. — Russ Clark

211 Cedar St. — Jerry Wallace
609 Cedar St. — Bob Ludlow
816 Cedar St. — Harry Rowley

223 Elwyn St. — Ray Burgess
619 Elwyn St. — Stuart Spiers

1403 Front St. — Jim Hoover

524 Gore St. — Jimmy Eccles
621 Gore St. — Richie Smith

83 Upper Granite Road — Bud Ruppel

913 Hall St. — Norman Boss

107 Hall Mines Rd.	Harley Breeze
307 Hall Mines Rd.	Teddy Cornfield
103 High St.	John Harlow
308 Hoover St.	George Greenwood
708 Hoover St.	Ken McBride
301 Houston St.	Ambrose Bain
700 Blk. Kootenay St.	Stan Castle
1307 Kootenay St.	Bill Barwis
407 Latimer St.	John Dingwall
416 Maple St.	Chub Greenwood
616 Mill St.	Wib Bentz
724 Mill St.	Harry Warner
914 Mill St.	Charles Lequereux
504 Nelson Ave.	Bob Andrew
805 Nelson Ave.	Ed Shardelow
324 Observatory St.	Tommy Wallace
412 Silica St.	Syd Horswill
416 Silica St.	Pat George
718 Silica St.	John Beattie
806 Silica St.	Mickey Prestley
816 Silica St.	Don Gibbon
910 Silica St.	Len Stewart
718 Stanley St.	Clare McDougall
1224 Stanley St.	Austin Brennan
1407 Stanley St.	Maurice Latornell
1419 Stanley St.	Cliff Craufurd

NELSON DISTRICT COMMUNITIES:

Balfour: Henry Hartridge

Bonnington: Robert Main
David Motley

Blewett: William Swift

Brilliant: Barry Cleeton

Kaslo: John Stubbs

Perry Siding: Theodore Beninger

Queens Bay: Matt Aylmer
Jim Hughes

Sheep Creek: Ray Hall

Slocan Park: Ronald Greavison

South Slocan: Evander Rogers

Vallican: Larry Flynn

Willow Point: Jack Campbell
Oscar Dorval
George Rasmussen

Ymir: John Grant
Dick Jones

Winlaw: Hugh McKean

NOTES

1. Bruce Hutchison, "Nelson Wishes We Understood It Better," *Vancouver Sun*, March 2, 1940, 11.

2. Art Joyce, "The Boer War: Part 1," *Nelson Daily News*, July 16, 1999.

3. Patricia A. Rogers and Floyd Low, *54th Bn Canadian Infantry, 1916–1919*. <http://members.tripod.com/appollon_2/> (August 14, 2003).

4. "Britain is Now 'Greater Britain of Stronger and More Powerful Empire' Spencer Tells the Legion and 111th," *Nelson Daily News*, October 5, 1939.

5. "Nelson Boy in Navy," *Nelson Daily News*, July 20, 1937.

6. Royal Air Force. *Royal Air Force Bomber Command 60th Anniversary: Campaign Diary*, 2002. <http://www.raf.mod.uk/bombercommand/diary/diary.html> (August 25, 2003).

7. All RCAF medal citations are available from: Air Force Association of Canada. *RCAF Personnel – Honours and Awards – 1939–1949*. <http://www.airforce.ca/index. php3?page=wwii> (September 4, 2003).

8. *Nelson Daily News*, June 1, 1940.

9. Shawn Lamb, "Nelson Drill Hall 'Symbolic' Building," *Nelson Daily News*, April 1, 1993.

10. Barry Broadfoot, *Six War Years, 1939–1945*: Memories of Canadians at Home and Abroad (Toronto: Doubleday, 1984), 66b [caption].

11. "Nelson Council Agrees Enemy Aliens Should Be Interned," *Nelson Daily News*, May 18, 1940.

12. "Nelson Council Will Urge Government Action Guard Against 'Fifth Column,'" *Nelson Daily News*, May 22, 1940.

13. "Iron Lungs Presented Hospital by Stibbs on Hospital Day," *Nelson Daily News*, May 13, 1940.

14. "Kootenay Lake's Fishing is 'Best in North America,'" *Nelson Daily News*, May 17, 1940.

15. "Inventions Board Studies His Proposed Aerial Bomb," *Nelson Daily News*, December 2, 1940.

16. John Armstrong, "Nelson's Gray Family Lost Both Sons in the War," *Nelson Daily News*, November 23, 1988.

17. Daphne Wilson, "Women in Canada in World War Two and How it Changed Your Life," in e-mail letter to author, November 18, 2003.

18. *Mountaineer* (Nelson, BC: Nelson High School, 1942), 2.

19. "'I'm All Right Now, Auntie,' Says Nelson's First Evacuee," *Nelson Daily News*, October 5, 1940.

20. "Mass Marks Anniversary of Death of Henry Hartridge; Killed Over Holland," *Nelson Daily News*, July 24, 1942.

21. "Nelson's 'Open House' Program for British and Anzac Airmen Being Publicized Through Empire," *Nelson Daily News*, November 27, 1941.

22. "Text of Tribute Paid Nelson in *Carry On Canada*," *Nelson Daily News*, September 25, 1941.

23. "Niven Article Tells Scotland of Nelson Plan," *Nelson Daily News*, March 5, 1942.

24. *Nelson Daily News*, February 19, 1942.

25. "Nelsonites Buy $118 Worth of War Savings Stamps in 'Sing Dictators Down' Program; Nearly 500 Attend," *Nelson Daily News*, February 24, 1941.

26. "Nelson Blackout Eerily Effective; Publicity is More Than Any Expected, *Nelson Daily News*, February 17, 1941.

27. "Nelson Boy on U.S. Warship Was in Thick of Pearl Harbor Bombing," *Nelson Daily News*, March 10, 1942.

28. W.D. MacDonald, letter to author, September 19, 2003.

29. "Jack Gray, Nelson Airman, Finds Thrills in Britain," *Nelson Daily News*, May 30, 1941.

30. Henry F. Humphries, videocassette interview, [Toronto, 1999].

31. Stuart E. Soward, *A Formidable Hero* (Toronto: Canav Books, 1987), 35, 57.

32. "Father of Airman Gray Was Broadcasting For Victory Loan Not Knowing Son Had Fallen," *Nelson Daily News*, March 5, 1942.

33. Wilson.

34. Edward Willett, *Wartime Rationing & Making Do.* <http://www. edwardwillett/Columns/warrationing.htm> 1995 (November 12, 2003).

35. "Nelson Salvage to Include Old German Cannon," *Nelson Daily News*, April 14, 1942.

36. "Nelson's 10,000 Heavy Machine-Guns," *Nelson Daily News*, November 21, 1942.

37. David Suzuki, *Metamorphosis: Stages in a Life* (Toronto: Stoddart, 1987), 71.

38. Eric Ramsden, "Mines Open, Logging Spurred in Nelson's Big War Effort," Vancouver *Province*, November 1, 1943.

39. Juno Beach Centre, *Canada in World War II: The Canadian Women's Army Corps*, 2003. <http://www.junobeach.org/e/4/can-tac-cwa-e.htm> (November 17, 2003).

40. Dorothy Howey, "Cpl. Edythe Thomson of Nelson Part of Competent Airwoman Team Enjoys New WD's Busy Life," *Nelson Daily News*, March 8, 1944.

41. M.D. Bradshaw, *Boys, Music and Mrs. F.*, (Nelson, BC: Nelson News Publishing, 1971), 12. Members of the Boys' Choir killed in World War II include: John Beattie, John Dingwall, Sydney Horswill, Robert Ludlow, Leonard Stewart, Wilfred "Jerry" Wallace.

42. Helen Ferguson Poisson, *Sing As You Go*: *Amy Ferguson and the Nelson Boys' Choir* (Helen Ferguson Poisson, 2002), 74.

43. Ibid.

44. "Tells of RCAF Sea Tragedy in Which Nelsonite Lost," *Nelson Daily News*, October 18, 1945.

45. Winnifred Linville, Letter to the Editor, *Nelson Daily News*, December 7, 2004.

46. "18 Candidates for Air Force Interviewed by Recruiting Party," *Nelson Daily News*, May 14, 1943.

47. Art Joyce, "Wartime Pressures Newlyweds," *Nelson Daily News*, January 3, 1997.

48. Wilson.

49. Logan Glendening, "Wartime Strains on Civilians," *Nelson Daily News*, January 27, 1944.

50. Garry Cleveland Myers, "Adopt Cheerful Attitude When Writing Soldier," *Nelson Daily News*, January 27, 1942.

51. "Kinsmen Milk for Britain Fund at $957," *Nelson Daily News*, June 16, 1943.

52. *Nelson Daily News*, August 25, 1943.

53. "Nelson Should Be Proud of Its Part in War," *Nelson Daily News*, August 10, 1943.

54. "Mayor Stibbs Awaits Visit by, or Word From Boeing Officials on Suggested Assembly Plant Here," *Nelson Daily News*, July 12, 1943.

55. Dawn Penniket, letter to author, October 14, 2003.

56. Andrew Haggins, "A World War II Experience," *Rear AG – 432 Sqdrn. Ex Air Gunners Short Bursts*. April, 2001. <http://angelfire.com/trek/rcaf/exag0104.html> (August 6, 2003).

57. Kathy Kiel, "Men of the 'News' Become the News," *Nelson Daily News*, November 10, 2004.

58. Society of Bomber Command Historians. Aircrew Memorial Association. *Daily Operations*. <http://www.rcaf.com/6group/Operations.html> (August 28, 2003); Aircrew Association. Metro Toronto Branch. *Dabous, Albert (Dabby), POW*, August 15, 2003. <http://www.torontoaircrew.com/Navigators/Dabous_1/dabous_1.html> (August 28, 2003).

59. J.L. Granatstein and Peter Neary, eds., *The Good Fight: Canadians and World War II* (Toronto: Copp Clark, 1995), 451.

60. Broadfoot, *Six War Years, 1939–1945*, 259.

61. Penniket.

62. Andrew Chung, "Coming Home," in The Dominion Institute, *The Memory Project*. 2003. <http://www.thememoryproject.com/peace_grant_cominghome.cfm> (January 4, 2004).

63. Penniket.

64. "Seaplane Fire Led to Death of Jim Eccles," *Nelson Daily News*, March 7, 1944.

65. John Blatherwick, *Awards to the Royal Canadian Navy*, July 20, 2001 <http://www.rcnvr.com/> (September 4, 2003).

66. J.L. Granatstein and Desmond Morton, *A Nation Forged in Fire: Canadians and the Second World War 1939–1945* (Toronto: Lester & Orpen Dennys, 1989), 145.

67. Penniket.

68. "Junior High Students Present Stirring Pageant to Large Crowd," *Nelson Daily News*, May 5, 1944.

69. Royal Air Force, *Royal Air Force Bomber Command 60th Anniversary: Campaign Diary*, 2002. <http://www.raf.mod.uk/bombercommand/diary/diary.html> August 25, 2003).

70. Les Allison and Harry Hayward, *They Shall Grow Not Old: A Book of Remembrance* (Brandon, MB: Commonwealth Air Training Plan Museum, 1991), 586.

71. "Nelson Seaman in Attack on Battleship," *Nelson Daily News*, May 2, 1944.

72. Whitby, Michael, *Lieutenant-Commander John Stubbs*, CFB Esquimalt Naval and Military Museum, 2000–2003. <http://www.navalandmilitarymuseum.org/resource/Resources_Frame.html?Stubbs.html&l> (August 27, 2003).

73. "Sigmn. John Norris of Nelson Tells How Rescuers Risked Capture to Aid *Athabaskan* Survivors, *Nelson Daily News*, June 24, 1944.

74. "Doukhobors Should be Treated as Conscientious Objectors Says Nelson Rehabilitation Committee," *Nelson Daily News*, June 23, 1943.

75. "Deport Sons of Freedom Says Esling," *Nelson Daily News*, February 16, 1944.

76. "180 Visitors See Excellent Display of V Bundles for Britain Work," *Nelson Daily News*, May 15, 1944.

77. Duncan Clark, "Recovery of Halifax LW 682," *The Aerodrome Magazine* (March 2001). <http://www3.sympatico.ca/scott.knox/pages/Herald.htm> (January 14, 2004).

78. Reginald H. Roy, *The Seaforth Highlanders of Canada*, 1919–1965 (Vancouver: Seaforth Highlanders of Canada, 1969), 291–309.

79. Arthur Gerald Chester, *The North Irish Horse In Italy*, 2001–2004. <http://www.geocities.com/vqpvqp/hih/narrative/italy6.html> (January 20, 2004).

80. Roy, *The Seaforth Highlanders of Canada*, 300.

81. Ilva Bleasdale, "Joe Dyck's Imitation of Hitler in Prison Camp Nearly Fatal; Women Prisoners Hardly Human," reprinted from *The British Columbian* in *Nelson Daily News*, June 16, 1945.

82. Kenneth A. Morrow, *A Boyhood in Nelson: Growing Up During the Depression* (Bellingham, WA: Kenneth A. Morrow, 2003), 218–21.

83. "Nelson Soldier's Landing Craft Hits Mine; Is Wounded by Mortar Shell," *Nelson Daily News*, July 26, 1944.

84. Bob Morrow, letter to author, October 15, 2003.

85. Audrey Heustis, e-mail letter to author, May 15, 2004.

86. E.L. Affleck, "The Aylmer Family of Queens Bay," in *Kootenay Outlook Reflections: A History of Procter, Sunshine Bay, Harrop, Longbeach, Balfour, Queens Bay* (Procter, BC: Procter-Harrop Historical Book Committee, 1988), 504-6.

87. Reginald H. Roy, with additional materials edited by D.M. Grubb, *Ready for the Fray: A History of the Canadian Scottish Regiment (Princess Mary's), 1920–2002* (Calgary: Bunker to Bunker, 2002), 276.

88. *The Valour & the Horror: In Desperate Battle: Normandy 1944*, Alderley Ventures, 1997. <http://www.valourandhorror.com/DB/CHRON/July_18.htm> (August 25, 2003).

89. G.W.L. Nicholson, *The Gunners of Canada: The History of the Royal Regiment of Canadian Artillery*, v. 2, *1919–1967* (Toronto: McClelland and Stewart, 1972), 316.

90. "Gnr. Peter Pearce, D.C.M., Carried on for Wounded Officer Under Heavy, Continuous Fire," *Nelson Daily News*, November 10, 1944.

91. Veterans Affairs Canada, *Canadian Virtual War Memorial*, Ottawa, ON, August 5, 2003. <http://www.vac-acc.gc.ca/general/sub.cfm?source=collections/virtualmem> (August 28, 2003).

92. Douglas E. Harker, *The Dukes: The Story of the Men Who Have Served in Peace and War with the British Columbia Regiment (D.C.O.), 1883–1973* (Vancouver: Mitchell Press, 1974), 236–38.

93. C.P. Stacey (ed.), *Official History of the Canadian Army in the Second World War*, v. 3, *The Victory Campaign: The Operations in North-West Europe, 1944–1945* (Ottawa: E. Cloutier, Queen's Printer, 1955–1960), 228.

94. Roy, *Ready for the Fray*, 304.

95. Terry Copp, "The March to the Seine, Part 30," *Legion Magazine* (March/April 2000). <http://www.legionmagazine.com/features/canadianmilitaryhistory/00-03.asp> (February 4, 2004).

96. L.A. Wrinch, *Report No. 143, Canadian Operations in Italy 4 Jun – 23 Feb 45*, Historical Section, Canadian Military Headquarters, Revised and reprinted at C.M.H.Q. in November 1946 by Colonel C.P. Stacey. <http://www.dnd.ca/hr/dhh/Downloads/cmhq/CMHQ143.PDF> (February 23, 2004).

97. "'McBride to Relieve McBride' Gives Thrill to Nelson Brothers Right in the Thick of Italian Fight," *Nelson Daily News*, February 16, 1944.

98. Letter from R.L. McBride, dated October 12, 1944.

99. "Zombies Number 4029 in B.C.," *Nelson Daily News*, November 23, 1944.

100. "Small Percentage 'Draft Dodgers,'" *Nelson Daily News*, November 16, 1944.

101. Bob Francis, "Gib Goucher of Nelson Just Misses Chance to Land Airborne Troops," *Nelson Daily News*, September 19,1944.

102. "PO. Peter Melneczuk 'Hits Silk' with Crew on Last Bombing Mission," *Nelson Daily News*, November 13, 1944.

103. "Nelson Soldier Has Close Call Doodle Bug Blast," *Nelson Daily News*, September 4, 1944.

104. "FO Carne, Nelson Aerial 'Newsboy' at Calcutta," *Nelson Daily News*, September 14, 1944.

105. "First Graduation Dinner at Nelson Great Success; Pupils Seek Courage for Next Chapter," *Nelson Daily News*, May 27, 1944.

106. "Mother, With One Son in Belgium and One in India, Makes Striking Appeal for Victory Loan," *Nelson Daily News*, November 10, 1944.

107. "Nelson District V-Loan Sales at $1,090,350; Gain 14 Pennants Believed Best Record in Canada," *Nelson Daily News*, November 20, 1944.

108. Tanna Allan, e-mail letter to author, May 18, 2004.

109. Don Thomas, "Canadian Forestry Corps," in *Canadian Military Engineers Throughout History (Echo Two)*. <http://users.uniserve.com/%7Eecho2/Don.htm#Forestry> (March 1, 2004).

110. "Honor to Nelson Mother: Second Medal for Sgt. Pat George, Who Gave Life Overseas," *Nelson Daily News*, January 24, 1946.

111. Royal Canadian Legion, Rockland & District Branch 554, *War Statistics* <http://rc1554.webcentre.ca/commem/War-stats.html> (January 10, 2004).

112. *Nelson Daily News*, June 1, 1945.

113. Robert A. Darlington and Fraser M. McKee, *The Canadian Naval Chronicle, 1939–1945: The Successes and Losses of the Canadian Navy in World War II* (St. Catharines, ON: Vanwell Publishing, 1996), 205.

114. Veterans Affairs Canada, *Groesbeek Canadian War Cemetery*. <http://www.vac-acc.gc.ca/general/sub.cfm?source=feature/Holland00/holschedule/groesbeek> (August 12, 2003).

115. Royal Canadian Air Force, *The R.C.A.F. Overseas: The Sixth Year* (Toronto: Oxford University Press, 1949), 120–21.

116. "Former Nelsonite Saw Nagasaki Atomic Bombing," *Nelson Daily News*, November 6, 1945.

117. Spencer Dunmore, *Above and Beyond: The Canadians' War in the Air, 1939–45* (Toronto: McClelland & Stewart, 1996), 341–43.

118. Soward,175.

119. "Smillie Recalls Leadership of Gray as Student," *Nelson Daily News*, November 14, 1945.

120. Soward, 27.

121. Ibid.,103.

122. "Nelson's Gray Family Lost Both Sons in War," *Nelson Daily News*, November 23, 1988.

123. E-mail letter from Stan Smith, October 20, 2004.

124. "Smillie Recalls…."

125. Carrigg, David. "Fascinating Stories Behind Service Medals," Vancouver Courier, November 9, 2003. <http://www.vancouver.com/ issues03/112103/news/112103nn7.html> (October 5, 2004).

126. Paula Shapleigh and Robert Moss. *"We Will Remember": War Monuments in Canada World Wide Web Site: British Columbia.* October, 2000. <http://www.stemnet.nf.ca/monuments/bc.htm> (March 31, 2004).

BIBLIOGRAPHY

100 Days, 100 Years: A Century of Nelson's Top News Stories. Nelson, B.C.: *Nelson Daily News,* 1997.

Bombs Away: Official Website of the 448th Bombardment Group. 2001– . <http://www.448bg.us/index.htm> (June 2, 2004).

Abbott, Kim. *Gathering of Demons: 407 Demon Squadron of the Royal Canadian Air Force, During Its First Year of Operations, Between May 8, 1941 and June 30, 1942, When It Was Engaged in Low Level Shipping Attacks Along the Coasts of Occupied Europe.* Perth, ON: Inkerman House, 1987.

Aircrew Association. Metro Toronto Branch. *Dabous, Albert (Dabby), POW.* August 15, 2003. < http://www.torontoaircrew.com/Navigators/Dabous_1/dabous_1.html > (August 28, 2003).

Air Force Association of Canada. *RCAF Personnel – Honours and Awards – 1939–1949.* <http://www.airforce.ca/index.php3?page=wwii> (September 4, 2003).

Allison, Les. *Canadians in the Royal Air Force.* Roland, MB: L. Allison, 1978.

Allison, Les, and Harry Hayward. *They Shall Grow Not Old: A Book of Remembrance.* Brandon, MB: Commonwealth Air Training Plan Museum, [1991].

Asmussen, John. *Bismarck & Tirpitz: Tirpitz.* 2000–2004. < http://www.bismarck-class.dk/tirpitz/tiroperationhist.html> (January 10, 2004).

Blatherwick, John. Awards to the Royal Canadian Navy. July 20, 2001. <http://www.rcnvr.com/> (September 4, 2003).

Braakhuis, Wilfried. The World At War: History of WW 1939-1945. Netherlands: Elite EngineerPublishing,1997–2002. <http://www.euronet.nl/users/wilfried/ww2/main.htm> (5 July 2004).

Bradshaw, M.D. *Boys, Music and Mrs. F.* Nelson, BC: Nelson News Publishing Co., 1971.

British Columbia. Ministry of Sustainable Resource Management. *BC Geographical Names.* 2001. <http://srmwww.gov.bc.ca/bcnames/> (May 3, 2004).

British Columbia Regiment. *A Proud History.* <http://www.bcregiment. com/> (August 25, 2003).

Broadfoot, Barry. *Six War Years, 1939–1945: Memories of Canadians at Home and Abroad.* Toronto, Doubleday, 1974.

Broadfoot, Barry. *Years of Sorrow, Years of Shame: The Story of the Japanese Canadians in World War II.* Toronto: Doubleday Canada, 1977.

Canadian Bank of Commerce. *War Service Records, 1939–1945; an Account of the War Service of Members of the Staff During the Second World War.* Toronto: The Bank, 1947.

Canadian War Museum. *Chronology of Canadian Military History: Canada and the Second World War.* April 2, 2003 <http://www. civilization.ca/cwm/chrono/1931crisis_e.html> (May 28, 2004).

Canadian War Museum. *Democracy at War: Canadian Newspapers and the Second World War: Canada and the War: The Canadian Armed Forces: Casualties.* September 19, 2003. <http://www.civilization.ca/cwm/ newspapers/canadawar/casualties_e.html> (December 30, 2003).

Carrigg, David. "Fascinating Stories Behind Service Medals," *Vancouver Courier*, November 9, 2003. <http://www.vancourier.com/ issues03/112103/news/112103nn7.html> (October 5, 2004).

Chester, Arthur Gerald. *The North Irish Horse in Italy.* <http://www. geocities.com/vqpvqp/nih/narrative/italy6.html> (January 20, 2004).

Chung, Andrew. "Coming Home." In The Dominion Institute, *The Memory Project*. 2003. <http://www.thememoryproject.com/peace_grant_cominghome.cfm> (January 4, 2004).

Clark, Duncan. "Recovery of Halifax LW 682." *The Aerodrome Magazine* (March 2001). <http://www3.sympatico.ca/scott.knox/pages/Herald.htm> (January 14, 2004).

Copp, Terry. "The March to the Seine, Part 30." *Legion Magazine* (March/April 2000). <http://www.legionmagazine.com/features/canadianmilitaryhistory/00-03.asp> (February 4, 2004).

Darlington, Robert A., and Fraser M. McKee. *The Canadian Naval Chronicle, 1939–1945: The Successes and Losses of the Canadian Navy in World War II*. St. Catharines, ON: Vanwell Publishing, 1996.

Depickere, Dave. *World War II Analyzed: The Canadians in the Falaise Pocket*. December 20, 2001. <http://users.pandora.be/dave.depickere/Text/D-DayText/falaise.html> (12 August 2003).

Dunmore, Spencer. *Above And Beyond: The Canadians' War in the Air, 1939–45*. Toronto: McClelland & Stewart, 1996.

Fleet Air Arm Archive. *Life of the Tracker: Story of the Escort Carrier HMS Tracker 1943–1945*. 2002. <http://www.fleetairarmarchive.net/Ships/TrackerTheStormyWestContinued.html> (March 25, 2004).

Granatstein, J.L., and Desmond Morton. *A Nation Forged In Fire: Canadians and the Second World War 1939–1945*. Toronto: Lester & Orpen Dennys, 1989.

Granatstein, J.L, and Peter Neary, eds. *The Good Fight: Canadians and World War II*. Toronto: Copp Clark, 1995.

Griffin, Anthony. "A Naval Officer's War," *Naval Officers Association of Canada*. <http://www.naval.ca/article/griffin/anavalofficerswar_ep3_byanthonygriffin.html> (February 18, 2004).

Haggins, Andrew. "A World War II Experience." *Rear AG – 432 Sqdrn. Ex Air Gunners Short Bursts*. April 2001. <http://www.angelfire.com/trek/rcaf/exag0104.html> (August 6, 2003).

Hall, Bob. "Lest We Forget … It's a Shame We Have." *Nelson Daily News*, June 7, 2001.

Harker, Douglas E. *The Dukes: The Story of the Men Who Have Served in Peace and War with the British Columbia Regiment (D.C.O.), 1883–1973*. Vancouver: Mitchell Press, 1974.

"History of the SSR." *Weyburn Review* (8 May 1985). <http://cap.estevan.sk.ca/SSR/nominal/history.html> (August 25, 2003).

"In Remembrance: The Crew of LW682." *The Aerodrome Magazine* (August 1999). <http://www3.sympatico.ca/scott.knox/pages/crew.htm> (August 28, 2003).

Johnson, Mac. "Burial in Belgium." *Legion Magazine* (January/February 1998). <http://www.legionmagazine.com/features/memoirspilgrimages/98-01b.asp> (August 28, 2003).

Joyce, Art. *Hanging Fire & Heavy Horses: A History of Public Transit in Nelson*. Nelson, BC: City of Nelson, 2000.

Juno Beach Centre. *Canada in World War II: The Canadian Women's Army Corps*. 2003. <http://www.junobeach.org/e/4/can-tac-cwa-e.htm> (November 17, 2003).

Kalmakoff, Jonathan J. *Doukhobor National Registration. Doukhobor Genealogy Website*, 1999–2004. <http://www.doukhobor.org/National-Registration.htm>. (January 12, 2004).

Kiel, Kathy. "Men of the 'News' Become the News." *Nelson Daily News*, November 10, 2004.

Kootenay Outlet Reflections: A History of Procter, Sunshine Bay, Harrop, Longbeach, Balfour, Queens Bay. Procter, BC: Procter-Harrop Historical Book Committee, 1988.

Lamb, Shawn. "Remembering Local Servicemen in European Graves." *Nelson Daily News*, May 16, 1995.

Law, C. Anthony. *White Plumes Astern: The Short, Daring Life of Canada's MTB Flotilla.* Halifax, NS: Nimbus, 1989.

McDougall, Robert L. *A Narrative of War: From the Beaches of Sicily to the Hitler Line with the Seaforth Highlanders of Canada, 10 July1943 – 8 June 1944.* Ottawa: Golden Dog Press, 1996.

Mission Museum. *The Westminster Regiment's "C" Company, "Mission's Own" in World War II.* Mission, BC <http://www.mission.museum. bc.ca/mm/localhist/milestones/milestones/westministar_regement2. html>. (August 25, 2003).

Morrow, Kenneth A. *A Boyhood in Nelson: Growing Up During the Depression.* Bellingham, WA: Kenneth A. Morrow, 2003.

Motiuk, Laurence. *Thunderbirds At War: Diary of a Bomber Squadron.* Nepean, ON: Larmot Associates, 1998.

The Naval Museum of Alberta. *Lt. Robert Hampton Gray, VC, DSC, MiD, RCNVR.* Calgary, AB: 2001. <http://www.navalmuseum.ab.ca/ gray.html> (August 27, 2003).

Naval Museum of Manitoba. *Motor Torpedo Boat Gallery.* <http://www.navalmuseum.mb.ca/mtb/> (September 12, 2003).

Naval Museum of Manitoba. *Wrens – A Proud Heritage: A Brief History of the Women's Royal Canadian Naval Service,* 25 April, 2003. <http:// www.naval-museum.mb.ca/history/exhib10.htm> (November 17, 2003).

Nelson, Mark. *Canadian Heroes: Private Henri Richard: Fôret de la Londe*. 1997.<http://www.multipointproductions.com/heroes/henr> (February 4, 2004).

Newham, Sara. "Nelson's Ties to Dieppe." *Nelson Daily News*, August 22, 2002.

Nicholson, G.W.L. *The Gunners of Canada: The History of the Royal Regiment of Canadian Artillery*, v. 2, *1919–1967*. Toronto: McClelland & Stewart, 1972.

Nicholson, G.W.L. *Official History of the Canadian Army in the Second World War*, v. 2, *The Canadians in Italy, 1943–1945*. Ottawa: E. Cloutier, Queen's Printer, 1955–1960.

Poisson, Helen Ferguson. *Sing As You Go: Amy Ferguson and the Nelson Boys' Choir*. [British Columbia]: Woolsock Press, 2002.

Rogers, Patricia A., and Floyd Low. *54th Bn Canadian Infantry, 1916-1919*. <http://members.tripod.com/apollon_2/> (August 14, 2003).

Roy, R.H.; with additional materials edited by D.M. Grubb. *Ready For the Fray: A History of the Canadian Scottish Regiment (Princess Mary's) 1920 to 2002*. Calgary: Bunker to Bunker, 2002.

Roy, Reginald H. *The Seaforth Highlanders of Canada, 1919–1965*. Vancouver: Seaforth Highlanders of Canada, 1969.

Royal Air Force. *Royal Air Force Bomber Command 60th Anniversary: Campaign Diary*. 2002. <http://www.raf.mod.uk/bombercommand/diary/diary.html> (August 25, 2003).

Royal Canadian Air Force. *The R.C.A.F. Overseas: The First Four Years*. Toronto, Oxford Univ. Press, 1944.

Royal Canadian Air Force. *The R.C.A.F. Overseas: The Sixth Year*. Toronto: Oxford Univ. Press, 1949.

Royal Canadian Legion, Branch 51. *Nelson Remembers: A Reflection of Peace*. Nelson *Daily News Supplement*, November 10, 1995.

Royal Canadian Legion, Rockland & District Branch 554. *War Statistics*. <http://rcl554.webcentre.ca/commem/War-stats.html> (January 10, 2004).

Shannon, Norman. "Valour Unlimited." *Legion* 44, no. 6 (November 1969): 14–15; 30.

Shapleigh, Paula, and Robert Moss. *"We Will Remember:" War Monuments in Canada World Wide Web Site: British Columbia*. October, 2000. <http://www.stemnet.nf.ca/monuments/bc.htm> (March 31, 2004).

Society of Bomber Command Historians. Aircrew Memorial Association. *Daily Operations*. <http://www.rcaf.com/6group/Operations.html> (August 28, 2003).

Soward, Stuart E. *A Formidable Hero*. Toronto: Canav Books, 1987.

Stacey, C.P. (ed). *Official History of the Canadian Army in the Second World War*, v. 3, *The Victory Campaign: The Operations in North-West Europe 1944–1945*. Ottawa: E. Cloutier, Queen's Printer, 1955–1960.

Stalag Luft I Online. <http://www.merkki.com/index.htm> (August 24, 2003).

Suzuki, David. *Metamorphosis: Stages in a Life*. Toronto: Stoddart, 1987.

Thomas, Don. "Canadian Forestry Corps." In *Canadian Military Engineers Throughout History (Echo Two)*. <http://users.uniserve.com/%7Eecho2/Don.htm#Forestry> (March 1, 2004).

The Valour & the Horror: In Desperate Battle: Normandy 1944. Alderley Ventures, 1997. <http://www.valourandhorror.com/DB/CHRON/July_18.htm> (August 25, 2003).

The Valour & the Horror: Women in the War. Alderley Ventures, 1997. <http://www.valourandhorror.com/DB/ISSUE/Women/> (April 25, 2004).

Veterans Affairs Canada. *Canadian Virtual War Memorial.* Ottawa, ON. 5 August, 2003. <http://www.vac-acc.gc.ca/general/sub. cfm?source=collections/virtualmem> (August 28, 2003).

Veterans Affairs Canada. *Groesbeek Canadian War Cemetery.* <http://www.vac-acc.gc.ca/general/sub.cfm?source=feature/Holland00/ holschedule/groesbeek> (August 12, 2003).

Veterans Affairs Canada. *Pilot Officer Wilbur Boyd Bentz.* Ottawa, ON. June 25, 1999. <http://www.vac-acc.gc.ca/general/sub. cfm?source=feature/belgium/bentz> (August 14, 2003).

Whalen, James M. "The Scrap That Made a Difference." *Legion Magazine* (November-December 1998). <http://www.legionmagazine. com/features/canadianreflections/98-11.asp> (August 19, 2003).

Whitby, Michael. *Lieutenant-Commander John Stubbs.* CFB Esquimalt Naval and Military Museum, 2000–2003. <http://www. navalandmilitarymuseum.org/resource/Resources_Frame.html?Stubbs .html&1> (August 27, 2003).

Willett, Edward. *Wartime Rationing & Making Do.* 1995. <http://www. edwardwillett.com/Columns/warrationing.htm> (November 12, 2003).

Wrinch, L.A. *Report No. 143, Canadian Operations in Italy, 4 Jun – 23 Feb 45.* Historical Section, Canadian Military Headquarters, Revised and reprinted at C.M.H.Q. in November 1946 by Colonel C.P. Stacey. <http://www.dnd.ca/hr/dhh/Downloads/cmhq/CMHQ143.PDF> (February 23, 2004).

Zuehlke, Mark. *The Liri Valley: Canada's World War II Breakthrough To Rome.* Chapter 17. <http://www.islandnet.com/pwacvic/zuehlk05. html>. Toronto: Stoddart, 2001 (August 25, 2003).

PERSONAL NAME INDEX

(Numbers in italics indicate a picture)